SCHAUM'S OUTLINE OF

THEORY AND PROBLEMS

of

PROGRAMMING

with

BASIC

•

by

BYRON S. GOTTFRIED, Ph. D.

Professor of Industrial Engineering
Systems Management Engineering and Operations Research
University of Pittsburgh

SCHAUM'S OUTLINE SERIES

McGRAW-HILL BOOK COMPANY

New York   St. Louis   San Francisco   Auckland   Düsseldorf   Johannesburg
Kuala Lumpur   London   Mexico   Montreal   New Delhi   Panama
Paris   São Paulo   Singapore   Sydney   Tokyo   Toronto

07-023842-1

8 9 10 11 12 13 14 15 16 17 18 19 20   **SH SH 8 7 6 5 4 3 2 1 0**

Library of Congress Cataloging in Publication Data

Gottfried, Byron S
Theory and problems of programming with Basic.
  (Schaum's outline series in computer science)
  Bibliography: p. 221
  1. Basic (Computer program language)   I. Title.
QA76.73.B3G67   001.6'424   75-2066
ISBN 0-07-023842-1

To Marcia, Sharon, Gail and Susan

Preface

Of the many programming languages that have been developed during the past 20 years, none is easier to learn than BASIC. Yet this remarkably simple language contains enough power and flexibility to be of interest to a wide variety of persons. The use of BASIC has become particularly common at the secondary school and junior college levels. Moreover, the availability of the language through most commercial timesharing systems has caused it to be widely used for many business, technical and scientific applications.

This book offers instruction in digital computer programming using the BASIC language. All of the principal features of BASIC are discussed. However, the objectives of the book are to teach the reader how to organize and write efficient computer programs and to stress the importance of good programming practice as well as to present the rules of BASIC.

The style of writing is deliberately elementary. This enables the book to be easily understood by a wide reader audience, ranging from high school students to practicing professionals. The book is particularly well suited to the advanced secondary or beginning college level, either as a textbook for an elementary programming course, a supplementary text for a more comprehensive course in analytical techniques, or as an effective self-study guide. For the most part, the required mathematical level does not go beyond high school algebra.

The text is organized into two parts of about equal length. Part I – "Basic BASIC" – contains the commonly used features of the language. A brief programming course can be taught from this material alone. Part II – "Advanced BASIC" – is concerned with more specialized features, such as subroutines, matrix statements and file manipulation.

The material is presented in such a manner that the reader can write complete, though elementary, BASIC programs as soon as possible. It is very important that the reader write such programs and run them on a computer concurrently with reading the text. This greatly enhances the beginning programmer's self-confidence and stimulates his interest in the subject. (Learning to program a computer is like learning to play the drums: it cannot be learned simply by studying a textbook!)

A large number of examples are included as an integral part of the text. These include a number of comprehensive programming problems as well as the customary drill type of exercises. In addition, a set of solved problems is included at the end of most chapters. The reader should study these examples and solved problems carefully as he reads each chapter and begins to write his own programs.

Sets of review questions, supplementary problems and programming problems are also included at the end of each chapter. The review questions enable the reader to test his recall of the material presented within the chapter. They also provide an effective chapter summary. Most of the supplementary problems and programming problems require no special mathematical or technological background. The student should solve as many of these problems as possible. (Answers to the supplementary problems are provided at the end of the text.) When using this book as a course text, it may also be advisable for the instructor to supplement the programming problems with additional assignments that reflect particular disciplinary interests.

I wish to express my gratitude to Mrs. Joanne Colella for patiently and diligently typing the entire manuscript, and to the Computer Center of the University of Pittsburgh for the computer time required to solve the numerous comprehensive programming examples. Also, I wish to thank my students who used early versions of the manuscript for their many constructive suggestions.

Finally, the reader who completes this book will have learned quite a lot about general computer programming concepts as well as the specific rules of BASIC. He should be completely convinced that programming with BASIC is not only *easy* but also *fun*!

Byron S. Gottfried

Contents

Complete Programming Examples

Part I
Basic BASIC

Chapter 1

Introductory Concepts

This book offers instruction in computer programming using the programming language called BASIC (Beginner's All-purpose Symbolic Instruction Code). We will see how a problem that is initially described in words can be analyzed, outlined and finally transformed into a working BASIC program. These concepts are demonstrated in detail by the many sample problems that follow.

1.1 Computer Characteristics

What is a digital computer and how does it operate?

A computer is an *information processing* machine. In order to function it must be given a unique set of instructions, called a *program*, for each particular task it is to perform. The program is stored in the computer's internal *memory* for as long as it is needed. Once a complete program has been stored in memory it can be *executed*, causing the desired operations to be carried out.

Normally, execution of a computer program causes the following to happen:

1. The necessary information, called the *input data*, is read into the computer and stored in another sector of the computer's memory.

2. The input data is processed to produce the desired results, which are known as the *output data*.

3. Finally, the output data (and perhaps a portion of the input data) is printed out onto a sheet of paper.

Example 1.1

Suppose we wish to use a computer to calculate the area of a circle using the formula

$$A = \pi r^2$$

given a value of the radius r. The steps involved would be as follows:

1. Read a numerical value for the radius.

2. Calculate a value for the area, using the above formula.

3. Print the values of the radius and the associated area.

4. Stop.

Each of these steps might correspond to one instruction in a BASIC program. Once the complete program has been executed it can be erased from memory, or it can be saved and run again, using a different value for the radius.

We can represent the entire procedure pictorially, as shown in Fig. 1.1. This is known as a *flowchart*. Flowcharts can be helpful in assisting the reader to visualize the flow of logic in a program.

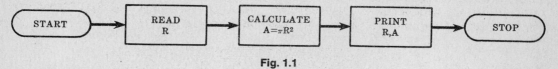

Fig. 1.1

We will consider what is meant by "reading" and "printing" in the next section. For now, however, let us take note of two important computer concepts: the computer's memory, and its ability to be programmed. Modern computers have memories that range in size from a few thousand to several hundred thousand *words*, where a word may represent an instruction, a numerical quantity or a set of characters. The size of a computer's memory is usually expressed as some multiple of $2^{10} = 1024$ words. This quantity is referred to as 1K. Thus a computer with a 48K memory will have $48 \times 1024 = 49{,}152$ words. Thus a great deal of information can be stored in the memory of even a small computer. Moreover, the unlimited number of different programs that can be written for a given computer is the principal reason for the computer's great versatility.

An additional computer characteristic is its extremely high speed. Simple tasks, such as adding two numbers, can be carried out in a fraction of a microsecond. (One microsecond, abbreviated 1 μs, is equivalent to 10^{-6}, or one millionth, of a second.) On a more practical level, the end-of-semester grades for all students in a large university can be processed in a few seconds of computer time, at a cost of about one dollar.

1.2   Modes of Operation

There are two different ways that a digital computer can be used. These are the *batch mode* and the *timesharing mode*. Both are very common. Each has its own advantages for certain types of problems.

Batch Processing

In *batch processing*, a number of jobs are read into the computer and are processed sequentially. (A *job* refers to a computer program and the sets of input data to be processed.) Usually the program and the data are recorded on punched cards. (Each character in an instruction or data item, and each digit in a numerical quantity, is represented on a punched card by an encoded set of holes. Every set of holes occupies one column of the punched card. A punched card will typically contain 80 columns. Thus as many as 80 characters or digits can be recorded on a single punched card.) Hence each job will be read into the computer via a mechanical cardreading device, and the output will be printed by means of a special printer.

Large quantities of information (both programs and data) can be transmitted into and out of the computer very quickly in batch processing. Therefore this mode of operation is well suited for jobs that require large amounts of computer time or are physically lengthy. On the other hand, the time required for a job to be processed in this manner usually varies from several hours to one or two days, even though the job may have required only a second or two of actual computer time. (The job must wait its turn before it can be read, processed and the results printed out.) Thus batch processing can be undesirable when it is necessary to process a simple job and return the results as quickly as possible.

Example 1.2

A student has 1000 different values for the radius of a circle and would like to calculate an area for each radius. To do so he must execute a computer program (such as the one described in Example 1.1) 1000 different times, once for each value of the radius. Batch processing will be used, since all of the calculations are to be carried out in rapid succession.

To process the data the student will read a deck of cards into the computer. The first part of the deck will contain the program, with one instruction per card. Following the program will be 1000 data cards, each of which will contain one value for the radius. The card deck is illustrated in Fig. 1.2.

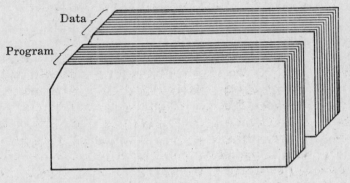

Data

Program

Fig. 1.2

After the deck of cards has been read into the computer there will be a delay of several hours before the program is executed and the input data processed. After the computation has been completed the results will be printed on a large sheet of paper. In this case the student will receive a listing that contains 1000 pairs of numbers. Each pair of numbers will represent a value for the radius and its corresponding area.

Timesharing

Timesharing involves the simultaneous use of the computer by several different users. Each user is able to communicate with the computer through a *typewriter terminal*, which may be connected to the computer by a telephone line or microwave circuit. (A commonly used typewriter terminal is shown in Fig. 1.3.) The terminals are usually located remotely from the computer — perhaps several hundred miles away. Because all of the terminals can be served at essentially the same time, each user will be unaware of the others and will seem to have the entire computer at his own personal disposal.

A single typewriter terminal serves as both input and output device. The program and the input data are typed into the computer via the keyboard, and the output data are transmitted from the computer to the typewriter terminal, where they are printed out. The transmission of data to and from the typewriter terminal is much slower, however, than the processing of the data by the computer. The processing may take 1 second, the transmission 5 minutes. (The cardreaders and printers used in batch processing are able to transmit data much more rapidly than are typewriter terminals.) It is

Fig. 1.3

this relative difference in speed that allows one computer to interact with several typewriter terminals simultaneously.

Timesharing is best suited for processing relatively simple jobs that do not require extensive data transmission or large amounts of computer time. Many of the computer applications that arise in schools and commercial offices have these characteristics. Such applications can be processed quickly, easily and at minimum expense using timesharing.

Example 1.3

A suburban high school has a computer timesharing facility consisting of 3 typewriter terminals. These terminals are connected to a large computer at a nearby university via telephone lines. Each terminal transmits data to or from the computer at a maximum speed of 10 characters per second. All 3 terminals can be used simultaneously, even though they are interacting with a single computer.

An additional 39 terminals are connected to the computer. Fifteen of these are located at 5 other high schools in the area, and the remaining 24 terminals are stationed at various places on the university campus. All 42 terminals can be (and frequently are) used at the same time. Hence a single computer is able to provide computational services for several educational institutions within a large metropolitan area. By sharing the computer in this manner, each institution is able to utilize the services of a large computer at a reasonable cost.

Example 1.4

A student has written a BASIC program that he wishes to execute in the timesharing mode. To do so, he must type his program into a typewriter terminal, one instruction at a time. Each instruction is typed on a separate line. The instructions are transmitted to the computer, where they are stored in memory as soon as they are typed.

After the entire program has been typed and stored in memory, the student can execute his program simply by typing the word RUN into the typewriter terminal. This will cause the input data to be read and the output data to be computed and then transmitted directly to the typewriter terminal.

An important feature of timesharing is the ability of the computer and the user to *interact* with one another during program execution. Thus a relatively small portion of a program may be executed and a message printed out, indicating the preliminary results that have been computed and requesting additional data from the user. Further execution of the program will be suspended until the additional data have been supplied.

In supplying the requested data, the user may be influenced by the preliminary results that have already been calculated. Thus he may wish to study the output before supplying any additional data. Moreover, the particular data supplied by the user may influence the manner in which the remainder of the program is executed. Hence the computer and the user are, in a sense, conversing with each other, since the information supplied by one of the participants may affect the subsequent actions of the other.

Programs that make use of this idea are said to be written in a *conversational mode*. Computerized games, such as tic-tac-toe, checkers and chess, are excellent examples of interactive (or conversational mode) programs.

Example 1.5

A student wishes to use a timesharing system to calculate the radius of a circle whose area has a value of 100. An interactive program is available which will calculate the area of a circle, given the radius. (Note that this is just the opposite of what the student wishes to do.) Therefore the student will proceed by trial-and-error, guessing a value for the radius and determining whether or not this value corresponds to the desired area. If not, the student will assume another value for the radius and calculate a new area, and so on. This trial-and-error procedure will continue until the student has found a value for the radius that yields an area sufficiently close to 100.

The student will communicate with the computer by means of a typewriter terminal. Once the communication link has been established and program execution begins, the message

    RADIUS=?

will be printed on the typewriter terminal. The student then enters a value for the radius. Let us assume that the student enters a value of 5 for the radius. The typewriter terminal will then respond by printing

AREA= 78.5398

DO YOU WISH TO REPEAT THE CALCULATION?

The student then types either YES or NO. If the student types YES, then the message

RADIUS=?

will again be printed, and the entire procedure is repeated. If the student types NO, then the message

GOODBYE

is printed on the typewriter terminal, and the communication link to the computer is automatically disconnected.

In Fig. 1.4 we see the information that is printed during a typical timesharing session, using the program described above. The information typed by the student has been underlined. An approximate value of $r = 5.6$ was determined after only 3 calculations.

Notice the manner in which the student and the computer appear to be conversing with one another. Also, note that the student waits until he sees a calculated area before deciding whether or not to carry out another calculation. If so, the new value that the student supplies for the radius will be influenced by the previous calculated results.

```
RADIUS=? 5
AREA= 78.5398

DO YOU WISH TO REPEAT THE CALCULATION? YES

RADIUS=? 6
AREA= 113.097

DO YOU WISH TO REPEAT THE CALCULATION? YES

RADIUS=? 5.6
AREA= 98.5204

DO YOU WISH TO REPEAT THE CALCULATION? NO

GOODBYE
```

Fig. 1.4

1.3   Introduction to BASIC

Many different kinds of languages have been developed for programming a digital computer. These languages differ considerably in their degree of difficulty, their general availability and their intended purpose.

BASIC is a digital computer programming language whose instructions resemble elementary algebraic formulas, augmented by certain English words, such as LET, GO TO, READ, PRINT, IF, THEN, etc. Thus BASIC is a simple, "people-oriented" language, in contrast to some other programming languages that are more cryptic and therefore more difficult to learn and use. Moreover, many people find that BASIC programming can be a lot of fun, in much the same way that some people enjoy solving crossword puzzles.

Because of its similarity to elementary algebra BASIC is particularly well suited to solving problems in science, mathematics and engineering. However, use of the language is by no means restricted to these areas. BASIC is also applied to a wide variety of problems in business, economics, psychology, medicine, library science — virtually any area that might require extensive manipulation of numerical data or character information. (By *character information* we mean nonnumerical symbols, letters, words, etc.) We will see a variety of elementary BASIC applications in the programming examples included in this book.

BASIC was originally developed at Dartmouth College by John Kemeny and Thomas Kurtz in the mid 1960's. The simplicity of the language attracted the attention of a number of commercial timesharing services, and it was not long before several of these services had adopted BASIC for the use of their customers. Most timesharing services now offer some version of BASIC, though there are some variations in the more advanced features. Nevertheless, the language has become sufficiently standardized so that anyone learning one version of BASIC (as presented in this book, for example) should have little difficulty in adapting to any other version.

As might be expected, BASIC is commonly thought of as a timesharing language. It is, in fact, the most widely used of all currently available timesharing languages. We will present the language from a timesharing point of view in this book. The reader should understand, however, that BASIC is also an effective batch-processing language, and its use should therefore be considered for batch as well as timesharing applications.

Structure of a BASIC Program

Each instruction in a BASIC program is written as a separate *statement*. Thus a complete BASIC program will be composed of a sequence of statements. These statements must appear in the order in which they will be executed unless a deliberate "jump" (i.e., a transfer of control) is indicated.

The following rules apply to all BASIC statements:

1. Every statement must appear on a separate line.†

2. A statement cannot exceed one line in length (i.e., cannot be "continued" from one line to the next).

3. Each statement must begin with a positive integer quantity, known as a *statement number* (or *line number*). No two statements can have the same statement number.

4. Successive statements must have increasing statement numbers.

5. Each statement number must be followed by a BASIC *keyword*, which indicates the type of instruction that is to be carried out.

6. Blank spaces may be inserted wherever desired in order to improve the readability of the statement.

It is also possible to include blank lines in a BASIC program. Every blank line must have a unique line number, however, and the line number must be followed by at least one blank space. (If a line number is followed immediately by a carriage return, then that line will be *deleted* from the program. We will discuss this further in Chapter 3.)

Example 1.6   Area of a Circle

Figure 1.5 presents a simple BASIC program to calculate the area of a circle whose radius is specified. The logic used to carry out the computation has already been discussed in Example 1.1. The program is so elementary, however, that its logical basis can be determined by simple inspection.

```
10 INPUT R
20 LET A=3.14159*R↑2
30 PRINT R,A
40 END
```

Fig. 1.5

We see that the program consists of four statements, each of which appears on a separate line. Every statement has its own statement number (or line number). These numbers increase successively from the beginning (top) to the end (bottom) of the program. The statements contain the BASIC keywords INPUT, LET, PRINT and END, respectively.

The purpose of the first statement (INPUT) is to enter a numerical value for the radius (R) from a typewriter terminal. The second statement (LET) causes the quantity πR^2 to be evaluated. This quantity will then be represented by the letter A. The third statement (PRINT) causes the numerical values for R and A to be transmitted to the typewriter terminal, where they are then printed. Finally, the last statement (END) is required in order to identify the end of the program.

Notice the symbols that are used in line 20 to represent arithmetic operations. Multiplication is indicated by an asterisk (*), and a vertical arrow (↑) is used to raise a quantity to a power. (This latter operation is known as *exponentiation*.) The other arithmetic operations, namely addition, subtraction and division, are represented in BASIC by a plus sign (+), a minus sign (−) and a slash (/), respectively.

---

†On most typewriter terminals, a line is equivalent to 72 characters. However, some typewriter terminals allow as many as 132 characters per line.

Execution of a BASIC Program

Once a BASIC program has been written it can be run on a great many different types and brands of computers. Except for a few minor differences that may exist from one version of BASIC to another, the language is machine-independent. This has been a significant factor in the widespread acceptance of BASIC.

The reason for this independence from a machine is that execution of a BASIC program is actually a two-step procedure. The first step, called *compilation*, causes the BASIC statements to be converted to the computer's own *machine-language* instruction set. (*Machine language* consists of a large number of very detailed instructions that are related to the computer's internal, electronic circuitry. Every computer has its own machine language. Programming in machine language is much more difficult than programming in a higher-level language, such as BASIC. Moreover, machine-language programs are not transferable from one type of computer to another.) Accordingly, the BASIC program is referred to as the *source* program. In the second step the resulting machine-language program, called the *object* program, is executed, causing the input data to be processed in the desired manner.

Usually the object program will be executed immediately after it has been compiled. The programmer will not be aware that two distinct steps have taken place, since he sees only the source program, the input data and the computed output data.

Some Advantages of BASIC

1. BASIC is "people-oriented." It is easy to learn and fun to use. Any well-organized person can learn to program in BASIC. An extensive background in mathematics is not necessary.

2. The language is flexible, allowing the programmer to alter an existing program with very little effort.

3. BASIC is well suited for use in a timesharing system, which offers the programmer the use of a large computer at minimum expense.

4. Except for minor differences between one version of BASIC and another, the language is machine-independent. Hence a BASIC program can be run on many different computers.

Review Questions

1.1 A digital computer can be thought of as what kind of a machine?

1.2 What is meant by a computer program?

1.3 What, in general, happens when a computer program is executed?

1.4 What is a computer memory? What kinds of information are stored in a computer's memory?

1.5 What terms are used to describe the size of a computer's memory? What are some typical memory sizes?

1.6   What time unit is used to express the speed with which elementary tasks are carried out by a computer?

1.7   What is meant by batch processing and timesharing?   Describe the advantages and disadvantages of each.

1.8   In what sense can a computer and a user interact with one another?   What is meant by a conversational mode program?

1.9   What does the word BASIC stand for?   What are the general characteristics of the BASIC language?

1.10   What is a BASIC statement?   In what order must the statements appear in a BASIC program?

1.11   Summarize the 6 rules that apply to all BASIC statements.

1.12   In BASIC, what are the symbols that are used to indicate addition, subtraction, multiplication and division?

1.13   What is meant by exponentiation?   What symbol is used in BASIC to represent exponentiation?

1.14   What is meant by compilation of a BASIC program?   What is a source program?   Object program?   Why are these concepts important?

1.15   Summarize the principal features of the BASIC language.

Solved Problems

1.16   Several elementary BASIC programs are presented below.   Explain the purpose of each program.

(a)   10 INPUT L,W
        20 LET A=L*W
        30 PRINT L,W,A
        40 END

   To calculate the area of a rectangle whose length and width are given.

(b)   10 INPUT A,B,C,D,E
        20 LET S=A+B+C+D+E
        30 PRINT A,B,C,D,E
        40 PRINT S
        50 END

   To calculate the sum of 5 numbers.   Note that the 5 numbers will be printed on one line, and the calculated sum on the next line.   (Each PRINT statement begins on a new line.)

(c)   10 INPUT A,B,C
        20 LET X1=(−B+(B↑2−4*A*C)↑.5)/(2*A)
        30 LET X2=(−B−(B↑2−4*A*C)↑.5)/(2*A)
        40 PRINT A,B,C,X1,X2
        50 END

To calculate values for x_1 and x_2 from the formulas

$$x_1 = \frac{-b + \sqrt{b^2 - 4ac}}{2a}$$

$$x_2 = \frac{-b - \sqrt{b^2 - 4ac}}{2a}$$

where the values for a, b and c are specified.

1.17 Write an elementary BASIC program for each of the situations described below.

(a) Calculate the radius of a circle whose area is known (see Example 1.6).

Since $A = \pi r^2$ we can solve for r, which yields

$$r = \sqrt{A/\pi}$$

Hence the desired program is

```
10 INPUT A
20 LET R=(A/3.141593)↑.5
30 PRINT A,R
40 END
```

(b) Calculate the length of a rectangle whose area and width are known [see Problem 1.16(a)].

```
10 INPUT A,W
20 LET L=A/W
30 PRINT A,W,L
40 END
```

(c) Calculate the product of 5 given numbers [see Problem 1.16(b)].

```
10 INPUT A,B,C,D,E
20 LET P=A*B*C*D*E
30 PRINT A,B,C,D,E
40 PRINT P
50 END
```

Supplementary Problems

1.18 Several elementary BASIC programs are presented below. Explain the purpose of each program.

(a)
```
10 INPUT B,H
20 LET A=(B*H)/2
30 PRINT B,H,A
40 END
```

(b)
```
10 INPUT L,W,
20 LET C=2*(L+W)
30 PRINT L,W,C
40 END
```

(c)
```
10 INPUT U,V
20 LET W=U+V
30 LET X=U−V
40 LET Y=U*V
50 LET Z=U/V
60 PRINT U,V
70 PRINT W,X,Y,Z
80 END
```

    (*d*)   10 INPUT X
           20 LET Y=1+X+(X↑2)/2+(X↑3)/6
           30 PRINT X,Y
           40 END

1.19   Write an elementary BASIC program for each of the situations described below.

(*a*) Calculate the circumference of a circle whose radius is given (see Example 1.6).

(*b*) Calculate the length of the hypotenuse of a right triangle whose base and height are given [see Problem 1.18(*a*)].

(*c*) Evaluate the formula

$$w = \frac{u - v}{u + v}$$

where u and v are given [see Problem 1.18(*c*)].

(*d*) Evaluate the formula

$$y = 100(1 + x + 2x^2 + 3x^3)$$

where x is specified [see Problem 1.18(*d*)].

1.20   Shown below is a BASIC program to calculate the area and perimeter of a rectangle and the length of the diagonal. Some of the statements are written incorrectly. Identify all errors.

          10 INPUT L,W
          20 LET A=L*W   30 LET P=2*(L+W)
          35 D=(L↑2+W↑2)↑.5
          25 PRINT L,W,A,P,D
          40 END

Chapter 2

Getting Started with BASIC

In this chapter we will examine several fundamental concepts of the BASIC language, such as numbers, variables and formulas. Then we will consider the six most commonly used BASIC statements, which allow us to do input/output and data manipulation operations and jump to other parts of a program whenever we wish. After completing this chapter the reader will be able to write his own BASIC programs for a variety of problem situations.

2.1 Numbers (Constants)

Numerical quantities are referred to in BASIC as *numbers* (or *constants*). Numbers can be expressed two different ways: as integer quantities (whole numbers, without a decimal point) or as decimal quantities (numbers that have a decimal point). The following rules apply to the writing of numbers:

1. Commas cannot appear anywhere in a number.

2. A number can be preceded by a + or − sign. (The number is understood to be positive if a sign does not appear.)

3. A number can contain an exponent, if desired. Exponential notation is similar to scientific notation, except that the base 10 is replaced by the letter E. (Thus the quantity 1.2×10^{-3} could be written in BASIC as 1.2E−3.) The exponent can be either positive or negative but cannot have a decimal point.

4. Most versions of BASIC allow a number to have as many as 8 or 9 significant figures.

5. Typically the magnitude of a number can be as large as 10^{38} and as small as 10^{-38}. (These values vary from one version of BASIC to another.) A value of zero is also permissible.

Example 2.1

The numerical quantities below are expressed as valid BASIC numbers. Note that each quantity (each row) can be written in several different ways.

0	+0	−0
1	+1	0.1E+1
−5280	−5.280E+3	−.5280E4
+1492	1492	1.492E+3
−.0000613	−6.13 E−5	−613 E−7
3000000	3E6	3 E+6

2.2   Strings

A *string* is a sequence of characters (i.e., letters, numbers and certain special characters, such as $+$, $-$, $/$, $*$, $=$, $\$$, ., etc.).   Blank spaces may be included in a string but not quotation marks.   The maximum number of characters that can be included in a string will vary from one version of BASIC to another.   In some versions a string cannot exceed 15 characters, while others allow as many as 4095 characters.

Strings are used to represent nonnumeric information — names, addresses, etc.   They are also used to label numerical output data and print out textual messages (applications that we will see later in the book).

Example 2.2

Here are several strings.

        SANTA CLAUS $19.95
        APOLLO—17   3730425
        X1=   THE ANSWER IS
        DO YOU WISH TO TRY AGAIN?
        TYPE A VALUE FOR C:

Note that each of the last two lines contains only one string.   Also note that a sequence of integers, such as 3730425, *does not* represent a numerical quantity when written as a string.

2.3   Variables

A *variable* is a name that represents a number or a string.   Each *numeric variable* must consist of a letter or a letter followed by an integer.   A *string variable* must be written as a letter followed by a dollar sign.   Most versions of BASIC also allow a string variable to be written as a letter, followed by an integer, followed by a dollar sign.

Example 2.3

Each of the following variables can represent a numerical quantity:

        A   K   X   C1   X5

Any of the following variables can represent a string:

        A$ K$ X$ C$ T$

In many versions of BASIC a string can also be represented by any of the following variables:

        A2$ K9$ X0$ C1$ X5$

2.4   Operators and Formulas (Expressions)

In BASIC we use special symbols, called *operators*, to indicate the arithmetic operations of addition, subtraction, multiplication, division and exponentiation.   These operators are

        Addition: +   (plus sign)
        Subtraction: −   (minus sign)
        Multiplication: *   (asterisk)
        Division: /   (slash)
        Exponentiation: ↑   (vertical arrow)

The operators are used to connect numbers and numerical variables, thus forming *formulas* (or *expressions*).

The indicated operations are carried out on the numeric terms in a formula, resulting in a single numerical value.   Hence *a formula represents a specific numerical quantity*.

Example 2.4

Several BASIC formulas are presented below:

        J+1
        A+B−C
        (2*X−3*Y)/(U+V)
        3.141593*R↑2
        B↑2−4*A*C

Each formula represents a numerical quantity. Thus if the variables A, B and C represent the numerical quantities 2, 5 and 3, respectively, the formula A+B−C will represent the quantity 4.

Strictly speaking, a formula can be composed of a single number or a single numeric variable as well as some combination of numbers, numeric variables and operators. It is important to understand, however, that *a numeric variable must be assigned some numerical quantity before it can appear in a formula.* Otherwise the formula could not be evaluated to yield a numerical value.

2.5 Hierarchy of Operations

Questions in meaning may arise when we have two or more operators in a formula. For example, does the formula 2*X−3*Y correspond to the algebraic term $(2x) - (3y)$ or to $2(x - 3y)$? Similarly, does A/B*C correspond to $a/(bc)$ or to $(a/b)c$? These questions can easily be answered once we have become familiar with the *hierarchy of operations* and the *order of execution* within a given hierarchical group.

The hierarchy of operations is

1. *Exponentiation.* All exponentiation operations are performed first.

2. *Multiplication and division.* These operations are carried out after all exponentiation operations have been performed. Multiplication does not necessarily precede division.

3. *Addition and subtraction.* These operations are the last to be carried out. Addition does not necessarily precede subtraction.

Within a given hierarchical group the operations are carried out from left to right.

Example 2.5

The formula

        A/B*C

is equivalent to the mathematical expression $(a/b)c$, since the operations are carried out from left to right.

Similarly, the formula

        B↑2−4*A*C

is equivalent to the mathematical expression $b^2 - (4ac)$. In this case the quantity B↑2 is formed initially, followed by the product 4*A*C (first 4*A, then (4*A)*C). The subtraction is performed last, resulting in the quantity (B↑2)−(4*A*C).

2.6 Use of Parentheses

There are many situations in which we will want to alter the normal hierarchy of operations in a formula. This is easily accomplished by inserting pairs of parentheses at the proper places within the formula. The operations within the innermost pairs of parentheses will then be performed first, followed by the operations within the second innermost pairs, and so on. Within a given pair of parentheses the natural hierarchy of operations will apply unless specifically altered by other pairs of parentheses imbedded inside the given pair.

We must remember always to use *pairs* of parentheses.   A careless imbalance of right and left parentheses is a common error.

Example 2.6

Suppose we want to evaluate the term

$$[2(a + b)^2 + (3c)^2]^{m/(n+1)}$$

A BASIC formula that corresponds to this algebraic term is

(2*(A+B)↑2+(3*C)↑2)↑(M/(N+1))

If there is some uncertainty in the order in which the operations are carried out, we can introduce additional pairs of parentheses, giving

((2*((A+B)↑2))+((3*C)↑2))↑(M/(N+1))

Both formulas are correct.   The first formula may be preferable, however, since it is less cluttered with parentheses and therefore easier to read.

2.7   Special Rules Concerning Formulas

Special problems can arise if a formula is not correctly written.   They can be avoided by applying these rules.

1. Preceding a variable by a minus sign is equivalent to multiplication by −1.

   Example 2.7

   The formula

   −X↑N

   is equivalent to −(X↑N) or −1*(X↑N), since exponentiation has precedence over multiplication. Hence if X and N are assigned values of 3 and 2, respectively, then −X↑N will yield a value of −9.

2. Except for the condition just described, operations cannot be implied.

   Example 2.8

   The algebraic expression $2(x_1 + 3x_2)$ must be written in BASIC as

   2*(X1+3*X2)

   with the multiplication operators shown explicitly.   The formulas 2(X1+3*X2) and 2*(X1+3X2) are incorrect.

3. A negative quantity can be raised to a power only if the exponent is an integer.   (Do not confuse the exponent in an *exponentiation formula* with the exponent that is a part of a *decimal number*.)

   To understand this restriction, we must see how exponentiation is carried out. If the exponent is an *integer* quantity, then the quantity to be exponentiated is multiplied by itself an appropriate number of times.

   On the other hand, suppose the exponent is a *decimal* quantity.   The procedure used with a decimal exponent is to compute the *logarithm* of the quantity being exponentiated, multiply this logarithm by the exponent and then compute the antilog. Since the logarithm of a negative number is not defined, we see that the operation is invalid if the quantity being exponentiated is negative.

   Example 2.9

   Consider the formula

   (C1+C2)↑3

   The quantity represented by (C1+C2) is multiplied by itself twice, thus forming the cubic expression.   Notice that it does not matter whether the quantity (C1+C2) is positive or negative.

However, the formula

$$(B\uparrow2-4*A*C)\uparrow.5$$

will be valid only if $B\uparrow2-4*A*C$ represents a positive quantity.

Finally, consider what happens when either A or N in the expression

$$A\uparrow N$$

is zero. If N has a value of zero, then $A\uparrow N$ will be assigned a value of 1, regardless of the value of A. If A has a value of zero and N is nonzero, however, $A\uparrow N$ will be evaluated as zero.

4. Numerical operations cannot be performed on strings or string variables.

Example 2.10

The formula

$$X\$-Y\$+\text{"DOLLARS"}$$

is not valid, since it is not meaningful to add or subtract character sets (strings).

2.8   Assigning Values—The LET Statement

The *LET statement* is used to assign a numerical or a string value to a variable. We can *define* a particular variable in a program by establishing its value in this manner.

A LET statement is composed of a statement number, followed by the keyword LET, followed by an *assignment* term that resembles a mathematical equation. The assignment term must consist of a variable, an equal sign and a formula, as shown in the examples below.

Example 2.11

```
10 LET X=12.5
20 LET C1=F3
30 LET A=3.141593*R↑2
40 LET N$="NAME"
50 LET T$=N$
```

In each of these statements the value of the term to the right of the equal sign is assigned to the variable on the left.

Note that the variable to the left of the equal sign and the term to the right must be of the same type (either numeric or string). In other words, a numerical value cannot be assigned to a string variable, and vice versa. Also, note that a string must be enclosed in quotation marks if it appears in a LET statement.

It is important to understand the difference between the assignment term that appears in the LET statement and an algebraic equation. Many assignment terms look like algebraic equations. On the other hand, there are certain legitimate assignment terms that would make no sense if viewed as algebraic equations.

Example 2.12

Consider the following LET statement, which is both correct and meaningful:

```
5 LET J=J+1
```

The assignment term J=J+1 obviously does not correspond to an algebraic equation, since the equation $j = j + 1$ makes no sense. What we are doing here is to increase the value of the numeric variable J by one unit. Thus the assignment term is entirely logical if we interpret it as follows: add one to the value represented by the variable J, and assign this new value to J. Note that this new value of J will replace the old value.

We will see that LET statements of this type are used quite often in BASIC.

Some versions of BASIC allow greater flexibility in writing LET statements than others. For example, in some versions of BASIC it is possible to assign the same value to two or more variables in a single LET statement. Moreover, the keyword LET can be omitted in certain versions of BASIC.

Example 2.13

The following LET statements would be permitted in *some* versions of BASIC:

```
10  LET A=B=C=5.089
20  A=L*W
30  X1=X2=(A+B)/(C+D)
40  LET A$=K$="TERMINATE"
```

Notice that the first, third and fourth statements involve multiple assignments and that the keyword LET has been omitted from the second and third statements.

2.9   Reading Input—The INPUT Statement

The *INPUT statement* is used to enter numerical or string data into the computer during program execution. The statement consists of a statement number, the keyword INPUT and a list of variables. Both numeric and string variables can be included in the list. The variables must be separated by commas.

Example 2.14

```
 5  INPUT A,B,C
10  INPUT N$,M$,X0,F5
15  INPUT P(I),Q(I),T$(I)
```

The variables shown in the last statement are called *subscripted variables*. We will discuss subscripted variables in Chapter 5.

When an INPUT statement is encountered during program execution, a question mark (?) is printed on the typewriter terminal, indicating a request for data. Normally the question mark appears at the start of a new line. Further execution of the program is suspended until the requested data have been supplied.

Once the question mark appears, the programmer (or program user) must supply the requested information by typing the appropriate data into the typewriter terminal, followed by a carriage return. The data will then be transmitted to the computer, and program execution will resume. Thus the INPUT statement can be particularly useful in conversational mode programming.

The following rules must be observed when entering the required input data:

1. The data items must correspond in number and in type to the variables listed in the INPUT statement (i.e., numbers must be supplied for numeric variables, strings for string variables). Extra data items will be ignored.

2. The data items must be separated by commas.

3. The data items must consist of numbers and strings. Formulas are not permitted.

4. Strings containing commas or beginning with blank spaces must be enclosed in quotation marks. Other strings may be enclosed in quotation marks if desired.

Example 2.15

Suppose that the statement

```
60  INPUT X,Y,C$
```

is encountered during execution of a BASIC program. This will cause a question mark to be printed at the start of a new line on the typewriter terminal. Further program execution will temporarily be suspended.

When the user sees the question mark, he proceeds to enter the required input data. Suppose the appropriate values for X, Y and C\$ are 5, -1.2×10^{-3} and NOVEMBER 27, 1937. The line of input data would then appear as

> ? 5,−1.2E−3,"NOVEMBER 27, 1937"

After the data have been typed, the user depresses the carriage return, causing the data to be transmitted to the computer. Execution of the remainder of the program then proceeds in the normal manner.

The INPUT statement is quite useful for elementary programs not requiring large quantities of input data. The entering of data via an INPUT statement, however, is relatively time-consuming, and data entered in this manner cannot be stored for subsequent use. (In most BASIC systems a *program* can be stored indefinitely and rerun whenever desired.) We will see another method for providing input data in Chapter 5.

2.10   Printing Output—The PRINT Statement

The *PRINT statement* is used to transmit numerical or string output data from the computer. The statement consists of a statement number, the keyword PRINT and a list of output items. The output items can be numbers, formulas or strings. Successive items must be separated by either commas or semicolons.

Example 2.16

```
100  PRINT A,B,C
110  PRINT "X=";X,"Y=";Y
120  PRINT "NAME:";N$,"ADDRESS:";A$
130  PRINT
140  PRINT K;C$(K);5*X0↑2/2;U(I)+V(I);P$
```

The variables C\$(K), U(I) and V(I) in the last statement are called *subscripted variables*. We will discuss subscripted variables in Chapter 5.

The following rules must be followed when writing a PRINT statement.

Line Spacing

1. Each PRINT statement begins a new line of output (an exception is discussed in rules 5 and 6 below). However, two or more lines of output will be generated by a single PRINT statement if the list of data items has a large number of entries.

   Example 2.17

   The PRINT statement

   > 50 PRINT C1,C2,C3,C4,C5,C6,C7,C8

   will cause the values of C1 through C5 to be printed on one line, and the values of C6 through C8 to be printed on the second line. Suppose, for example, that C1 through C8 represent the following values:

   ```
   C1=3
   C2=−12
   C3=6.5
   C4=5000
   C5=0
   C6=.0047
   C7=−8
   C8=7.2E−15
   ```

   The output would appear as

   ```
   3            -12          6.5          5000         0
   0.0047       -8           7.20000E-15
   ```

2. If a PRINT statement does not contain any data items, then a blank line will appear. This is a useful way to control the vertical spacing of output data.

Example 2.18

The PRINT statements

        40 PRINT C1,C2,C3,C4
        50 PRINT
        60 PRINT C5,C6,C7,C8

will cause the values of C1 through C4 to be printed on one line and C5 through C8 to be printed on another line, with a blank line between them.

If C1 through C8 have the same values indicated in Example 2.17, then the output resulting from the above three print statements will appear as

    3   -12   6.5   5000

    0   0.0047   -8   7.20000E-15

Significant Figures

3. Numerical output quantities will appear as follows:

In most versions of BASIC, an integer quantity that contains 8 or less digits will be printed as an integer number. If an integer quantity exceeds 8 digits, it will be rounded to 6 significant figures and printed as a decimal number with an exponent.

A decimal quantity will be printed as a decimal number. If the quantity contains more than 6 digits (including any leading zeros to the right of the decimal point), it will be rounded to 6 digits. An exponent will be shown if the magnitude of the number exceeds 999999, or is less than 0.1 and contains more than 6 significant figures.

Example 2.19

Suppose a BASIC program contains the variables A, B, C, D, E and F, which have been assigned the following values:

        A=1234567
        B=123456789
        C=-0.001234
        D=0.000012345
        E=-1234.5
        F=1234567.89

The statements

        100 PRINT A,B,C
        110 PRINT D,E,F

would generate the following two lines of output:

        1234567   1.23457E+8   -0.001234
        1.23450E-5   -1234.5   1.23457E+6

Strings

4. Strings must be enclosed in quotation marks. (See Example 2.20, below.)

Spacing of Output Items Within a Line

5. If the data items in the output list are separated by commas, then each line of output will be divided into 5 zones of equal length, and one output value will be printed in each zone.

Example 2.20

A BASIC program contains the statement

65 PRINT "NAME",N$,X,.5*(C1+C2)

If the variables have been assigned the values

N$=CINNAMON   C1=7
X=39   C2=11

then the above PRINT statement will generate the following line of output:

N AME   CINNAMØN   39   9

Other illustrations of the use of commas in a PRINT statement are shown in Examples 2.17, 2.18 and 2.19.

If a comma follows the *last* item in the data list, then the next output quantity (i.e., the first output quantity in a subsequent PRINT statement) will be printed on the same line providing sufficient space is available. (Note that this produces an exception to rule 1 on page 19.)

Example 2.21

The statements

100 PRINT A,B,C,
110 PRINT D,E,F

will cause the values of A, B, C, D and E to be printed on one line, followed by the value of F on the next line.

If A, B, C, D, E and F have been assigned the same numerical values as in Example 2.19, the output resulting from the above PRINT statements will appear as follows:

1234567   1•23457E+8   -0•001234   1•23450E-5   -1234•5
1•23457E+6

(Compare with the results in Example 2.19.)

As many as 4 commas can appear consecutively if desired. The effect of each comma is to position the print mechanism of the typewriter terminal at the start of the next zone. Thus it is possible to print widely spaced data in this manner.

Example 2.22

A BASIC program contains the statements

120 PRINT A,B,C,D,E
130 PRINT F,,,,G

If the variables have been assigned the following values

A=1   C=3   E=5   G=7
B=2   D=4   F=6

then the above statements will generate the following lines of output:

1   2   3   4   5
6   7

6. If semicolons are used rather than commas to separate numerical data items in an output list, then the output values will be spaced more closely together. The particular spacing will depend on the number of digits or characters in each output item. By using semicolons in this manner it is possible to print more than 5 output quantities on each line.

Example 2.23

A BASIC program contains the statement

100 PRINT A1;A2;A3;A4;A5;A6;A7;A8

If the variables have been assigned the following values

A1=11	A5=15
A2=12	A6=16
A3=13	A7=17
A4=14	A8=18

then the above PRINT statement will generate the following line of output

$$11 \quad 12 \quad 13 \quad 14 \quad 15 \quad 16 \quad 17 \quad 18$$

If a semicolon follows a string or a string variable in an output list, then the string will be printed without any trailing spaces, and the next output item will be printed immediately beyond the string.

Example 2.24

A BASIC program contains the statement

    200 PRINT "X=";X,"Y=";Y

If the variables are assigned the values X=12 and Y=−5, then the above statement will generate the following line of output:

$$X=12 \qquad\qquad Y=-5$$

In many BASIC programs an INPUT statement is preceded by a PRINT statement that contains a string. The purpose of the PRINT statement is to produce a message describing the required input data. If the string is followed by a semicolon, then the question mark generated by the INPUT statement will appear at the end of the printed message.

Example 2.25

A BASIC program has been written to compute the area and circumference of a circle. The first step in executing the program is to read in a value of the radius. Hence the program will contain the statements

    10 PRINT "RADIUS=";
    20 INPUT R

These two statements will cause the following line of output to be printed by the typewriter terminal:

    RADIUS=?

The user then types a value for R (the radius) into the terminal (as shown in Example 1.5).

Finally, it should be understood that the effect of placing a semicolon after the last entry in the data list is the same as the placement of a comma in this position (i.e., the next printed quantity will appear on the same line). We have just seen an illustration of this in Example 2.25.

2.11   The END Statement

The *END statement* indicates the end of a BASIC program. The statement consists simply of a statement number followed by the keyword END. It must be the last statement in the program, and it must have the highest statement number.

One use of the END statement is shown in Example 1.6. For another such illustration, see Example 2.26.

2.12   Writing Complete BASIC Programs

By now we have learned how to read data into the computer, perform arithmetic calculations and write out the results. Hence we can carry out all of the major steps in a complete (though simple) BASIC program.

In Chapter 3, we will discuss the mechanics of entering a program into the computer, editing the program and executing the program. For now we will be concerned only with writing simple programs. Example 2.26 illustrates such a program. The reader is urged to write a few other programs of this nature on his own. (Several suggestions are given at the end of this chapter.)

Example 2.26   Roots of a Quadratic Equation

We wish to calculate the roots of a quadratic equation, using the well-known formulas

$$x_1 = \frac{-b + \sqrt{b^2 - 4ac}}{2a} \qquad x_2 = \frac{-b - \sqrt{b^2 - 4ac}}{2a}$$

Let us assume that the values of a, b and c are such that $b^2 - 4ac$ will always be positive. Therefore we need not worry about calculating the square root of a negative number.

The steps to be followed are these:

1. Read numerical values for a, b and c.

2. Calculate a value for $\sqrt{b^2 - 4ac}$.

3. Calculate values for x_1 and x_2, using the above formulas.

4. Print the values for a, b, c, x_1 and x_2.

5. Stop.

A corresponding flowchart is shown in Fig. 2.1.

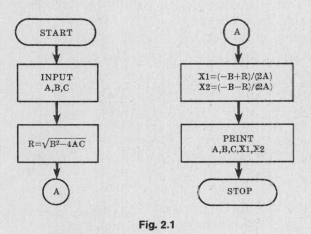

Fig. 2.1

If we make use of the material presented earlier in this chapter, it is quite simple to write a complete BASIC program to carry out the calculations. Step 1 can be implemented by means of a PRINT and an INPUT statement, and Steps 2 and 3 can be accommodated by LET statements. PRINT statements will be required for Step 4 and an END statement for Step 5. The desired BASIC program is shown in Fig. 2.2.

```
10 PRINT "ENTER VALUES FØR A, B AND C"
20 INPUT A,B,C
30 LET R=(B↑2-4*A*C)↑.5
40 LET X1=(-B+R)/(2*A)
50 LET X2=(-B-R)/(2*A)
60 PRINT
70 PRINT "A=";A,"B=";B,"C=";C
80 PRINT "X1=";X1,"X2=";X2
90 END
>RUN

ENTER VALUES FØR A, B AND C
 ?2,5,3

A= 2            B= 5            C= 3
X1=-1           X2=-1.5
```

Fig. 2.2

At the bottom of Fig. 2.2 is the output generated by the program for $a = 2$, $b = 5$ and $c = 3$. (We will discuss the method for executing a BASIC program in Chapter 3.) We see that x_1 has a value of -1, and x_2 a value of -1.5.

2.13   Program Comments—The REM Statement

The most common way to introduce remarks (comments) into a BASIC program is to make use of the *REM* (*REMARK*) *statement*. This statement consists of a statement number followed by the keyword REM and a textual message. REM statements can be inserted anywhere in a BASIC program.

Example 2.27

A typical REM statement is shown below:

    5 REM PROGRAM TO CALCULATE THE ROOTS OF A QUADRATIC EQUATION

This statement would provide an appropriate heading for the program presented in Example 2.26.

REM statements do not provide any executable instructions for the computer. They are, however, listed with all the other statements in a BASIC program, in correct sequential order. Thus they offer the programmer a convenient means to *document* a program (i.e., to provide a program heading, to identify important variables and to distinguish the major logical segments of a program). We will see numerous illustrations of the use of REM statements in subsequent examples.

Surrounding the REM statement with blank lines causes the remarks of the REM statement to stand out clearly from the rest of the program, thus adding to the clarity of the program documentation.

Sometimes it is desirable to add a comment explaining a certain key statement in a BASIC program. This can, of course, be accomplished with a REM statement. An even more desirable method, however, might be to place the comment on the same line as the statement. A comment of this type must be preceded by an apostrophe in order to distinguish it from the end of the statement. Such a comment cannot exceed the remaining length of the line.

Example 2.28

Add the comments CALCULATE FIRST ROOT and CALCULATE SECOND ROOT to the fourth and fifth statements, respectively, of the program shown in Fig. 2.2.

The fourth and fifth statements will appear as

    40 LET X1=(-B+R)/(2*A)   'CALCULATE FIRST ROOT
    50 LET X2=(-B-R)/(2*A)   'CALCULATE SECOND ROOT

2.14   Transferring Control—The GO TO Statement

Normally the statements in a BASIC program are executed in the same order as they appear, one after another. Sometimes, however, it is necessary to "jump" to some other part of the program, thus altering the normal sequence of execution. This can be accomplished by means of the *GO TO statement*. We usually refer to such a jump as an *unconditional branching* operation, or as a *transfer of control*. Hence the GO TO statement allows us to transfer control to any other statement in a BASIC program (including a REM statement).

The GO TO statement consists of a statement number, followed by the keywords GO TO and the number of the statement to which control will be transferred.

Example 2.29

A BASIC program contains the following GO TO statement.

    100 GO TO 10

Thus the computer is instructed to execute statement number 10 next.

We will consider branching operations in much more detail in Chapter 4. For now we will restrict our attention to one simple but important application of the GO TO statement.

2.15   Repetitious Program Execution

Many situations arise that require the use of a BASIC program to process several sets of data, one after the other. This can easily be accomplished by ending the program with a transfer of control back to the "read input" statements, thus causing successive sets of input data to be read into the computer and then processed. (Note that we are referring to the *logical* ending of the program, not the *physical* ending. The last *physical* statement in the program must still be the END statement.) This procedure continues until all of the input data have been processed, at which time the user terminates his connection to the computer.

The transfer of control is usually carried out by means of a GO TO statement. Example 2.30 illustrates.

Example 2.30   Roots of a Quadratic Equation

Let us modify the BASIC program presented in Example 2.26 so that we can process several sets of input data (i.e., several different radii) sequentially. If we examine the program shown in Fig. 2.2 we see that the modification can easily be carried out if we add a "GO TO 10" statement immediately before the END statement.

The modified program is shown in Fig. 2.3. Note that we have added an empty PRINT statement and a GO TO 10 statement near the end of the program. The purpose of the empty PRINT statement is to separate the output data from the successive input messages. Also, note that we have added a REM statement at the beginning of the program and that comments have been added to lines 40 and 50.

```
5    REM PRØGRAM TØ CALCULATE THE RØØTS ØF A QUADRATIC EQUATIØN
10   PRINT "ENTER VALUES FØR A, B AND C"
20   INPUT A,B,C
30   LET R=(B↑2-4*A*C)↑.5
40   LET X1=(-B+R)/(2*A)     'CALCULATE FIRST RØØT
50   LET X2=(-B-R)/(2*A)     'CALCULATE SECØND RØØT
60   PRINT
70   PRINT "A=";A,"B=";B,"C=";C
80   PRINT "X1=";X1,"X2=";X2
90   PRINT
100  GØ TØ 10
110  END
>RUN


ENTER VALUES FØR A, B AND C
 ?2,6,1

A= 2          B= 6          C= 1
X1=-0.177124  X2=-2.82288

ENTER VALUES FØR A, B AND C
 ?3,3,0

A= 3          B= 3          C= 0
X1=-9.93411E-9            X2=-1.

ENTER VALUES FØR A, B AND C
 ?1,3,1

A= 1          B= 3          C= 1
X1=-0.381966  X2=-2.61803
```

Fig. 2.3

At the bottom of Fig. 2.3 we see the output resulting from three different sets of values for a, b and c. (Notice that the second value for x_1 is calculated as -9.9×10^{-9} rather than zero, which is the exact answer.)   The connection to the computer was terminated after processing the third set of data, though the procedure could have been continued as long as we had wished.

2.16   Closing Remarks

By now we have learned enough about BASIC so that the reader can organize and write complete, though elementary, programs of his own.   Later chapters will show how to write programs that are more interesting, challenging and sophisticated.

Review Questions

2.1   Name two different ways that numbers (constants) can be written in BASIC.

2.2   Summarize the grammatical rules for writing numbers.

2.3   Present a detailed comparison between a number written in scientific notation and a number written in BASIC as a decimal quantity with an exponent.

2.4   What is a string?   What are strings used for?

2.5   Summarize the grammatical rules for writing numeric and string variables.

2.6   What are the arithmetic operators used in BASIC?   What is their natural hierarchy?   In what order are operations carried out within a hierarchical group?

2.7   What is a formula (expression) in BASIC?   What does a formula represent?

2.8   How can the natural hierarchy of operations be altered in a formula?

2.9   Cite a particular problem that can arise in exponentiation operations.   Present the reason for the problem, and describe how the problem can be avoided.

2.10   What is the purpose of the LET statement?

2.11   Summarize the grammatical rules for writing a LET statement.

2.12   Discuss the similarities and differences between a LET statement and an algebraic equation.

2.13   In what ways are the rules for writing a LET statement relaxed in some versions of BASIC?

2.14   What is the purpose of the INPUT statement?

2.15   What happens when an INPUT statement is encountered during execution of a BASIC program?

2.16   Summarize the grammatical rules for writing an INPUT statement.

2.17   Cite two disadvantages in the use of INPUT statements for entering data into the computer.

2.18   What is the purpose of the PRINT statement?

2.19   Summarize the grammatical rules that apply to each of the following aspects of the PRINT statement:

(a) The generation and spacing of lines of output.

(b) The appearance of numerical output quantities and the maximum number of significant figures.

(c) The treatment of strings.

(d) The spacing of numerical quantities and strings within a line of output.

2.20 In what way can a PRINT statement be used in conjunction with an INPUT statement when reading data into the computer?

2.21 What is the purpose of the END statement? What are the rules associated with its use?

2.22 What is the purpose of the REM statement? What rules govern its use?

2.23 What is meant by program documentation? How can program documentation be carried out in BASIC?

2.24 What is the purpose of the GO TO statement? How is it written?

2.25 Name one statement that *must* be present in every BASIC program. Where will this statement appear? What can be said about its statement number?

2.26 Exactly what advantage is there in writing a BASIC program that can be executed repetitiously? Is a significant amount of programming effort required to write a program in this manner?

Solved Problems

2.27 Express each of the following quantities as a BASIC number.

Quantity	BASIC Number
7,350	7350 or 7.35E+3
−12	−12
10^6	1000000 or 1E+6
$-2,053.18 \times 10^3$	−2053180 or −2.05318E+6
0.00008291	0.00008291 or 8.291E−5
9.563×10^{12}	9.563E+12
1/6	0.16666667

2.28 Each of the following BASIC numbers is written incorrectly. Identify the errors.

Number	Error
7,104	comma not allowed
−+4920	double sign not allowed
2.665E+42	exponent is too large in magnitude
0.333333333333	too many significant figures
4.63E−0.8	exponent cannot contain a decimal point

2.29 Each of the following items represents a BASIC string. Identify which, if any, are written incorrectly.

String	Error
TWENTY-SEVEN	correct
2+5=7	correct
ENTER ALL INPUT DATA	too long for some versions of BASIC
75.50	correct
SYMBOL IS "X"	quotation marks are not allowed

2.30 Each of the following represents a numeric variable. Identify which, if any, **are** written incorrectly.

Variable	Error
XR	second character, if present, must be an integer
Q	correct
C23	too many characters
8C	first character must be a letter; second character, if present, must be an integer
BIGC	too many characters
J8	correct
A$	second character, if present, must be an integer

2.31 Each of the following represents a string variable. Identify which, if any, **are** written incorrectly.

Variable	Error
N$	correct
C	dollar sign is missing
Z$3	last character must be a dollar sign; some versions of BASIC allow only 2 characters
Z3$	may be correct, though some versions of BASIC allow only 2 characters
E$	correct

2.32 Write a BASIC formula that corresponds to each of the following **algebraic expressions.**

Algebraic Expression	BASIC Formula
$3x + 5$	3*X+5
$i + j - 2$	I+J−2
$x^2 + y^2$	X↑2+Y↑2
$(x + y)^2$	(X+Y)↑2
$a/b + c/d$	A/B+C/D or (A/B)+(C/D)
$(u + v)^{k-1}$	(U+V)↑(K−1)
$(4t)^{1/6}$	(4*T)↑.16666667 or (4*T)↑(1/6)

2.33 Write a LET statement for each of the following situations.

(a) Assign a value of 2.54 to the variable C.

       10 LET C=2.54

(b) Assign a value of 12 to the variable X.

       20 LET X=12

(c) Assign the value represented by the variable N to the variable N1.

       30 LET N1=N

(d) Assign the string JANUARY 31 to the variable A$.

       40 LET A$="JANUARY 31"

(e) Assign the string represented by the variable S$ to the variable T$.

       50 LET T$=S$

(f) Assign the value represented by the formula (A↑2+B↑2+C↑2) to the **variable F.**

       60 LET F=A↑2+B↑2+C↑2

(g) Increase the value assigned to the variable C7 by 0.01.

       70 LET C7=C7+.01

(h) Assign the value represented by the formula (I+J) to the **variable I.**

       80 LET I=I+J

2.34 Write a multiple LET statement for each of the following situations.

    (a)   Assign a value of −37.5 to the variables C1, C2 and C3.

          10 LET C1=C2=C3=−37.5

    (b)   Assign the string ∗∗∗∗∗ERROR∗∗∗∗∗ to the variables P5\$ and P7\$.

          20 LET P5\$=P7\$="∗∗∗∗∗ERROR∗∗∗∗∗"

    (c)   Assign the value represented by the formula (I+J)/K to the variables M and N.

          30 LET M=N=(I+J)/K

    Note that multiple LET statements are not available in all versions of BASIC.

    In some versions of BASIC, the keyword LET can be omitted, i.e.

          30 M=N=(I+J)/K

2.35 Write a LET statement that corresponds to each of the following algebraic equations.

    (a) $z = (x/y) + 3$

          10 LET Z=X/Y+3

    (b) $z = x/(y+3)$

          20 LET Z=X/(Y+3)

    (c) $w = (u+v)/(s+t)$

          30 LET W=(U+V)/(S+T)

    (d) $f = \left[\dfrac{2ab}{c+1} - \dfrac{t}{3(p+q)}\right]^{1/3}$

          40 LET F=(2∗A∗B/(C+1)−T/(3∗(P+Q)))↑.33333333

    (e) $r = \dfrac{6.8(a+b)^2/c - 7.2a/\sqrt{b+c}}{(a+c)^{1/n}}$

          50 LET R=(6.8∗(A+B)↑2/C−7.2∗A/(B+C)↑.5)/(A+C)↑(1/N)

2.36 Two complicated algebraic equations are shown below. Replace each equation with several simple equations and write the corresponding LET statements.

    (a) $t = \left[\dfrac{2ab}{c+1} - \dfrac{r}{7(p+q)}\right]^{1/n}$

        $t_1 = \dfrac{2ab}{c+1}$ 10 LET T1=2∗A∗B/(C+1)

        $t_2 = \dfrac{r}{7(p+q)}$ 20 LET T2=R/(7∗(P+Q))

        $t = (t_1 - t_2)^{1/n}$ 30 LET T=(T1−T2)↑(1/N)

    (b) $f = \dfrac{[6.8(a-b)^2/c - 7.2a/\sqrt{b+c}]^{1/7}}{[(c-a)^m + b^n]^{1/3}}$

        $f_1 = 6.8(a-b)^2/c$ 10 LET F1=6.8∗(A−B)↑2/C

        $f_2 = 7.2a/\sqrt{b+c}$ 20 LET F2=7.2∗A/(B+C)↑.5

        $f_3 = (c-a)^m + b^n$ 30 LET F3=(C−A)↑M+B↑N

        $f = (f_1 - f_2)^{1/7}/f_3^{1/3}$ 40 LET F=(F1−F2)↑(1/7)/F3↑(1/3)   or

                                   40 LET F=(F1−F2)↑.14285714/F3↑.33333333

2.37 Write an appropriate statement, or set of statements, for each situation described below.

(a) Enter numerical values for X1, X2 and X3, and a string value for X$. All of the data are to be typed on one line of a typewriter terminal.

      10 INPUT X1,X2,X3,X$

(b) Enter numerical values for X1, X2 and X3 on one line of a typewriter terminal, and a string value for X$ on the next line.

      10 INPUT X1,X2,X3
      15 INPUT X$

(c) Enter numerical values for X1 and X2 on one line of a typewriter terminal, and a numerical value for X3, followed by a string value for X$, on the next line.

      10 INPUT X1,X2
      15 INPUT X3,X$

(d) Print the values of C1, C2, C3, C4 and C5 on one line of a typewriter terminal.

      50 PRINT C1,C2,C3,C4,C5

(e) Print the values of A1, A2 and A3 on one line of a typewriter terminal, and the values of B1, B2 and B3 on another line, with a blank line separating them.

      60 PRINT A1,A2,A3
      65 PRINT
      70 PRINT B1,B2,B3

(f) Print the values of A1, A2, A3, B1, B2 and B3 all on one line, as closely spaced as possible.

      50 PRINT A1;A2;A3;A4;A5;A6

(g) Print the values of X, Y and Z on one line. Precede each numerical value with an appropriate label.

      100 PRINT "X=";X,"Y=";Y,"Z=";Z

or

      100 PRINT "X=";X;"Y=";Y;"Z=";Z

(h) Print the values of N$ and N next to one another, followed by the value of the formula $A↑2+B↑2$.

      120 PRINT N$;N;A↑2+B↑2

or

      120 PRINT N$;N,A↑2+B↑2

(i) Print the strings LEFT and RIGHT near the left and right edges of the paper.

      150 PRINT "LEFT",,,,"RIGHT"

(j) Print the message ROOTS OF SIMULTANEOUS EQUATIONS on one line, centered on the page as closely as possible.

      200 PRINT, "ROOTS OF SIMULTANEOUS EQUATIONS"

(k) Print a message indicating a request for the numerical value of C, then enter a numerical value for C.

      5 PRINT "C=";
      10 INPUT C

2.38 Show how the input data will appear in each of the following situations.

(a) 10 INPUT X1,X2,X3,X$

where $X1=4.83\times10^{-3}$ $X3=941.55$
        $X2=-537$ $X\$=BUCS$

?4.83E−3,−537,941.55,BUCS

or

?.00483,−537,941.55,BUCS

(b)   10 INPUT X$,X1
      20 INPUT X2,X3

where the variables have the same values as in part (a).

?BUCS,4.83E−3
?−537,941.55

(c)   30 INPUT A,A$,A1

where $A=350$ $A1=-8.05$
        $A\$=APRIL\ 12,\ 1969$

?350,"APRIL 12, 1969",−8.05

2.39 Show how the printed output will appear in each of the following situations.

(a)   10 PRINT "NAME ",N$,(X+Y)↑2/3,T4

where $N\$=GEORGE$ $Y=8.2$
        $X=27.6$ $T4=-5.83\times10^{-4}$

NAME   GEØRGE   427·213   −0·000583

(b)   10 PRINT "NAME ";N$;(X+Y)↑2/3;T4

where the variables have the same values as in part (a).

NAME GEØRGE 427·213 −0·000583

(c)   12 PRINT A1,A2,A3,A4
      14 PRINT B1,B2,B3 B4

where $A1=7.43\times10^{3}$ $B1=-2.55\times10^{-8}$
        $A2=-4373665.8$ $B2=0.843\times10^{7}$
        $A3=0.0006066183$ $B3=400.33$
        $A4=-3136687$ $B4=10^{-3}$

7430   −4·37367E+6   6·06618E−4   −3136687
−2·55000E−8   8430000   400·33   0·001

(d)   12 PRINT A1;A2;A3;A4;
      14 PRINT B1;B2;B3;B4

where the variables have the same values as in part (c).

7430 −4·37367E+6 6·06618E−4 −3136687 −2·55000E−8 8430000 400·33
0·001

2.40 In each of the following cases show how the comment (or remark) can be placed in a BASIC program.

(a)   Add the program heading AREA AND CIRCUMFERENCE OF A CIRCLE

10 REM AREA AND CIRCUMFERENCE OF A CIRCLE

(b) Add the comments AREA and CIRCUMFERENCE to the statements

40 LET A=P*R↑2

and

50 LET C=2*P*R

```
40 LET  A=P*R↑2   'AREA
50 LET  C=2*P*R   'CIRCUMFERENCE
```

2.41 Several GO TO statements are shown below. Identify which, if any, are written incorrectly.

Statement	Error
10 GO TO 50	correct
120 GO TO M	the statement number to which control is transferred must be a positive integer, not a variable
80 GO TO 25	correct
50 GO TO 50	a GO TO statement cannot transfer control to itself.

Supplementary Problems

2.42 Answer the following questions for the version of BASIC that is used at your particular school or office.

(a) How many significant figures can be included in a number?

(b) How many characters can appear in a string (i.e., what is the maximum string length)?

(c) Can a string variable be written as a letter followed by a digit and a dollar sign (e.g., C1$)?

(d) Can the keyword LET be omitted from a LET statement (e.g., 10 A=B+C)?

(e) Are multiple assignments permitted in a single LET statement (e.g., 10 LET X=Y=Z=13)?

2.43 Express each of the following quantities as a BASIC number.

(a) 5

(b) 8000

(c) -1.8033×10^{-9}

(d) 1/3

(e) $-7,328,500$

(f) 0.2851×10^4

(g) 0.2851×10^{10}

(h) $-16,752.47$

2.44 Some of the following constants are written incorrectly. Identify all errors.

(a) +0.250

(b) 5076

(c) 3 E−2

(d) 3.8822E−7.3

(e) −77777777

(f) 1,000,000

(g) 2.53E+99

(h) 64E+6

(i) 0.833333333333E−2

(j) −00263

(k) 4.48E

(l) 0.83333333−E2

2.45 Some of the following strings are written incorrectly. Identify all errors.

(a) $1,995.00

(b) JULY 4, 1776

(c) BEGINNER'S ALL-PURPOSE SYMBOLIC INSTRUCTION CODE

(d) 4 O'CLOCK

(e) "NUTS!"

(f) 2X+4Y=Z

2.46   Each of the following represents either a numeric or a string variable. Some are written incorrectly. Determine the type of variable in each correct case, and identify all errors.

(a) J   (c) J\$ (e) \$J6   (g) XSTAR   (i) P⁻   (k) 5T   (m) Z0

(b) J6   (d) J\$6   (f) J6\$ (h) C10   (j) N3   (l) Y*   (n) M 5

2.47   Write a BASIC formula that corresponds to each of the following algebraic terms.

(a) t^{n+1}

(b) $(x+3)^{1/k}$

(c) $2(a/b)^{1/3}$

(d) $1.87(u+v) - 5.088(x/y + 2z^2)$

(e) $1 - x + x^2/2 - x^3/6 + x^4/24 - x^5/120$

(f) $\dfrac{2(p/q)^{k-1}}{(r-3t)^{1/m}}$

(g) $(i+j-1)^2/5$

(h) $\left[\dfrac{(x_1+x_2)^m(y_1+y_2)^n}{(x_1/y_1)^{m+n}(x_2/y_2)^{m-n}}\right]^{1/mn}$

2.48   What is required of each variable that appears on the right side of the equal sign in a LET statement?

2.49   Write a LET statement for each of the following situations.

(a) Assign a value of 758.33 to the variable P.

(b) Assign the value represented by the variable A to the variable B.

(c) Assign the string PITTSBURGH, PA. to the variable F\$.

(d) Assign the string represented by the variable M\$ to the variable N\$.

(e) Assign the value of the formula X/(A+B−C) to the variable Y3.

(f) Decrease the value assigned to the variable K by 2.

(g) Double the value assigned to the variable C5.

(h) Assign the value of the formula (A↑2+B↑2)↑.5 to the variables B and C.

2.50   Write a LET statement that corresponds to each of the following algebraic equations.

(a) $w = \dfrac{(a+3)b^n}{2.7(c-d/b)+1}$

(b) $f = \left\{\dfrac{(a/b)^n/(c-d)^m}{[d/(b-a)^{n+m}]}\right\}^{1/(n+m)}$

(c) $y = \dfrac{a_1 - a_2x + a_3x^2 - a_4x^3 + a_5x^4}{c_1 - c_2x + c_3x^2 - c_4x^3}$

(d) $P = rA(1+r)^n/[(1+r)^n - 1]$

2.51   Each of the equations in Problem 2.50 above will have resulted in a lengthy LET statement. Replace each statement with an equivalent sequence of short, simple LET statements.

2.52   Write an algebraic equation that corresponds to each of the following LET statements.

(a) 10 LET F=A+2*B/C↑.5

(b) 20 LET F=A+(2*B/C)↑.5

(c) 30 LET F=(A+2)*(B/C)↑.5

(d) 40 LET F=((A+2)*B/C)↑.5

(e) 50 LET G=P*Q/R*S/T

2.53   What particular difficulty might be experienced in executing the statement

15 LET X=(Y−Z)↑.25

2.54   Consider the statement

25 LET P=−Q↑4

If Q=2, what value will be assigned to P?

2.55   Consider the statement

   35 LET P=Q↑4

If Q=−2, what value will be assigned to P? (Compare with the answer to Problem 2.54 above.)

2.56   Write an appropriate statement, or set of statements, for each situation described below.

   (a) Enter numerical values for A, B and C, and string values for M$ and N$. All of the data are to be typed on one line of a typewriter terminal.

   (b) Enter the values for A, N$ and B on one line of a typewriter terminal, and the values for M$ and C on the next line.

   (c) Enter numerical values for A, B and C, and string values for M$ and N$. Each value is to be typed at the start of a new line.

   (d) Print a message saying

   ENTER VALUES FOR A,B,C,M$ AND N$

   and then enter the requested data on the same line as the printed message.

   (e) Print the message described in part (d). Then enter the requested data on the next line.

   (f) Print the values of A, B, C, M$ and N$ on one line of a typewriter terminal, with normal spacing between each item.

   (g) Print the values of A, B, C, M$ and N$ on one line of a typewriter terminal, spacing the items as closely as possible.

   (h) Print the values of A, B and C on one line of a typewriter terminal, spacing the items as closely as possible. Allow for subsequent output to begin on the same line, immediately after the value for C.

   (i) Print the values of A, B, C, (A+B+C)/3, (A*B*C)↑(1/3) and (A↑2+B↑2+C↑2)↑.5 on one line of a typewriter terminal. Follow this with a blank line, then a third line with the value of M$ printed near the left margin and the value of N$ printed near the right.

   (j) Print the numerical values of A, B and C on one line of a typewriter terminal. Precede each number with an appropriate descriptive label.

   (k) Print the values of M$ and N$ on separate lines of a typewriter terminal, with a blank line between them. Precede the value of M$ with the label NAME: and precede N$ with the label SOCIAL SECURITY NUMBER: Center the output on the page as closely as possible.

2.57   Show how the input data will appear in each of the following situations.

   (a)   5 INPUT A,B,C
         10 INPUT M$,N$

   where   A = 0.0000062   M$ = SHARON
           B = 27.5 × 10^{-12} N$ = GAIL
           C = −1000

   (b) 20 INPUT P1,P2,T$

   where   P1 = −743.08   T$ = SUSAN
           P2 = 0.00987

   (c) 25 INPUT A$,B$,C$

   where   A$ = NEW YORK   C$ = SAN FRANCISCO
           B$ = CHICAGO

   (d) 15 INPUT P,P$,Q,Q$

   where   P = 2,770,543   Q = 48.8 × 10^9
           P$ = DECEMBER 29, 1963   Q$ = ELEVEN O'CLOCK

2.58   Show how the printed output will appear in each of the following situations.

   (a) 100 PRINT A;B;C;P;P1;P2;Q

where $A = 0.0000062$ $P1 = -743.08$
              $B = 27.5 \times 10^{-12}$ $P2 = 0.00987$
              $C = -1000$ $Q = 48.8 \times 10^9$
              $P = 2,770,543$

(b)   110 PRINT A,B,C,P,P1,P2,Q

where the variables have the same values as in part (a).

(c)   120 PRINT A+B*C,P/Q,P1/P2

where the variables have the same values as in part (a).

(d)   130 PRINT M$,P$,Q$

where   M$ = SHARON
            P$ = DECEMBER 29, 1963
            Q$ = ELEVEN O'CLOCK

2.59   In each of the following cases show how the comment (or remark) can be placed in a BASIC program.

(a)   Add the program heading AVERAGING OF AIR POLLUTION DATA

(b)   Insert the remark BEGIN LOOP TO CALCULATE CUMULATIVE SUM

(c)   Add the comment CALCULATE AVERAGE VALUE to the statement

         80 LET A=S/N

(d)   Add the comment READ A DATA POINT to the statement

         20 INPUT X,T

2.60   Several GO TO statements are shown below. Identify which, if any, are written incorrectly.

(a)   100 GO TO 12   (d)   55 GO TO 400
(b)   75 GO TO K+1   (e)   20 GO TO "60"
(c)   30 GO TO 30

Programming Problems

2.61   Prepare a flowchart for the program shown in Example 2.30. Compare with the flowchart for Example 2.26, shown in Fig. 2.1.

2.62   Write a complete BASIC program for each of the following problem situations.

(a)   A temperature reading, in Fahrenheit degrees, is to be read into the computer and converted into Centigrade degrees, using the formula

$$°C = \frac{5}{9}(°F - 32)$$

(b)   A piggy bank contains n_1 half-dollars, n_2 quarters, n_3 dimes, n_4 nickels and n_5 pennies. How much money is in the bank, in terms of dollars?

2.63   Develop an outline, draw a flowchart, and then write a complete BASIC program for each of the following problems. Write each program in such a manner that it can be used to process several sets of data sequentially. Be sure that all output data is clearly labeled.

(a)   Calculate the volume and area of a sphere using the formulas

$$V = 4\pi r^3/3$$
$$A = 4\pi r^2$$

where r is the radius of the sphere.

(b) The pressure, volume and temperature of a mass of air are related by the formula

$$PV = 0.37\,m(T + 460)$$

where P = pressure, pounds per square inch,
         V = volume, cubic feet,
         m = mass of air, pounds,
         T = temperature, °F.

If an automobile tire containing 2 cubic feet of air is inflated to 28 pounds per square inch at room temperature, how much air is in the tire?

(c) If a, b and c represent the three sides of a triangle, then the area of the triangle is

$$A = \sqrt{s(s-a)(s-b)(s-c)}$$

where $s = (a + b + c)/2$. Also, the radius of the *largest inscribed* circle is given by

$$r_i = A/s$$

and the radius of the *smallest circumscribed* circle is

$$r_c = abc/(4A)$$

Calculate the area of the triangle, the area of the largest inscribed circle and the area of the smallest circumscribed circle for each of the following sets of data:

a	11.88	5.55	10.00	13.75	12.00	20.42	7.17	173.67
b	8.06	4.54	10.00	9.89	8.00	27.24	2.97	87.38
c	12.75	7.56	10.00	11.42	12.00	31.59	6.66	139.01

(d) Suppose that P dollars are invested at an annual interest rate of i (expressed as a decimal). If the interest is reinvested, after n years the total amount of money, A, can be determined as $A = P(1 + i)^n$. (This is known as the *law of compound interest*.)

If \$5000 is invested at 6%, compounded annually, how much will have accumulated after 10 years?

If the interest is compounded quarterly rather than annually, the above equation must be changed to read $A = P(1 + i/4)^{4n}$.

If the same \$5000 is invested at an annual rate of 6%, compounded quarterly, how much will have accumulated after 10 years?   Compare this answer with the result obtained earlier (for interest compounded annually).

(e) The increase in population of a bacteria culture with time is directly proportional to the size of the population. Thus the larger the population, the faster the bacteria will increase in number. Mathematically the population at any time can be expressed as

$$P = P_0[1 + 0.0289\,t + (0.0289\,t)^2/2 + (0.0289\,t)^3/6$$
$$+ (0.0289\,t)^4/24 + \cdots + (0.0289\,t)^n/n!]$$

where t = time in hours beyond a reference time
         P_0 = bacteria population at the reference time
         P = bacteria population at time t.

Calculate the population multiplication factor (P/P_0) at 2, 5, 10, 20 and 50 hours beyond the reference time. Include the first 10 terms of the series (i.e., let $n = 9$).

Chapter 3

Running a BASIC Program

Now that we have learned to write simple BASIC programs, let us see how these programs can be read into the computer and executed. In particular, we will be concerned with procedures for entering, listing, running, storing and editing a program in a typical timesharing system. We will also consider methods for detecting and correcting the different types of errors that can occur in an improperly written program.

In this book our attention will be restricted to the timesharing mode, since most BASIC programs are implemented in this manner. A BASIC program can, however, also be run in the batch mode (though the READ and DATA statements must be used in place of the INPUT statement, as described in Chapter 5). The reader who may wish to learn the details of batch processing can do so by reading a programming manual for his particular computer once he has become familiar with the material in this book.

3.1 The Timesharing Terminal

We have already learned that a programmer must communicate with a computer through a typewriter terminal, such as the one shown in Fig. 1.3, when operating in the timesharing mode. (Typewriter terminals are also referred to as timesharing terminals, Teletype[†] terminals, typewriter consoles, timesharing consoles, etc.) Many of these devices have a built-in telephone dialup unit. Those typewriter terminals that do not contain such a unit can be wired to an external acoustic coupler, which can be used with an ordinary telephone handset. Thus any typewriter terminal can be connected to a computer via telephone lines. Some typewriter terminals also contain a paper-tape reader/punch, as shown in Fig. 1.3.

Figure 3.1 shows a closeup of the keyboard for the terminal presented in Fig. 1.3. Other typewriter terminals have keyboards that are quite similar, if not identical. We will refer to certain of these keys in subsequent sections of this chapter.

Fig. 3.1

[†]*Teletype* is a registered trademark of the Teletype Corporation, though the word is commonly used to refer to any typewriter terminal.

3.2 Logging In

The first step in communicating with a computer through a timesharing terminal is to establish a connection to the computer. This is accomplished by means of the *login* (or *logon*) procedure. The following description is representative of a login procedure, though there will be minor variations from one version of BASIC to another.†

If the connection is to be made via a telephone line, the login procedure begins by the user dialing a specified telephone number (after turning on the power to the terminal). The computer will then respond by typing a brief message and requesting that the user "log in" (i.e., identify himself by specifying a project number, etc.). The user must then type LOGIN (or LOGON, or simply LOG), followed by the desired information. It may then be necessary for the user to type BASIC, indicating that the user wishes to work with BASIC rather than some other language.

The procedure is similar, though simpler, when the terminal is wired directly to the computer (i.e., *hardwired*), thus not requiring a telephone line connection. In this case the procedure normally begins when the user types LOGIN, followed by his project number.

Example 3.1

A student at a large university wishes to run a BASIC program from a telephone-dialup typewriter terminal. The student's assigned project number is 123456. The login procedure is described below.

1. The student turns on the power switch of his typewriter terminal. (On the terminal shown in Fig. 1.3, the power switch is located near the right front of the keyboard.)

2. The student then dials the appropriate telephone number, and the computer responds by typing
    PLEASE LOGIN.

3. The student types the word LOG after the period, and then depresses the RETURN key. The computer responds by typing
    JOB 27 TTY42
    #

4. The student then enters his project number, 123456, after the # sign and again depresses the RETURN key. The computer then types
    08-FEB-73   THUR   21:11:46

    indicating the date, day and time, respectively.

5. The word BASIC is then typed by the student, after the period. This causes the BASIC system to be accessed from the computer's library of programming languages.

6. The computer types
    NEW OR OLD --->

    and the student must respond accordingly. If the student wanted to access a BASIC program that had previously been stored in the computer's library, he would type OLD. In this case, however, the student wishes to enter a new program. He therefore types the word NEW after the arrow.

7. Finally, the computer types
    NEW FILE NAME --->

    and the user responds by typing the name of the new program — in this case, SAMPLE. (Typically, a program name will consist of 1 to 6 characters, beginning with a letter.) The student is now ready to begin typing in his program.

A listing of the entire login procedure is shown in Fig. 3.2. Those items that were typed by the student have been underlined.

†The procedures described in this chapter apply specifically to the DECsystem-10 computer, as currently implemented at the University of Pittsburgh.

```
PLEASE LØGIN.

.LØG
JØB 27        TTY42
#123456
08-FEB-73        THUR        21:11:46

.BASIC

NEW ØR ØLD-->NEW
NEW FILE NAME-->SAMPLE
```

Fig. 3.2

If an error is made in transmitting the required information to the computer during the login procedure, then an appropriate message will be typed and the user will be asked to enter the information again.

Example 3.2

Referring to the situation described in Example 3.1, suppose the student had typed BASIV instead of BASIC during the login procedure (the V key is next to the C key on most terminal keyboards). The computer would respond by typing

      ?BASIV

The student would then type BASIC after the period, and the login procedure would be continued. The entire login procedure is shown in Fig. 3.3. Again, the student responses are underlined.

```
PLEASE LØGIN.

.LØG
JØB 32      TTY 42
#123456
08-FEB-73     THUR      21:37:07

.BASIV

?BASIV

.BASIC

NEW ØR ØLD-->NEW
NEW FILE NAME-->SAMPLE
```

Fig. 3.3

```
PITT DEC-1055/A   54A.31 21:11:46

PLEASE LØGIN ØR ATTACH.

.LØG
JØB 27 PITT DEC-1055/A   54A.31 TTY 42
#115421/160531
PASSWØRD:
ALLØCATIØN REMAINING: 9.8 UNITS
2111      08-FEB-73        THUR

.R BASIC

NEW ØR ØLD-->NEW
NEW FILE NAME-->EX3.1
```

Fig. 3.4

Many timesharing systems issue each user a separate *password* that must be supplied with the project number. The password is keyed in, but the typing is suppressed by the computer, thus maintaining confidentiality. The user will not be allowed to log in if he does not supply the correct password for a given project number.

A listing of a login procedure requiring a password is shown in Fig. 3.4. As before, the user-supplied responses have been underscored.

3.3 Entering a Program

Once the login procedure has been completed, the user may type in his program, one statement (one line) at a time. To do so, the user must wait for the computer to type the symbol

      >

at the start of a line. (This is known as *prompting*.) The user then types in a BASIC statement, starting with the statement number (line number). The typed information will not be transmitted to the computer, however, until the RETURN key has been depressed. Once this is done the printing head will move to the start of the next line, and the computer will request the next statement by printing another > symbol.

This procedure is continued until all of the program statements have been entered and transmitted to the computer. When the computer generates the symbol > after the last statement, the user may respond with a command specifying what should be done with the program (e.g., RUN, LIST, SAVE, etc.). We will discuss these commands later in this chapter.

When typing a program into the computer the instructions need not be entered in the same order that they will be executed. The computer will rearrange the instructions by increasing statement numbers once the entire program has been entered. (Remember that it is the ordering of the statement numbers that determines the sequence with which the statements will be executed.)

Example 3.3

A programmer who has just completed the login procedure wishes to enter a program into his computer. In his haste to enter and run the complete program, the programmer forgot to type the first two statements. The programmer realized his mistake before he was finished, however, and then typed in the missing statements. This is entirely permissible, since the program will be properly rearranged within the computer's memory.

A listing of the statements, in the order that they were entered, is shown in Fig. 3.5.

```
>20 PRINT "RADIUS=";
>30 INPUT R
>40 LET A=P*R↑2
>50 LET C=2*P*R
>60 PRINT "R=";R,"A=";A,"C=";C
>70 GØ TØ 20
>80 END
>5  REM PRØGRAM TØ CALCULATE AREA AND CIRCUMFERENCE ØF A CIRCLE
>10 LET P=3.1415927
>
```

Fig. 3.5

3.4   Correcting Errors

It is practically impossible for a programmer to write a complete program and enter it into the computer without making an occasional mistake. Therefore we must have a way to correct typing errors, and to add, delete or change a statement once it has been transmitted to the computer. In this section we will see that all of these operations can easily be accomplished in BASIC.

Incorrectly typed characters can be deleted by depressing the DELETE key (on some terminals, the RUBOUT key). The most recent character will be deleted by depressing the DELETE key once; depressing it twice will cause the two most recent characters to be deleted, and so on. Such deletions must, however, be made before the line containing the errors is transmitted to the computer (by depressing the RETURN key). After the desired characters have been deleted the programmer may proceed to type in the correct characters.

Example 3.4

A programmer wishes to enter the BASIC program shown in Fig. 3.5 into the computer. While typing the first statement, however, the programmer accidentally types a U in place of an I. Thus the line appears as follows:

>20 PRU

Realizing his mistake immediately, the programmer depresses the DELETE key once, and then proceeds to type in the remainder of the statement.

The entire typed line will appear as

>20 PRU\U\INT "RADIUS=";

Note that the deleted character (U) is shown between a pair of backward slashes. The backward slashes are typed automatically when the DELETE key is first used and when its use is first discontinued. It is important to understand, however, that the backward slashes and the deleted character will not be transmitted to the computer. Thus the computer will interpret the line of type as

20 PRINT "RADIUS=";

as desired.

Example 3.5

Let us again consider the typing error discussed in the previous example. Now, however, we assume that the programmer has not noticed his error until he has typed a few more characters. Thus the typed line will appear as

>20 PRUNT "RA

when the error is discovered. The programmer must therefore depress the DELETE key 7 times in order to delete everything from (and including) the letter U, and then retype the rest of the statement correctly.

The first typed line will appear as follows:

>20 PRUNT "RA\AR" TNU\INT "RADIUS=";

Again we see that the deleted characters are enclosed by a pair of backward slashes. The slashes are printed automatically when the DELETE key is first used and when it is first discontinued. Note that the deletions run "backward," i.e., the first character to be deleted is the letter A, followed by the letter R, etc., until the U has been deleted. Since these characters are not transmitted to the computer, the typed line will be stored in the computer as

20 PRINT "RADIUS=";

Sometimes a typing error is not noticed until an entire line (or most of it) has been typed. In such a situation it may be very cumbersome to delete one character at a time with the DELETE (or RUBOUT) key. A better procedure is to delete the entire line, replacing it with a new line. If the line has not been transmitted to the computer it can be deleted by depressing the ALTMODE or ESCAPE key (labeled ESC in Fig. 3.1). Once a line has been transmitted it can be replaced simply by entering a new line having the same statement number as the old line.

Example 3.6

In entering the program shown in Fig. 3.5, suppose that the programmer had typed

>20 PRUNT "RA

and then realized he had made a mistake (by typing a U instead of an I). He could delete the incorrect line by depressing the ESC key, and then retype the line correctly.

Alternatively, he could depress the RETURN key, thus entering the incorrect, incomplete statement into the computer. He would then proceed to type the correct statement, i.e.

>20 PRINT "RADIUS=";

When the RETURN key is again depressed the new statement will be entered into the computer, thus replacing the previous (incorrect) statement having the same statement number.

An entire statement can be deleted from a BASIC program simply by typing the statement number and then depressing the RETURN key.

Example 3.7

Suppose that the program shown in Fig. 3.5 has been entered into the computer, and the programmer then decides to delete the REM statement. He merely types

>5

and then depresses the RETURN key, thus deleting statement number 5 (the REM statement).

3.5 Processing a Program

A program is ready to be processed once it has been entered into the computer and all known mistakes have been corrected. Usually we will want to type out (i.e., *list*) the program, store (i.e., *save*) the program for later use and, of course, execute (i.e., *run*) the program. These operations are easily carried out by typing the words LIST, SAVE and RUN. The programmer can issue these commands in whatever order he may desire.

```
PITT DEC-1055/A  54B.01B 18:21:29

PLEASE LØGIN ØR ATTACH.

.LØGIN
JØB 42 PITT DEC-1055/A  54B.01B TTY42
#115421/160531
PASSWØRD:
ALLØCATIØN REMAINING: 9.8 UNITS
1821    15-FEB-73      THUR

.R BASIC


NEW ØR ØLD-->NEW
NEW FILE NAME-->CIRCLE

>20 PRUNT\TNU\INT RADIUS
>30 INPUT R
>40 LET A=P*R↑2
>50 LET C=2*P*R
>60 PRINT "R=";R,"A=";A,"C=";C
>70 GØ TØ 20
>80 END
>5  REM PRØGRAM TØ CALCULATE AREA AND CIRCUMFERENCE ØF A CIRCLE
>10 LET P=3.1416\6\5927
>65 PRINT
>20 PRINT "RADIUS=";
>35 IF R=0 THEN 80
>LIST

CIRCLE          18:27           15-FEB-73

5   REM PRØGRAM TØ CALCULATE AREA AND CIRCUMFERENCE ØF A CIRCLE
10 LET P=3.1415927
20 PRINT "RADIUS=";
30 INPUT R
35 IF R=0 THEN 80
40 LET A=P*R↑2
50 LET C=2*P*R
60 PRINT "R=";R,"A=";A,"C=";C
65 PRINT
70 GØ TØ 20
80 END

>SAVE

>RUN

CIRCLE          18:28           15-FEB-73


RADIUS=? 15
R= 15        A= 706.858     C= 94.2478

RADIUS=? 6.82
R= 6.82      A= 146.123     C= 42.8513

RADIUS=? 37.4
R= 37.4      A= 4394.33     C= 234.991

RADIUS=? 0


TIME:  0.21 SECS.

>BYE
JØB 42, USER [115421,160531]  LØGGED ØFF TTY42    1829  15-FEB-73
SAVED ALL FILES (25 BLØCKS)
CPUTIME 0:01   DISK R+W=77+15   CØNNECT=8 MIN   UNITS=0.0101
```

Fig. 3.6

Example 3.8   Area and Circumference of a Circle

A program similar to the one shown in Fig. 3.5 has been entered into the computer, and the programmer then wishes to print out, store and execute the program. The programmer therefore types the word LIST after the *original* program listing (which may contain error corrections, statements out of order, etc.). This causes the corrected statements to be listed in the proper order.

Once the complete listing has been printed out by the computer, the programmer types the words SAVE and RUN in order to store and execute the program, respectively. Finally, the programmer types BYE after the execution has terminated, thus terminating his connection to the computer.

A listing of the entire timesharing session is shown in Fig. 3.6. The information provided by the programmer (except for the actual program statements) has been underlined as before. Notice that the original program statements contain error corrections in statements 10 and 20, and that the initial statement 20 has been replaced with a later, corrected statement. Also, we see that the statements have not been typed in the sequence in which they will be executed.

Once the programmer types LIST we see that the title of the program (which happens to be CIRCLE) is printed, followed by a properly sequenced listing of the program statements. The input and output data associated with the execution of the program are shown after the command RUN. Finally, the last few lines contain statistical information that is provided by the logout procedure resulting from the BYE command (we will say more about this in Section 3.6).

After the programmer has logged out he can no longer communicate with the computer (unless, of course, he subsequently logs in again). The program CIRCLE will be stored for subsequent use, however, as a result of the SAVE command. (The program will probably be stored on a magnetic disk or tape rather than in the computer's main memory, though the programmer need not be concerned with this.)

If a previously stored program is to be processed rather than a newly entered program, then the programmer must type OLD rather than NEW after the login procedure. The computer will respond with

OLD FILE NAME --->

The programmer will then type in the name of the stored program. From this point on the program can be processed in the manner described earlier.

Example 3.9

Suppose that the program CIRCLE, discussed in Example 3.8, is to be executed after having previously been stored. Figure 3.7 below shows a listing of the complete timesharing session, including the login and logout procedures. Notice that the commands are very similar to those shown in Fig. 3.6, the only difference being the use of the word OLD instead of NEW.

The BASIC language also allows us to process a program in other ways. For example we can delete a previously stored program by typing UNSAVE, or we can obtain a listing of the names of all stored programs by typing CATALOG. Collectively, the commands used to process a program are called *system commands* (or *editing commands*). Although the number of available editing commands will differ from one version of BASIC to another, virtually all versions of the language contain the essential features described above. A summary of the more commonly used system commands is presented in Appendix C.

3.6   Logging Out

We have already seen that the procedure required to terminate the connection to the computer (i.e., the logout procedure) is initiated by typing the word GOODBYE (or simply BYE). Once this command has been issued the computer will respond by typing some summary statistics for the current timesharing session. Included in the statistics are the date, the number of *files* (i.e., programs and data sets) that have been saved, the length of the connection (timewise), the amount of actual computer time used and, usually, the cost. The logout procedure is illustrated in Examples 3.8 and 3.9 (see Figs. 3.6 and 3.7) as well as in Example 3.10 below.

```
PITT DEC-1055/A   54B.01B 20:13:09

PLEASE LOGIN OR ATTACH.

.LOGIN
JOB 62 PITT DEC-1055/A   54B.01B TTY 42
#115421/160531
PASSWORD:
ALLOCATION REMAINING: 9.8 UNITS
2013   15-FEB-72        THUR

.R BASIC


NEW OR OLD-->OLD
OLD FILE NAME-->CIRCLE

>RUN

CIRCLE         20:14          15-FEB-73


RADIUS=? 17.45
R= 17.45       A= 956.623     C= 109.642

RADIUS=? 12.7
R= 12.7        A= 506.707     C= 79.7965

RADIUS=? 32.6
R= 32.6        A= 3338.76     C= 204.832

RADIUS=? 0


TIME:  0.20 SECS.

>BYE
JOB 62, USER [115421,160531]  LOGGED OFF TTY 42    2015  15-FEB-73
SAVED ALL FILES (25 BLOCKS)
CPUTIME 0:01   DISK R+W=98+6   CONNECT=3 MIN   UNITS=0.0078
```

Fig. 3.7

Example 3.10

A programmer has just completed processing of his program and has therefore typed the word BYE. The computer responds by typing the three lines of information shown in Fig. 3.8, and then breaking the connection to the typewriter terminal immediately thereafter.

```
>BYE
JOB 27, USER [115421,160531]  LOGGED OFF TTY 42    2128   8-FEB-73
SAVED ALL FILES (15 BLOCKS)
CPUTIME 0:07   DISK R+W=856+8   CONNECT=17 MIN   UNITS=0.0240
```

Fig. 3.8

The first line of output states that the user whose account number is 115421, 160531 has logged out from terminal number 42 at 9:28 P.M. (i.e., 2128 hours) on February 8, 1973. The second line shows that 15 "blocks" of information have been saved (where one "block" contains 640 characters in this particular version of BASIC). In line 3 we see that 0.07 seconds of computer time (actually, central processor time) were required to process this program; that information was read from a magnetic disk storage device 856 times and written onto the disk 8 times; and that the entire timesharing session lasted 17 minutes at a charge 0.0240 "units." (A "unit" is approximately equivalent to one hour of central processor time, at costs that typically range from $75 to $300.)

3.7 Error Diagnostics

Programming errors often remain undetected until an attempt is made to execute the program. Once the RUN command has been issued, however, the presence of certain errors will become readily apparent, since such errors will prevent the program from being *compiled*, i.e., transformed into a machine-language program. Some particularly common errors of this type are a reference to an undefined variable or an undefined statement number, right- and left-hand parentheses that do not balance, failure to terminate the program with an END statement, etc. Such errors are called *grammatical* (or *syntactical*) errors.

Most versions of BASIC will generate a diagnostic message when a grammatical error has been detected. These messages are not always completely straightforward in their meaning, but they are nevertheless helpful in identifying the nature and location of the error.

Example 3.11

Figure 3.9 shows a BASIC program similar to that presented in Fig. 3.6, except that several grammatical errors have deliberately been introduced. The diagnostic messages that are generated by issuing the RUN command are clearly shown. Notice that the errors in lines 40 and 80 and the omission of the END statement have been found. However, the error in line 50 (reference to the variable B rather than P) has gone undetected.

```
EX3.11          22:19          18-FEB-73

5   REM PRØGRAM TØ CALCULATE AREA AND CIRCUMFERENCE ØF A CIRCLE
10  LET P=3.1415927
20  PRINT "RADIUS=";
30  INPUT R
40  LET A=(P*R↑2
50  LET C=2*B*R
60  PRINT "R=";R,"A=";A,"C=";C
70  PRINT
80  GØ TØ 15

> RUN

EX3.11          22:19          18-FEB-73

?  ILLEGAL FØRMULA IN LINE 40
?  UNDEFINED LINE NUMBER 15 IN LINE 80

?  NØ END INSTRUCTIØN

TIME:  0.18 SECS.
```

Fig. 3.9

Grammatical and typing errors are usually very obvious when they occur. Much more insidious, however, are *logical* errors. Here the program correctly conveys the programmer's instructions, free of grammatical or typing errors, but the programmer has supplied the computer with a logically incorrect set of instructions.

Sometimes a logical error will result in a condition that can be recognized by the computer. Such a situation might result from the generation of an excessively large numerical quantity (exceeding the largest permissible number that can be stored in the computer), or from an attempt to compute the square root of a negative number, etc. Diagnostic messages will be generated in situations of this type, making it easy to identify and correct the errors. These diagnostic messages are called *run-time* diagnostics, to distinguish them from the *compile-time* diagnostics described earlier.

Example 3.12

Figure 3.10 shows a BASIC program for computing the real roots of the quadratic equation

$$ax^2 + bx + c = 0$$

using the quadratic formula

$$x = \frac{-b \pm \sqrt{b^2 - 4ac}}{2a}$$

The program is completely free of grammatical errors. However, the program is unable to accommodate negative values for $b^2 - 4ac$ (see rule 3, Section 2.7). Furthermore, numerical difficulties may be encountered if the variable a has a very small or a very large numerical value (see rule 5, Section 2.1).

Following the listing of the program we see the output that is generated for $a = 1$, $b = 2$ and $c = 3$, and for $a = 10^{-30}$, $b = 10^{10}$ and $c = 10^{36}$. In the first case we obtain a negative value for $b^2 - 4ac$. This is the reason for the first two diagnostic messages (notice that the computation proceeds using the absolute value of $b^2 - 4ac$). The second set of data results in an excessively large value for x_2, thus causing the overflow message.

By comparing Figs. 3.9 and 3.10 we see that run-time diagnostics are preceded by a percent sign (%), whereas compile-time diagnostics are preceded by a question mark (?). This is a convenient means of identifying at what stage in the computation the error was detected.

```
EX3.12          22:05        22-FEB-73

10 REM REAL ROOTS OF A QUADRATIC EQUATION
20 INPUT A,B,C
30 IF A=0 THEN 90
40 LET D=B↑2-4*A*C
50 LET X1=(-B+D↑.5)/(2*A)
60 LET X2=(-B-D↑.5)/(2*A)
70 PRINT "A=";A,"B=";B,"C=";C,"X1=";X1,"X2=";X2
80 GO TO 20
90 END

> RUN

EX3.12          22:05        22-FEB-73


? 1,2,3

% ABSOLUTE VALUE RAISED TO POWER IN LINE 50

% ABSOLUTE VALUE RAISED TO POWER IN LINE 60
A= 1          B= 2          C= 3          X1= 0.414214  X2=-2.41421
? 1E-30,1E10,1E36

% OVERFLOW IN LINE 60
A= 1.00000E-30            B= 1.00000E+10            C=
  1.00000E+36   X1=-8.32000E+32            X2=-1.70141E+38
? 0,0,0


TIME: 0.50 SECS.
```

Fig. 3.10

3.8   Logical Debugging

We have just seen that grammatical errors and certain types of logical errors will cause diagnostic messages to be generated when compiling or executing a program. Errors of this type are very easy to find and correct. Usually, however, logical errors are much more difficult to detect, since the output resulting from a logically incorrect program may appear to be error-free.   Moreover, logical errors are often hard to find even when they are known to exist (as, for example, when the computed output is obviously incorrect).   Thus a good bit of "detective work" may be required in order to find and correct errors of this type. Such detective work is known as *logical debugging*.

Detecting Errors

The first step in attacking logical errors is to find out if they are present.   This can sometimes be accomplished by testing a new program with data that will yield a known answer.   If the correct results are not obtained, then the program obviously contains errors. Even if the correct results are obtained, however, one cannot be absolutely certain that the program is error-free, since some errors cause incorrect results only under certain circumstances (as, for example, with certain values of the input data or with certain program options).   Therefore a new program should receive thorough testing before it is considered to be debugged.   This is especially true of complicated programs or programs that will be used extensively by others.

As a rule, a calculation will have to be carried out by hand, with the aid of a slide rule or a desk calculator, in order to obtain a known answer.   For some problems, however, the amount of work involved in carrying out a hand calculation is prohibitive.   (A problem requiring a few minutes of time on a large computer may require several weeks to solve by hand!)   Therefore a sample problem cannot always be developed to test a new program. Though logical debugging of such programs can be particularly difficult, the programmer can often detect logical errors by studying the computed results carefully to see if they are reasonable.

Correcting Errors

Once it has been established that a program contains a logical error, some resourcefulness and ingenuity may be required to find the error.   Error detection should always begin with the programmer carefully reviewing each logical group of statements in the program. Armed with the knowledge that an error exists somewhere, the programmer can often spot the error by such careful study.   If the error cannot be found, it sometimes helps to set the program aside for a while.   It is not unusual for an overly intent programmer to miss an obvious error the first time around.

If an error has not been found after repeated inspection of the program, then the programmer should proceed to rerun the program, printing out a large quantity of intermediate output.   This is sometimes referred to as *tracing*.   Often the source of error will become evident once the intermediate calculations have been carefully examined.

When a programmer has tried all the tricks he can think of and still has not found an error, he may be inclined to suspect either a machine error or a compilation error.   Though rare, such errors do occur.   (Machine errors are sometimes intermittent, whereas a compilation error will be consistent and therefore reproducible.)   In most instances, however, a suspected compilation or machine error will turn out to be a logical programming error once the problem has finally been resolved.   Thus the programmer should avoid the temptation to "cry wolf" whenever he encounters a stubborn error, lest he end up with egg on his face as well as errors in his program.

Finally, the reader should recognize the fact that logical errors are inescapable in computer programming, though a conscientious programmer should make every attempt to minimize their occurrence.   Thus the programmer should anticipate that a certain amount of debugging will be required as a part of the overall effort in writing a realistic, meaningful BASIC program.

Example 3.13

A student has written a BASIC program to evaluate the formula

$$y = \left(\frac{x-1}{x}\right) + \frac{1}{2}\left(\frac{x-1}{x}\right)^2 + \frac{1}{3}\left(\frac{x-1}{x}\right)^3 + \frac{1}{4}\left(\frac{x-1}{x}\right)^4 + \frac{1}{5}\left(\frac{x-1}{x}\right)^5$$

To simplify the programming the student has defined a new variable, u, as

$$u = \left(\frac{x-1}{x}\right)$$

so that the formula becomes

$$y = u + \frac{1}{2}u^2 + \frac{1}{3}u^3 + \frac{1}{4}u^4 + \frac{1}{5}u^5$$

The complete BASIC program is shown in Fig. 3.11.

```
10 PRINT "X=";
20 INPUT X
30 LET U=X-1/X
40 LET Y=U+(U/2)↑2+(U/3)↑3+(U/4)↑4+(U/5)↑5
50 PRINT "Y=";Y
60 END
>RUN


EX3.13          21:25           05-MAY-74

X= ?2
Y= 2.20971



TIME:  0.08 SECS.
```

Fig. 3.11

The student knows that y should have a value of about 0.69 when $x = 2$. However, the program results in a calculated value of $y = 2.20971$ when $x = 2$, as seen in Fig. 3.11. The student concludes, therefore, that the program contains logical errors, which must be found and corrected.

By carefully inspecting his program the student became aware that statement number 30 results in a value of $u = 1.5$ when $x = 2$, whereas the correct value should be $u = 0.5$. The reason for the error is the omission of parentheses in statement 30, which *should* read

        30 LET U=(X−1)/X

The student then corrected his program and reran it for a value of $x = 2$. The PRINT statement (line 50) was also changed so that the calculated value of u is printed out along with the calculated value of y.

```
10 PRINT "X=";
20 INPUT X
30 LET U=(X-1)/X
40 LET Y=U+(U/2)↑2+(U/3)↑3+(U/4)↑4+(U/5)↑5
50 PRINT "U=";U,"Y=";Y
60 END
>RUN


EX3.13          21:27           05-MAY-74

X= ?2
U= 0.5          Y= 0.567384



TIME:  0.07 SECS.
```

Fig. 3.12

```
10 PRINT "X=";
20 INPUT X
30 LET U=(X-1)/X
40 LET Y=U+(U↑2)/2+(U↑3)/3+(U↑4)/4+(U↑5)/5
50 PRINT "U=";U,"Y=";Y
60 END
>RUN


EX3.13          21:29           05-MAY-74

X= ?2
U= 0.5          Y= 0.688542



TIME:  0.08 SECS.
```

Fig. 3.13

When the program was executed the value of u was calculated correctly, but the value of y was still incorrect, as seen in Fig. 3.12. Therefore the student concluded that the program contains an additional error, which must be located somewhere in statement number 40.

After some additional study the student discovered that statement number 40 is indeed incorrect. This statement should be written

$$40 \text{ LET } Y=U+(U\uparrow2)/2+(U\uparrow3)/3+(U\uparrow4)/4+(U\uparrow5)/5$$

(Note that the pairs of parentheses are actually not necessary because of the natural hierarchy of operations.) The program was then corrected, as shown in Fig. 3.13. At the bottom of Fig. 3.13 we see that the value of y corresponding to $x = 2$ is correctly calculated as $y = 0.688542$.

3.9   Closing Remarks

We have on several occasions stated that BASIC programming is both easy to learn and fun to do. The reader is now in a position to find out for himself if this is indeed the case, by running a few of his own programs (such as those suggested at the end of Chapter 2).

The rules presented in the last two chapters should not be memorized — they will quickly become second nature with repeated practice. Thus the reader will learn that BASIC programming is much like playing the drums. It cannot be learned simply by reading a book; rather, it is a skill that is gradually acquired through repeated practice.

Review Questions

3.1   Name several commonly used synonyms for a typewriter terminal.

3.2   Describe, in general terms, the login and logout procedures used with BASIC.

3.3   What is meant by prompting? How is prompting indicated on a typewriter terminal when entering or processing a BASIC program?

3.4   How is a line of information that has been typed on a typewriter terminal transmitted to the computer?

3.5   Suppose a BASIC program is entered into the computer with certain of the statements in the wrong places. How can this situation be corrected?

3.6   How can one or more characters be deleted from a line of text on a typewriter terminal? How can an entire line be deleted?

3.7   How can an incorrect statement be changed once it has been transmitted to the computer?

3.8   How can a statement be deleted from a BASIC program once it has been transmitted to the computer?

3.9   How can a BASIC program be listed on a typewriter terminal?

3.10   How can a BASIC program be stored within the computer's memory (or on a magnetic device) for later use?

3.11   How is a BASIC program executed?

3.12   Suppose a BASIC program has been stored on a magnetic storage device and is to be retrieved for subsequent processing.   How can the program be accessed?

3.13   Describe the purpose of each of the following system commands: BYE, CATALOG, GOODBYE, LIST, NEW, OLD, RUN, SAVE, UNSAVE.

3.14   What is meant by a syntactical error?

3.15   How do grammatical errors and logical errors differ from one another?

3.16   Name some common grammatical errors.

3.17   Name some common logical errors.

3.18   What is meant by diagnostic messages?   How can compile-time diagnostics be distinguished from run-time diagnostics?

3.19   Are diagnostic messages generated in response to logical programming errors?

3.20   What is meant by logical debugging?   Name some common debugging procedures.

3.21   In what way is learning to program with BASIC like learning to play the drums?

Supplementary Problems

The following "problems" are concerned with information gathering rather than actual problem solving.

3.22   Familiarize yourself with the typewriter terminals used at your school or office.
   (*a*)   Where is the ON/OFF switch?
   (*b*)   Does the unit have a built-in telephone dialup unit?   If so, how does it operate?
   (*c*)   Does the unit have a paper-tape reader/punch?
   (*d*)   Which key causes one or more characters to be deleted from a line of text?   An entire line to be deleted?
   (*e*)   Which key causes a typed line to be transmitted to the computer?
   (*f*)   Can the unit be operated in a LOCAL mode (i.e., as a stand-alone device, disconnected from a computer)?   If so, how is this done?

3.23   Determine the exact login and logout procedures that are used at your particular school or office. Exactly what information is required to log in?   What is the meaning of the information provided by the computer during the login and logout procedures?

3.24   What are the BASIC system commands in use at your school or office?   Familiarize yourself with those that were not discussed in this chapter.

3.25   How can compile-time diagnostics be distinguished from run-time diagnostics in the version of BASIC used at your particular school or office?

3.26   How are timesharing costs determined at your particular school or office?   What is the actual cost of one timesharing unit?   (*Note*: it is especially important that this question be answered by the student who receives free access to a computer through an educational institution.   Most students have no idea of the equivalent commercial cost of using a computer!)

Programming Problems

3.27   Log in to your computer system, determine the names of any programs that may have been saved under your account number and log out.

3.28   Enter the program shown in Fig. 3.6 for calculating the area and circumference of a circle. Be sure to correct any typing errors. List the program after it has been read into the computer. When you are sure that it is correct, execute the program several times using whatever values you wish for the radius. Verify that the computed answers are correct by comparing them with hand calculations. (Note that the execution is terminated by entering a value of zero for the radius.)

3.29   Enter, correct, list, execute and save the programs for a few of the following problems:

(a) The temperature conversion problem described in Prob. 2.62(a).

(b) The piggy-bank problem described in Prob. 2.62(b).

(c) Computation of the volume and area of a sphere, as described in Prob. 2.63(a).

(d) Computation of the mass of air in an automobile tire, as described in Prob. 2.63(b).

(e) Computation of the area of a triangle, areas of the largest inscribed circle and the smallest circumscribed circle, as described in Prob. 2.63(c).

(f) The compound-interest problem, as described in Prob. 2.63(d).

(g) Computation of the growth of a bacteria culture, as described in Prob. 2.63(e).

Chapter 4

Branching and Looping

The programming problems we have considered so far have been of the "adding machine" variety. That is, the calculations were always carried out in a fixed order. However, the remarkable versatility of the digital computer lies not in its ability to carry out a specified sequence of calculations in a short period of time. Rather, it is the ability of the computer to make logical decisions and then carry out an appropriate set of orders, based on the outcome of those decisions, that renders the computer so useful. Let us now turn our attention to this important topic.

We have already learned that *unconditional branching* operations (i.e., a transfer of control, or "jump," from one part of a program to another) can be carried out in BASIC by means of the GO TO statement (see Section 2.14). Another situation that arises frequently is a transfer to one of two different portions of a program, depending on the outcome of a comparison between two quantities. Such an operation, called a *conditional branch,* allows logical decisions to be carried out within the computer.

Looping is another operation that is often required in a computer program. This involves repeating some portion of the program either a specified number of times or until some particular condition has been satisfied. The repeated portion of the program (the loop) may contain a conditional branching operation that determines whether the loop will be terminated or executed at least one more time. If the loop is to be executed again, then control is transferred back to the start of the loop. Hence the instructions in the repeated portion of the program need not be written more than once.

In this chapter we will see how branching and looping operations can be carried out in BASIC. This opens the door to a much broader and more interesting class of programming problems.

4.1 Relational Operators

In order to carry out a conditional branching operation in BASIC we must have a way to express conditions of equality and inequality. This is accomplished through the use of the *relational operators*. These operators are

Equal to:	$=$
Not equal to:	$<>$
Less than:	$<$
Less than or equal to:	$<=$
Greater than:	$>$
Greater than or equal to:	$>=$

The relational operators are used to connect numerical quantities (i.e., numbers, variables or formulas) or strings, thus forming conditions that are either satisfied or unsatisfied.

Example 4.1

Several conditions involving numerical quantities are shown below. Each condition will be either satisfied or unsatisfied, depending on the numerical values of the variables.

$$X=27$$
$$N<=.001$$
$$C>(C1+C2)\uparrow 2$$
$$A+B<C+D$$
$$P<>Q$$
$$Z>=X*Y$$

Thus the last condition will be satisfied if the value of Z is greater than or equal to the value of $X*Y$, otherwise it will be unsatisfied.

Inequality conditions involving strings are interpreted as "comes before" or "comes after" rather than "less than" or "greater than." Moreover, trailing blanks are ignored when comparing strings.

Example 4.2

Several conditions involving strings are presented below. Each condition will be either satisfied or unsatisfied, depending on the particular strings that are assigned to the string variables.

$$N\$="SMITH"$$
$$P\$<>Q\$$$
$$C\$<G\$$$

The first condition will be satisfied if the string assigned to N$ is SMITH; otherwise it will be unsatisfied. The second condition will be satisfied only if the string assigned to P$ is different from that assigned to Q$. In order for the last condition to be satisfied, the string assigned to C$ must come earlier in an alphabetized list than the string assigned to G$.

4.2 Conditional Branching — The IF-THEN Statement

The *IF-THEN statement* is used to carry out a conditional branching operation. The statement consists of the words IF and THEN, separated by a relation, and followed by the number of a remote statement. When executing the IF-THEN statement control will be transferred to the remote statement if the relation is satisfied; otherwise, the statement following IF-THEN will be executed next. (Note that control can be transferred to *any* remote statement within a program, including a REM statement.)

Example 4.3

Shown below is a portion of a BASIC program which includes an IF-THEN statement.

```
15...
...
50 IF I>=100 THEN 80
55 LET I=I+1
60 GO TO 15
...
80...
```

The manner in which the program is executed will depend on the relation

$$I>=100$$

contained in the IF-THEN statement. If the relation is satisfied (i.e., if the value of I is greater than or equal to 100), then statement number 80 will be executed next. If the relation is not satisfied (i.e., if the value of I is less than 100), then statement number 55 will be executed next.

Notice the way the IF-THEN statement is used in conjunction with the GO TO statement in this example to form a loop.

Many versions of BASIC allow use of the words GO TO rather than THEN.

Example 4.4

Shown below is an IF-GO TO statement involving strings.

    45 IF N$="SHARON" GO TO 120

(It should be clear that the use of GO TO rather than THEN has nothing to do with the type of relation, i.e., numerical vs. string.)

Example 4.5   Roots of an Equation

Computers are frequently used to solve algebraic equations that cannot be solved by elementary methods. Consider, for example, the equation

$$x^5 + 3x^2 - 10 = 0$$

This equation cannot be rearranged to yield an exact solution for x. Hence we will determine the solution by a repeated trial-and-error procedure (i.e., an *iterative* procedure) that successively refines an initially crude guess.

Computational Procedure

We begin by rearranging the equation into the form

$$x = \sqrt[5]{10 - 3x^2}$$

Our procedure will then be to guess a value for x, substitute this value into the right-hand side of the rearranged equation and thus calculate a new value for x. This new value will then be substituted into the right-hand side, and still another value obtained for x, and so on. The procedure will continue until either the successive values of x have become sufficiently close (i.e., the method has *converged*), or a specified number of iterations has been exceeded (thus preventing the computation from continuing indefinitely in the event that the computed results do not converge).

To see how the method works, suppose we choose an initial value of $x = 1.0$. Substituting this value into the right side of the equation, we obtain

$$x = \sqrt[5]{10 - 3(1.0)^2} = 1.47577$$

We then substitute this new value of x into the equation, resulting in

$$x = \sqrt[5]{10 - 3(1.47577)^2} = 1.28225$$

Continuing the procedure, we obtain

$$x = \sqrt[5]{10 - 3(1.28225)^2} = 1.38344$$

$$x = \sqrt[5]{10 - 3(1.38344)^2} = 1.33613$$

and so on. Note that the successive values for x appear to be converging to some final answer.

The Program Outline

In order to write a BASIC program outline, let us define the following symbols.

      X = the value of x substituted in the right-hand side of the equation
     X1 = the newly calculated value of x
      I = an iteration counter (I will increase by one unit at each successive iteration)
      N = the maximum permissible number of iterations.

We will continue the computation until either

(a) the difference in successive values of x becomes less than 0.00001, or

(b) the iteration counter (I) has reached its maximum allowable value (N).

We can now write an outline of our BASIC program as follows.

1. Read X, N

2. Initialize the counter (set I=1).

3. Compute a value for X1 using the formula

$$X1=(10-3*X\uparrow2)\uparrow.2$$

4. Print the newly calculated values for I and X1. (By printing out the results of each iteration in this manner we can actually see whether or not the computation is converging.)

5. Test to see if $|X-X1|$ (i.e., the absolute value of successive values of x) is less than 0.00001.

    (a) If $|X-X1|<0.00001$, then go to step 7 (print final answers).

    (b) If $|X-X1|\geq0.00001$, then proceed to step 6 below.

6. Test to see if I=N (note that the value of I will be less than N in the early stages of the computation).

    (a) If I=N, then go to step 8 (print a message indicating that the computation has not converged).

    (b) If I<N, then increase I by one unit (i.e., I=I+1), let the recently calculated value for X1 be called X, and go back to step 3, thus beginning the next iteration.

7. Print the final values of X1 and I, and then go to step 9 (stop).

8. Print a message indicating that the computation has not converged, followed by the most recent value for I and N.

9. Stop.

A flowchart of the computational procedure is shown in Fig. 4.1.

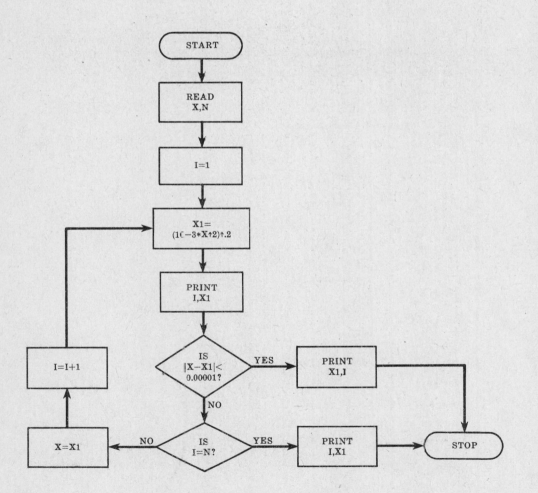

Fig. 4.1

The BASIC Program

In Fig. 4.2 we see a complete BASIC program that corresponds to the above outline and flowchart. The program contains two IF statements, in lines 60 and 70. (For illustrative purposes both the IF-THEN and the IF-GO TO forms have been used.) Notice that the program reads in an initial value for X and a value for N, but the convergence criterion (i.e., the value 0.00001) is a fixed constant within the program. The convergence criterion could have been treated as an input quantity if we had wished. Also, notice the use of the letters ABS in line 60. This refers to a BASIC library function that determines the absolute value of the quantity $(X-X1)$. (We will discuss library functions in Chapter 5, Section 5.1.) Finally, we see that we could have experienced some difficulty with this program if the formula

$$10-3*X\uparrow2$$

in line 40 resulted in a negative quantity. A test for such a condition could have been included in the program.

```
>LIST

EX 4.5           17:51           03-MAR-73

10   REM AN ITERATIVE METHOD FOR COMPUTING ROOTS OF AN EQUATION
20   INPUT X,N
25   PRINT
30   LET I=1
40   LET X1=(10-3*X↑2)↑.2
50   PRINT "I=";I,"X1=";X1
60   IF ABS(X-X1)<.00001 THEN 110
70   IF I=N GO TO 160
80   LET X=X1
90   LET I=I+1
100  GO TO 40
110  PRINT
120  PRINT "THE FINAL ANSWER IS X=";X1
130  PRINT
140  PRINT "NUMBER OF ITERATIONS REQUIRED =";I
150  GO TO 190
160  PRINT
165  PRINT "COMPUTATION HAS NOT CONVERGED AFTER ";I;" ITERATIONS"
170  PRINT
180  PRINT "LAST VALUE OF X =";X1
190  END

>RUN

EX 4.5           17:52           03-MAR-73


? 1, 25

I= 1          X1= 1.47577
I= 2          X1= 1.28225
I= 3          X1= 1.38344
I= 4          X1= 1.33613
I= 5          X1= 1.35951
I= 6          X1= 1.34826
I= 7          X1= 1.35375
I= 8          X1= 1.35109
I= 9          X1= 1.35238
I= 10         X1= 1.35175
I= 11         X1= 1.35206
I= 12         X1= 1.35191
I= 13         X1= 1.35198
I= 14         X1= 1.35195
I= 15         X1= 1.35196
I= 16         X1= 1.35195

THE FINAL ANSWER IS X= 1.35195

NUMBER OF ITERATIONS REQUIRED = 16


TIME:  0.36 SECS.
```

Fig. 4.2

Following the program listing we see a set of output that is generated for an initial guess of $x = 1.0$. Notice that the computation has converged to the solution $x = 1.35195$ after 16 iterations. From the printed output we can actually see the successive values of x become closer and closer, leading to the final converged solution.

Figure 4.3 shows the output that is generated when convergence is not obtained. In this case we have specified a maximum value of only 10 iterations (N=10), which is not sufficient to obtain a converged solution from the starting value $x = 1.0$. The lack of convergence is clearly indicated by the printed message.

```
> RUN

EX 4.5            17:53          03-MAR-73


? 1, 10

I = 1             X1= 1.47577
I = 2             X1= 1.28225
I = 3             X1= 1.38344
I = 4             X1= 1.33613
I = 5             X1= 1.35951
I = 6             X1= 1.34826
I = 7             X1= 1.35375
I = 8             X1= 1.35109
I = 9             X1= 1.35238
I = 10            X1= 1.35175

COMPUTATION HAS NOT CONVERGED AFTER  10  ITERATIONS

LAST VALUE OF X = 1.35175



TIME:  0.26 SECS.
```

Fig. 4.3

4.3 Multiple Branching — The ON-GO TO Statement

Multiple branching can be carried out in BASIC by means of the *ON-GO TO statement*. This statement contains a numeric variable or formula, and two or more numbers of remote statements. Control will be transferred to the first remote statement if the variable or formula has a value of 1, to the second remote statement if the variable or formula has a value of 2, etc.

Example 4.6

A typical ON-GO TO statement is shown below.

    30 ON K GO TO 15,40,25,40,60

Control will be transferred to statement number 15 if K has a value of 1, to statement 40 if K has a value of 2 or 4, to statement 25 if K equals 3 and to statement 60 if K equals 5.

If the variable or formula has a value that is not integral, then the decimal portion of the number will be ignored (i.e., the number will be *truncated*).

Example 4.7

Suppose the variable K in Example 4.6 had been assigned a value of 3.67. The .67 would be ignored, and K would be considered to have a value of 3. Hence control would be transferred to statement number 25.

Notice that the value originally assigned to K has been *truncated — not rounded*.

Most versions of BASIC allow use of the word THEN in place of GO TO.

Example 4.8

A typical ON-GO TO statement is shown below.

> 50 ON A↑2+B↑2 GO TO 20,150,180

In most versions of BASIC the above statement could also be written as

> 50 ON A↑2+B↑2 THEN 20,150,180

4.4 The STOP Statement

The *STOP statement* is used to terminate the computation at any point in the program. It is equivalent to a GO TO statement that transfers control to the END statement. The statement consists simply of a statement number, followed by the word STOP.

It is important to understand the distinction between the STOP and END statements. The STOP statement can appear *anywhere* in a BASIC program, except at the very end. More than one STOP statement may appear. On the other hand, the END statement *cannot* appear anywhere *except* at the end of the program, hence it cannot be used more than once in any given program. (Recall that every BASIC program *must* end with an END statement.)

The use of the STOP statement, as well as the ON-GO TO statement, is illustrated in Example 4.9 below.

Example 4.9   Calculating Depreciation

Let us consider how to calculate the yearly depreciation for a depreciable item (e.g., a building, piece of machinery, etc.). There are 3 different methods for calculating depreciation, known as the *straight-line* method, the *double declining balance* method and the *sum-of-the-years'-digits* method. We wish to write a BASIC program that will allow us to select any one of these methods for each set of calculations.

Computational Procedure

The computation will begin by reading in the original (undepreciated) value of the item, the life of the item (the number of years over which it will be depreciated) and an integer that indicates which method of depreciation will be used. The yearly depreciation and the remaining (depreciated) value of the item will then be calculated and printed out for each year.

The *straight-line* method is the simplest to use. In this method the original value of the item is divided by its life (total number of years). The resulting quotient will be the amount by which the item depreciates each year. For example, if an $8000 item is to be depreciated over 10 years, then the annual depreciation would be $8000 ÷ 10 = $800, and the item would decrease by $800 every year. Notice that the annual depreciation is the same each year.

When using the *double declining balance* method, the value of the item will decrease by a constant *percentage* each year. (Hence the *actual amount* of the depreciation, in dollars, will vary from one year to the next.) To obtain the depreciation factor we divide 2 by the life of the item. This factor is multiplied by the value of the item at the beginning of each year (*not the original* value of the item) to obtain the annual depreciation.

Suppose, for example, that we wish to depreciate an $8000 item over 10 years, using the double declining balance method. The depreciation factor will be $2 ÷ 10 = 0.20$. Hence the depreciation for the first year will be $0.20 × $8000 = 1600. The second year's depreciation will be $0.20 × ($8000 − $1600) = 0.20 × ($6400) = 1280, the third year's depreciation will be $0.20 × $5120 = 1024, and so on.

In the *sum-of-the-years'-digits* method the value of the item will decrease by a percentage that is different each year. The depreciation factor will be a fraction whose denominator is the sum of the digits from 1 to N, where N represents the life of the item (e.g., for a ten-year lifetime the denominator will be $1 + 2 + 3 + \cdots + 9 + 10 = 55$). For the first year the numerator will be N, for the second year it will be (N−1), for the third year (N−2), and so on. The yearly depreciation is obtained by multiplying the depreciation factor by the *original* value of the item.

To see how the sum-of-the-years'-digits method works, we again depreciate an $8000 item over 10 years. The depreciation for the first year will be $(10/55) × $8000 = 1454.55, for the second year it will be $(9/55) × $8000 = 1309.09, and so on.

The Program Outline

We begin by defining the following symbols.

V = the value of the item

N = the number of years over which the item will be depreciated (the lifetime)

I = an integer that indicates which method will be used to calculate the depreciation

   (a) I=1 indicates straight-line depreciation

   (b) I=2 indicates the double declining balance method

   (c) I=3 indicates the sum-of-the-years'-digits method

J = a counter that indicates which year is currently being considered

$D1,D2,D3$ = the annual depreciation calculated by each of the three methods.

Our BASIC program will follow the outline presented below.

1. Read V,N,I

2. Print a message indicating which method will be used to calculate the depreciation.

3. Set J=0

4. Calculate D1=V/N

$$F1 = \frac{V}{N*(N+1)/2}$$

(F1 is used in the sum-of-the-years'-digits method. Note that the sum of the digits $1 + 2 + 3 + \cdots + N$ is equal to $N*(N+1)/2$.)

5. Increment J (i.e., J=J+1).

6. Calculate the yearly depreciation and the new value for the item by the appropriate method, and print the results.

   (a) If I=1, then:

      (i) Calculate V=V−D1

      (ii) Print J,D1,V

      (iii) If J<N, go to step 5; otherwise, stop.

   (b) If I=2, then:

      (i) Calculate D2=(2/N)*V

           V=V−D2

      (ii) Print J,D2,V

      (iii) If J<N, go to step 5; otherwise, stop.

   (c) If I=3, then:

      (i) Calculate F2=N−J+1

           D3=F1*F2

           V=V−D3

      (ii) Print J,D3,V

      (iii) If J<N, go to step 5; otherwise, stop.

A corresponding flowchart is shown in Fig. 4.4.

The BASIC Program

In Fig. 4.5 we see a complete BASIC program for carrying out the computation. Notice that the program contains two ON-GO TO statements, in lines 90 and 210. (We could just as easily have used ON-THEN, the logic would be identical.) Each of these statements provides us with a conditional three-way branch in this particular problem. We also see the use of the STOP statement, in lines 340 and 450. As an alternative we could have written GO TO 560 in place of the STOP statements.

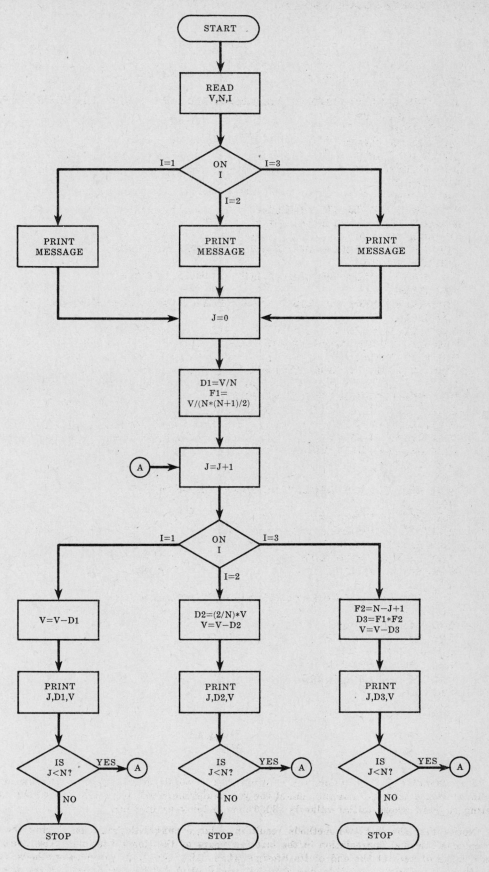

Fig. 4.4

```
EX 4.9              13:57          25-AUG-73

10    REM COMPUTATION OF DEPRECIATION BY THREE DIFFERENT METHODS
20    PRINT "V=";
30    INPUT V
40    PRINT "N=";
50    INPUT N
60    PRINT "I=";
70    INPUT I
80    PRINT
90    ON I GO TO 100,120,140
100   PRINT "STRAIGHT-LINE METHOD"
110   GO TO 150
120   PRINT "DOUBLE DECLINING BALANCE METHOD"
130   GO TO 150
140   PRINT "SUM-OF-THE-YEARS'-DIGITS METHOD"
150   PRINT
160   PRINT "END OF YEAR","DEPRECIATION","CURRENT VALUE"
170   LET J=0
180   LET D1=V/N
190   LET F1=V/(N*(N+1)/2)
200   LET J=J+1
210   ON I GO TO 300,400,500
215
300   REM STRAIGHT-LINE METHOD
305
310   LET V=V-D1
320   PRINT J,D1,V
330   IF J<N THEN 200
340   STOP
345
400   REM DOUBLE DECLINING BALANCE METHOD
405
410   LET D2=(2/N)*V
420   LET V=V-D2
430   PRINT J,D2,V
440   IF J<N THEN 200
450   STOP
455
500   REM SUM-OF-THE-YEARS'-DIGITS METHOD
505
510   LET F2=N-J+1
520   LET D3=F1*F2
530   LET V=V-D3
540   PRINT J,D3,V
550   IF J<N THEN 200
560   END
```

Fig. 4.5

Figures 4.6(a), (b) and (c) show the output that is obtained with the straight-line method, the double declining balance method and the sum-of-the-years'-digits method, respectively. In each case we are depreciating an item whose initial value is $8000 over a ten-year lifetime.

Notice that the last two methods result in a large annual depreciation during the early years, but a very small annual depreciation in the last few years of the item's lifetime. Also, we see that the item has a value of zero at the end of its lifetime when using the first and third methods, but a finite value remains when using the double declining balance method. (The appearance of the number 2.47955E$-$5 rather than zero in Fig. 4.6(c) is caused by numerical roundoff errors.)

```
V=? 8000                                    V=? 8000
N=? 10                                      N=? 10
I=? 1                                       I=? 2

STRAIGHT-LINE METHØD                        DØUBLE DECLINING BALANCE METHØD

END ØF YEAR   DEPRECIATIØN  CURRENT VALUE   END ØF YEAR    DEPRECIATIØN   CURRENT VALUE
1             800           7200            1              1600           6400
2             800           6400            2              1280           5120
3             800           5600            3              1024           4096
4             800           4800            4              819.2          3276.8
5             800           4000            5              655.36         2621.44
6             800           3200            6              524.288        2097.15
7             800           2400            7              419.43         1677.72
8             800           1600            8              335.544        1342.18
9             800           800             9              268.435        1073.74
10            800           0               10             214.748        858.993


TIME:  0.45 SECS.                           TIME:  0.43 SECS.
```

            (a)   (b)

```
                    V=? 8000
                    N=? 10
                    I=? 3

                    SUM-ØF-THE-YEARS'-DIGITS METHØD

                    END ØF YEAR   DEPRECIATIØN   CURRENT VALUE
                    1             1454.55        6545.45
                    2             1309.09        5236.36
                    3             1163.64        4072.73
                    4             1018.18        3054.55
                    5             872.727        2181.82
                    6             727.273        1454.55
                    7             581.818        872.727
                    8             436.364        436.364
                    9             290.909        145.455
                    10            145.455        2.47955E-5


                    TIME:  0.31 SECS.
```

                              (c)

                           Fig. 4.6

4.5 Building a Loop — The FOR-TO Statement

We have already seen that a loop can be built in BASIC by using the IF-THEN and the GO-TO statements. This is convenient when it is not known in advance how many times the loop must be repeated. Often, however, we do know in advance how many times a loop should be executed. Under these circumstances the loop can be built most easily by using the FOR-TO and the NEXT statements.

The *FOR-TO statement* specifies how many times the loop will be executed. It must always be the first statement in the loop. Included in the FOR-TO statement is a nonsubscripted (ordinary), numeric variable, called the *running variable,* whose value changes each time the loop is executed. The number of executions is determined by specifying initial and final values for the running variable.

Example 4.10

A typical FOR-TO statement is shown below.

        50 FOR I=1 TO 10

In this example I is the running variable. The first time the loop is executed I will be assigned a value of 1. I will increase by 1 unit each time the loop is repeated, until I has reached its final value of 10 during the last execution. The execution will be terminated once I has exceeded its final value of 10. Hence the loop defined by the above FOR-TO statement will be executed 10 times.

The running variable will always increase by 1 unit if the FOR-TO statement contains no instructions to the contrary. We can, however, increment the running variable by some value other than 1 if we wish. This is accomplished by adding a STEP clause to the FOR-TO statement, as illustrated in the next example.

Example 4.11

Suppose we want to execute a loop 50 times, and we require that the running variable increase by 2 units after each successive execution. We could write

        75 FOR J=1 TO 99 STEP 2

Thus the running variable J would be assigned a value of 1 during the first pass, a value of 3 during the second pass, 5 during the third pass, etc., until J would take on a value of 99 during the 50th (last) pass.

The running variable need not be restricted to positive integer values, it can take on negative and fractional values if desired. Furthermore, the running variable can be made to *decrease* with each successive execution of the loop. (This is accomplished by specifying a negative quantity in the STEP clause.) Finally, the initial, final and STEP values assigned to the running variable can be expressed as variables or formulas as well as numbers.

Example 4.12

Shown below are several illustrations of valid FOR-TO statements.

        30 FOR X=−1.5 TO 2.7 STEP 0.1
        15 FOR I=N TO 0 STEP −1
        55 FOR K=N1 TO N2 STEP N3
        80 FOR F=A/2 TO (B+C)↑2 STEP K+1

Some versions of BASIC allow use of the word BY rather than STEP.

Example 4.13

In some versions of BASIC the FOR-TO statement shown in Example 4.11 could also be written as

        75 FOR J=1 TO 99 BY 2

4.6 Closing a Loop — The NEXT Statement

Just as a loop always begins with a FOR-TO statement, it always ends with a *NEXT statement*. The complete loop is comprised of all statements included between the FOR-TO and the NEXT statements.

The NEXT statement consists of a statement number, followed by the keyword NEXT, followed by a running variable name. This running variable must be the same as the running variable that appears in the corresponding FOR-TO statement.

Example 4.14

Shown below is the skeletal structure of a loop that is built using the FOR-TO and NEXT statements.

        50 FOR I=1 TO 10
        . . .
        90 NEXT I

The loop will consist of all statements from statement number 50 to statement number 90, and it will be executed 10 times.

Several rules must be kept in mind when constructing a FOR-TO...NEXT loop. These rules are summarized below.

1. The running variable can appear in a statement inside the loop, but its value cannot be altered.

2. If the initial and final values of the running variable are equal and the step size is nonzero, then the loop will be executed once.

3. The loop will not be executed at all under the following three special conditions.

   (a) The initial and final values of the running variable are equal and the step size is zero.

   (b) The final value of the running variable is less than the original value, and the step size is positive.

   (c) The final value of the running variable is greater than the original value, and the step size is negative.

   (Usually the conditions described in rules 2 and 3 occur only by accident.)

4. Control can be transferred out of a loop but not in. (The transfer out can be accomplished by a GO TO, IF-THEN or ON-GO TO statement.)

Example 4.15

Consider the skeletal structure of the loop shown below.

```
120 FOR X=0 TO 0.5 STEP 0.01
       . . .
165        LET Z=X+Y
170        IF Z>Z1 THEN 250
       . . .
195 NEXT X
       . . .
250 PRINT X,Y,Z
```

This example illustrates the use of the running variable (X) within the loop (specifically, in statement 165). We also see that statement 170 causes control to be transferred outside the loop if the value of Z is greater than the value of Z1. Finally, we see that the running variable that appears in the NEXT statement (X) is the same as the running variable in the FOR-TO statement, as required.

Notice that the statements within the loop, between FOR-TO and NEXT, are indented to the right. This is not required but it is good programming practice, since the indentation allows the statements within the loop to be easily identified.

The FOR-TO...NEXT loop structure is frequently used in many different types of problem situations. A typical problem involving the use of such a loop is shown in the example below.

Example 4.16 Averaging of Air Pollution Data

The level of air pollution can be expressed in terms of the air quality, i.e., the number of particles of a particular pollutant per cubic centimeter of air. Hence the higher the value for air quality, the greater the pollution level. Measurements of air quality are made several times a day in most large cities.

Suppose we are given a table containing N measurements of air quality at different times during the day, as shown in Table 4.1. (Note that the time is given in 24-hour cycles, i.e., 13:00 refers to 1:00 P.M. Also, note that N=20 in this example.) We would like to calculate an average (mean) value of air quality for the entire period. This can be accomplished by first calculating an average value for each time interval (i.e., the time period between successive readings), and then calculating a weighted overall average from the individual averages.

Table 4.1

Time	Air Quality	Time	Air Quality
0:00	12.2	13:00	46.6
2:00	12.5	14:00	43.1
4:00	11.9	15:00	39.2
6:00	13.5	16:00	44.7
7:00	22.4	17:00	62.9
8:00	31.4	18:00	88.0
9:00	57.7	19:00	71.4
10:00	84.4	20:00	59.0
11:00	68.0	22:00	43.5
12:00	51.6	24:00	28.7

Computational Procedure

Let us first introduce the following symbols.

$T1$ = the time at the start of a given time interval
$T2$ = the time at the end of the given time interval
$Q1$ = the air quality at the start of the given time interval
$Q2$ = the air quality at the end of the given time interval
$Q3$ = the average air quality within the given time interval

The computation will proceed as follows.

1. Calculate the average air quality within each time interval using the formula

   $$Q3 = (Q1+Q2)/2$$

2. Multiply each average air quality by the corresponding time interval $(T2-T1)$ and add up all of these products, i.e.,

   $$S = [Q3*(T2-T1)]_1 + [Q3*(T2-T1)]_2 + \cdots + [Q3*(T2-T1)]_{N-1}$$

   In the above formula S refers to the sum of the individual products, and the subscripts $1, 2, \ldots, N-1$ refer to the various time intervals. (Note that there will be $N-1$ time intervals, since there are N values of Q and T.)

3. Divide this sum by the *overall* time interval (the time of the last reading minus the time of the first reading) to obtain the time-averaged value.

   $$A = S/(T9-T0)$$

   where A refers to the time-averaged air quality, and $T0$ and $T9$ refer to the times of the first and last readings, respectively.

(The reader who has studied numerical calculus will recognize this problem as an elementary exercise in numerical integration. The method is known as the *trapezoidal rule*.)

The Program Outline

We can now write the following detailed outline of the computational procedure.

1. Read N.

2. Set S equal to zero before reading any of the actual data.

3. Read the first set of data (i.e., the initial values for T1 and Q1).

4. Set T0 equal to T1. (This is a way of "tagging" the time of the first reading. We will need this value in step 7 below.)

5. Perform the following calculations $(N-1)$ times.

   (*a*) Read T2 and Q2.

   (*b*) Calculate Q3.

   (*c*) Add the product Q3*(T2-T1) to S.

(d) Set T1 equal to T2 and Q1 equal to Q2, in preparation for the next time interval. (In other words, the values for T and Q at the *end* of a *given* time interval become the values for T and Q at the *start* of the *next* time interval.)

6. Set T9 equal to the last value of T2.

7. Calculate A.

8. Print A and the overall time interval, (T9-T0).

9. Stop.

A flowchart corresponding to the above outline is shown in Fig. 4.7. Notice that the FOR-TO...NEXT loop is enclosed within a dashed rectangle.

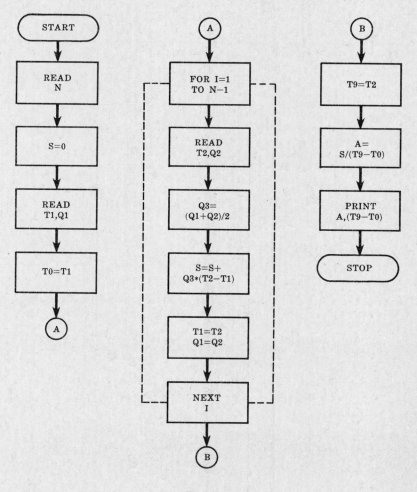

Fig. 4.7

The BASIC Program

Figure 4.8 shows a complete BASIC program that corresponds to the outline presented above. We see that the cumulative sum S is formed by the FOR-TO...NEXT loop consisting of statements 100 through 160. Notice that the program does not require that the complete list of input data be stored internally in order to calculate this cumulative sum. (We will see a convenient way to store a complete list, if we should choose to do so, in the next chapter.)

The lower portion of Fig. 4.8 shows the input values and the calculated results corresponding to the data in Table 4.1. We see that the overall average air quality is 41.5 for the given 24-hour period. (Note that the answer will not be accurate to more than 3 significant figures, since this is the accuracy of the input data.)

```
EX 4.16         21:57         14-MAR-73

10    REM AVERAGING OF AIR POLLUTION DATA
20    PRINT "N=";
30    INPUT N
40    LET S=0
50    PRINT
60    PRINT "  T      Q"
70    PRINT
80    INPUT T1,Q1
90    LET T0=T1
100   FOR I=1 TO N-1
110      INPUT T2,Q2
120      LET Q3=(Q1+Q2)/2
130      LET S=S+Q3*(T2-T1)
140      LET T1=T2
150      LET Q1=Q2
160   NEXT I
170   LET T9=T2
180   LET A=S/(T9-T0)
190   PRINT
200   PRINT "AVERAGE AIR QUALITY=";A;"TIME INTERVAL=";T9-T0;"HOURS"
210   END

>RUN

EX 4.16         21:53         14-MAR-73


N=? 20

   T    Q

?  0,   12.2
?  2,   12.5
?  4,   11.9
?  6,   13.5
?  7,   22.4
?  8,   31.4
?  9,   57.7
? 10,   84.4
? 11,   68.0
? 12,   51.6
? 13,   46.6
? 14,   43.1
? 15,   39.2
? 16,   44.7
? 17,   62.9
? 18,   88.0
? 19,   71.4
? 20,   59.0
? 22,   43.5
? 24,   28.7

AVERAGE AIR QUALITY= 41.5354 TIME INTERVAL= 24 HOURS


TIME:  0.63 SECS.
```

Fig. 4.8

4.7 Nested Loops

One loop can be imbedded within another (i.e., *nested*) if desired. In fact, there can be several levels of nesting. The rules for writing single loops also apply to nested loops. In addition, the following restrictions must be observed.

1. Each nested loop must begin with its own FOR-TO statement and end with its own NEXT statement.

2. An outer loop and an inner (nested) loop cannot have the same running variable.

3. Each inner (nested) loop must be *completely* imbedded within an outer loop (i.e., the loops cannot overlap).

4. Control can be transferred from an inner (nested) loop to a statement in an outer loop or to a statement outside of the entire nest. However, control cannot be transferred to a statement within a nest from a point outside the nest.

Example 4.17

Shown below is the skeletal structure of a program containing a nested loop.

```
100 FOR I=0 TO N STEP 2
        . . .
120         FOR J=I TO N
                . . .
160         NEXT J
        . . .
200 NEXT I
```

Notice that the inner loop (statements 120 through 160) is completely imbedded within the outer loop (statements 100 through 200). Each loop begins and ends with its own FOR-TO and NEXT statements, and each loop has its own running variable. Note, however, that the running variable of the outer loop (I) is used as the *initial value* for the running variable of the inner loop (J). This is permissible, since the value of I is not altered within the inner loop.

A nest of loops provides a convenient means of carrying out repeated sets of calculations. An example follows.

Example 4.18   Generation of Fibonacci Numbers and Search for Primes

The Fibonacci numbers are members of an interesting sequence in which each number is equal to the sum of the previous 2 numbers. In other words

$$F_i = F_{i-1} + F_{i-2}$$

where F_i refers to the ith Fibonacci number. The first 2 Fibonacci numbers are defined to equal 1, i.e.,

$$F_1 = 1$$
$$F_2 = 1$$

Hence

$$F_3 = F_2 + F_1 = 1 + 1 = 2$$
$$F_4 = F_3 + F_2 = 2 + 1 = 3$$
$$F_5 = F_4 + F_3 = 3 + 2 = 5$$

and so on.

All of the Fibonacci numbers are positive integer quantities, and some of them will be *primes*. A positive prime number is an integer that is divisible, without a remainder, only by 1 or by itself. For example, 5 is a prime number because the only quantities that can be divided evenly into 5 are 1 and 5. On the other hand, 8 is not a prime because 8 is divisible by 2 and 4 as well as by 1 and 8.

Computational Procedure

It is very easy to calculate the first N Fibonacci numbers using the above formula. However, the procedure for determining whether or not a number is prime requires some explanation.

Suppose we want to determine if a given integer whose value is greater than 2 can be divided evenly by a smaller integer. Let us call the given integer F and the divisor J. The procedure is to calculate a quotient, Q, as

    Q=F/J

We then calculate a *truncated* quotient, Q1, as

    Q1=INT(Q)

The letters INT refer to a BASIC library function that will determine the largest integer that does not exceed Q. (We will say more about BASIC library functions in the next chapter.) Thus if Q has a value of 5.3, then Q1 will have a value of 5.

If Q and Q1 have the same value, then F is evenly divisible by J. Furthermore, if F is evenly divisible by *any* value of J, from J=2 to J=F−1, then F cannot be prime. Hence F will be a prime number only if Q and Q1 *are not equal* for J = 2, 3, ..., F−1.

The Program Outline

Let us refer to F as a given Fibonacci number (i.e., F_i), F1 as the previous Fibonacci number (F_{i-1}) and F2 as the second previous Fibonacci number (F_{i-2}). We can now write an outline of our program as follows.

1. Read N.

2. Set F1 and F2 equal to 1.

3. Print F1 and F2, identifying each as a prime.

4. Do the following calculations for $I = 3, 4, \ldots, N$.

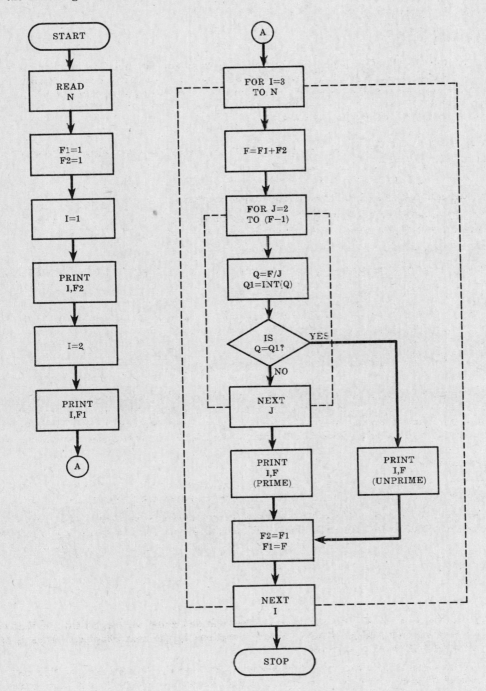

Fig. 4.9

```
10   REM GENERATIØN ØF FIBØNACCI NUMBERS AND SEARCH FØR PRIMES
20   PRINT "N=";
30   INPUT N
40   PRINT
50   PRINT "GENERATIØN ØF FIBØNACCI NUMBERS AND SEARCH FØR PRIMES"
60   PRINT
70   LET F1=1
80   LET F2=1
90   PRINT "I=";1,"F=";1;" (PRIME)"
100  PRINT "I=";2,"F=";1;" (PRIME)"
110  FØR I=3 TØ N    '(GENERATE FIBØNACCI NUMBERS)
120     LET F=F1+F2
130     FØR J=2 TØ F-1   '(TEST FØR A PRIME NUMBER)
140        LET Q=F/J
150        LET Q1=INT(Q)
160        IF Q=Q1 THEN 200
170     NEXT J
180     PRINT "I=";I,"F=";F;" (PRIME)"
190     GØ TØ 210
200     PRINT "I=";I,"F=";F
210     LET F2=F1
220     LET F1=F
230  NEXT I
240  END

> RUN
```

```
N=? 30

GENERATIØN ØF FIBØNACCI NUMBERS AND SEARCH FØR PRIMES

I= 1          F= 1    (PRIME)
I= 2          F= 1    (PRIME)
I= 3          F= 2    (PRIME)
I= 4          F= 3    (PRIME)
I= 5          F= 5    (PRIME)
I= 6          F= 8
I= 7          F= 13   (PRIME)
I= 8          F= 21
I= 9          F= 34
I= 10         F= 55
I= 11         F= 89   (PRIME)
I= 12         F= 144
I= 13         F= 233   (PRIME)
I= 14         F= 377
I= 15         F= 610
I= 16         F= 987
I= 17         F= 1597   (PRIME)
I= 18         F= 2584
I= 19         F= 4181
I= 20         F= 6765
I= 21         F= 10946
I= 22         F= 17711
I= 23         F= 28657   (PRIME)
I= 24         F= 46368
I= 25         F= 75025
I= 26         F= 121393
I= 27         F= 196418
I= 28         F= 317811
I= 29         F= 514229   (PRIME)
I= 30         F= 832040

TIME:   71.91 SECS.
```

Fig. 4.10

(a) Calculate a value for F using the formula

$$F = F1 + F2$$

(b) Do the following for $J = 2, 3, \ldots, F-1$. (Test for a prime number.)

   (i) Calculate values for Q and Q1, and test to see if they are equal.

   (ii) If Q and Q1 are equal for any value of J, then F cannot be a prime number. Hence print I and F, and proceed directly to step 4(c) below.

   (iii) If Q and Q1 are unequal for *all* values of J, then F must be a prime number. Hence print I and F, identifying F as a prime, and proceed to step 4(c) below.

(c) Update F1 and F2 (i.e., assign the current value of F1 to F2, then assign the current value of F to F1), in preparation for calculating a new Fibonacci number (i.e., a new value for F).

5. Stop.

A corresponding flowchart is shown in Fig. 4.9.

The BASIC Program

A complete BASIC program corresponding to the above outline is shown in Fig. 4.10. Notice that the program contains a nest of loops. The purpose of the inner loop (statements 130-170) is to determine whether or not each Fibonacci number is a prime, whereas the outer loop (statements 110-230) causes the desired sequence of Fibonacci numbers to be generated. Note the conditional transfer of control out of the inner loop when Q=Q1 (statement 160).

The lower portion of Fig. 4.10 shows the output that is generated when the program is executed for a value of N=30. We see that 11 of the first 30 Fibonacci numbers are primes. It is also noteworthy that the execution required about 72 seconds of computer time, which is much greater than any of the previous programming examples in this book. Thus we see that programs that contain nested loops can require significant quantities of computer time.

Review Questions

4.1   Is logical decision making an important attribute of a digital computer? Explain the reasons for your answer.

4.2   What is meant by a transfer of control within a BASIC program?

4.3   What is a conditional branching operation? How does this operation differ from an unconditional branching operation?

4.4   What is a looping operation? What is the purpose of such an operation?

4.5   Name the six relational operators used in BASIC. What is their purpose?

4.6   What is the purpose of the IF-THEN statement?

4.7   Summarize the rules for writing an IF-THEN statement, and explain what happens when this statement is executed.

4.8   How does the IF-THEN statement differ from the GO TO statement? Can these two statements be used together to carry out a common logical operation?

4.9   What is meant by an iterative procedure?

4.10 What is the purpose of the ON-GO TO statement?

4.11   How does the ON-GO TO statement differ from the IF-THEN statement?

4.12   Summarize the rules for writing an ON-GO TO statement, and explain what happens when this statement is executed.

4.13   Exactly what happens to a number when it is truncated?

4.14   What is the purpose of the STOP statement?   How does this statement differ from an END statement?

4.15   What is the purpose of the FOR-TO statement?   What is the purpose of the running variable? The STEP clause?

4.16   Can the running variable in a FOR-TO statement take on fractional or negative values?

4.17   Can the running variable be made to decrease in value with each successive execution of the loop?

4.18   What is the purpose of the NEXT statement?   What is required of the running variable that appears in this statement?

4.19   Indicate two different ways that a loop can be structured in BASIC.   For what kind of situation is each type of loop best suited?

4.20   Can the running variable appear in a statement that is contained within a FOR-TO...NEXT loop? Can the value of the running variable be altered in such a statement?

4.21   Under what conditions will a FOR-TO...NEXT loop be executed only once?   Not at all?

4.22   What restrictions apply to a transfer of control into or out of a FOR-TO...NEXT loop?

4.23   Why are the statements that appear in a FOR-TO...NEXT loop frequently indented?   Is such indentation necessary?

4.24   What is meant by nested loops?

4.25   Summarize the rules that apply to a nest of FOR-TO...NEXT loops.   Compare with the rules that apply to a single such loop.

Solved Problems

4.26   Each of the following is a condition that involves the use of relational operators. Identify which, if any, are written incorrectly.

Condition	Error
X="DATE"	A numeric variable cannot be compared with a string.
K↑2>=100	Correct.
N$<>A+B	A string variable cannot be compared with a numeric quantity.
P$="123456"	Correct.
T$=R$+S$	Formulas involving strings or string variables are not allowed.

4.27 Several IF-THEN statements are shown below. Identify which, if any, are written incorrectly.

Statement	Error
20 IF K↑2>=100 THEN 50	Correct.
20 IF (K↑2>=100) THEN 50	Correct.
20 IF K↑2>=100 GO TO 50	Not all versions of BASIC allow use of GO TO in place of THEN.
65 IF X+Y<>Z THEN M	The statement number to which control is transferred must be a positive integer, not a variable.
100 IF G$="MAY 13" THEN 45	Correct.
35 GO TO 150 IF J=3	Incorrect grammatical structure (statement must begin with IF).
50 IF X1<=50 THEN X=X+5	Incorrect grammatical structure (THEN can be followed only by a statement number).

4.28 The skeletal structures of several IF-THEN...GO TO loops are shown below. Identify which, if any, are written incorrectly.

(a)   20...
        . . .
        60 IF N>N1 THEN 110
        . . .
        85 LET N=N+1
        90 GO TO 20
        . . .
        110...

   Correct.

(b)   35 LET P=0
        . . .
        50...
        . . .
        75 IF P<=0 THEN 125
        80 GO TO 50
        . . .
        125...

   Control will always be transferred to statement 125, since P is initially assigned a value of zero and this value is not subsequently altered.

(c)   15...
        . . .
        45 INPUT X
        50 IF X<50 THEN 90
        . . .
        85 STOP
        90...
        . . .
        110 GO TO 15

   Correct.

(d)   110 C=5
      . . .
      130. . .
      . . .
      160 IF C<=0 THEN 200
      170 C=C+5
      180 GO TO 130
      . . .
      200. . .

The loop will continue indefinitely, since C will never be less than or equal to zero.

4.29 Several ON-GO TO statements are shown below. Identify which, if any, are written incorrectly.

Statement	*Error*
15 ON X3 GO TO 25,15,25,40	Correct.
100 ON 2*(C1+C2)/N GO TO K1,K2,K3	The statement numbers to which control is transferred must be positive integers, not variables.
55 ON J+K THEN 120,90,150	Not all versions of BASIC allow use of THEN in place of GO TO.
80 ON T GO TO 25	At least 2 different statement numbers must be given.
20 ON N$ GO TO 50,70,50,90	A string variable cannot appear in an ON-GO TO statement.
60 ON P(I) GO TO 10,120	Correct. (Note that P(I) is a *subscripted* variable. We will discuss subscripted variables in Chapter 5.)

4.30 Several FOR-TO statements are shown below. Identify which, if any, are written incorrectly.

Statement	*Error*
20 FOR N=J TO 3*(K+1) STEP J1	Correct.
50 FOR N=0 TO −100 STEP −5	Correct.
75 FOR X(I)=1 TO 100	A subscripted variable cannot be used as a running variable.
35 FOR K=K1 TO 100 STEP K1	Correct.
65 FOR N$=1 TO 19 STEP 2	A string variable cannot be used as a running variable.
100 FOR I=J TO K STEP I	The running variable cannot appear in the STEP clause.

4.31 The skeletal structures of several FOR-TO. . . NEXT loops are shown below. Identify which, if any, are written incorrectly.

(a)   20 FOR I=1 TO 100 STEP J
      . . .
      80 NEXT J

The running variable in the NEXT statement (J) is not the same as the running variable in the FOR-TO statement (I).

(b)   50 FOR N=N1 TO N2
      . . .
      75. . .
      . . .
      90 NEXT N
      . . .
      120 IF N=10 THEN 75

Control cannot be transferred into a loop.

(c)   100 FOR K=3 TO −3 STEP −1
. . .
130 PRINT X↑K
. . .
150 NEXT K

    Correct, providing a value has been assigned to X.   (Notice that the running variable appears within the PRINT statement, but its value is not altered.)

(d)   25 FOR X=0 TO 1 STEP 0.05
    . . .
   50   FOR Y=0 TO 10 STEP 0.1
      . . .
   75   NEXT X
    . . .
100 NEXT Y

    The loops overlap.

(e)   100 FOR I=1 TO M
    . . .
  125   FOR J=1 TO N
      . . .
  135   FOR K=1 TO M+N
        . . .
  160   NEXT K
      . . .
  180   NEXT J
      . . .
  200   FOR J=1 TO N
      . . .
  225   NEXT J
      . . .
  235   FOR K=1 TO M+N
      . . .
  240   NEXT K
    . . .
250 NEXT I

    Correct.

Supplementary Problems

4.32 Each of the following is a condition that involves the use of a relational operator.   Identify which, if any, are written incorrectly.

  (a) J>=J1+J2   (d) X<.01

  (b) C=C+1   (e) P2<>T$

  (c) N$="END"   (f) A/B<=C/D

4.33 In order that the condition

        P$<Q$

be satisfied, what is required of the strings represented by the variables P$ and Q$?

4.34 Several IF-THEN statements are shown below. Identify which, if any, are written incorrectly.

(*a*)   30 IF K<>K1 THEN 10   (*e*)   150 IF P=P1 THEN K

(*b*)   50 IF J<100 THEN J=J+1   (*f*)   100 IF B↑2<>(4*A*C) THEN 150

(*c*)   120 IF X>=Y+Z GO TO 200   (*g*)   45 IF X↑2<0 THEN 20

(*d*)   75 IF M$="DATE" THEN 50

4.35 Write one or more BASIC statements to accommodate each situation described below.

(*a*) If K has a value less than 15, then transfer control to statement number 50; otherwise execute the next statement.

(*b*) If N$ represents the string "OPTION A," then transfer control to statement number 70; otherwise transfer control to statement number 150.

(*c*) If X has a value equal to or greater than 100, then transfer control ahead to statement 200; otherwise increment J by one unit, read a new value for X, and return to statement 60.

(*d*) If J has a value of zero, then transfer control to statement 150; otherwise add the value of J to the value of S and return to statement 20.

4.36 The skeletal structures of several IF-THEN...GO TO loops are shown below. Identify which, if any, are written incorrectly.

(*a*)   20...
        ...
        120 IF K$="END" THEN 200
        130 PRINT A,B,C
        140 GO TO 20
        ...
        200 STOP

(*b*)   10 INPUT N
        20 LET T=0
        30 LET J=1
        40 INPUT T1
        50 LET T=T+T1
        60 IF J=N THEN 150
        70 LET J=J+1
        80 GO TO 30
        ...
        150 PRINT J,T
        160 END

(*c*)   10 LET X=100
        ...
        50...
        ...
        100 IF X>=100 THEN 200
        110 LET X=X−5
        120 GO TO 50
        ...
        200...

(*d*)   10 LET X=100
        ...
        50...
        ...
        100 IF X>100 THEN 200
        110 LET X=X−5
        120 GO TO 50
        ...
        200...

(*e*)   10 LET X=100
        ...
        50...
        ...
        100 IF X=0 THEN 200
        110 LET X=X−5
        120 GO TO 50
        ...
        200...

4.37 Several ON-GO TO statements are shown below. Identify which, if any, are written incorrectly.

(*a*)   50 ON N$ GO TO 10,70,120   (*e*)   150 ON ((A+B)/C)↑2 GO TO 170,190,225

(*b*) 100 ON A GO TO 50,20,50,200,120   (*f*)   45 ON K−3 THEN 65,90

(*c*)   75 ON X1 GO TO 100,25,75,150   (*g*)   80 GO TO 50,120,150 ON (X+Y)

(*d*) 100 ON N GO TO N1,N2,N3,N4,N5

4.38 Consider the following ON-GO TO statement (which is grammatically correct):

            75 ON J−K GO TO 100,50,20,150

What will happen when this statement is executed if

(a) J=2 and K=3?   (d) J=5 and K=0?

(b) J=4.5 and K=0.75?   (e) J=−1 and K=−2.8?

(c) J=1 and K=−1?

4.39 Several FOR-TO statements are shown below. Identify which, if any, are written incorrectly.

(a) 100 FOR C=.1*A TO .25*(A+B) STEP P/2   (d) 125 FOR X=V(1) TO V(2) STEP V(3)

(b)   65 FOR X↑2=0 TO 100 STEP 20   (e)   30 FOR J1=25 TO −25 STEP −5

(c)   80 FOR K$=P$ TO Q$ (f)   45 FOR A=12 TO 0 STEP 0.1

4.40 Write an appropriate pair of FOR-TO and NEXT statements (i.e., write the skeletal structure of a FOR-TO...NEXT loop) for each situation described below.

(a) A loop is to be repeated 200 times.

(b) A loop is to be repeated 200 times, except that control will be transferred out of the loop to statement 175 if the value of the variable X becomes less than 0.001.

(c) A loop will be repeated as many times as necessary for the running variable to increase from 1 to 73, assuming that the running variable is increased by 3 units each time the loop is executed.

(d) A loop will be repeated as many times as necessary for the running variable to increase from 0.5 to a value given by the formula A↑3−10. Each time the loop is executed the running variable will increase by the value given by the formula A+B.

4.41 The skeletal structures of several FOR-TO...NEXT loops are shown below. Identify which, if any, are written incorrectly.

(a)   10 FOR K=K1 TO K2   (d) 100 FOR X=0 TO 1 STEP .02
          ...   ...
      50   K=K+1   150   FOR X=0 TO 5 STEP .05
          ...   ...
      90 NEXT K   200 NEXT X

(b)   10 FOR C1=0 TO 50 STEP 5   (e)   50 FOR P=1 TO 50
          ...   ...
      35   FOR C2=0 TO C1   80   FOR Q=2 TO 100 STEP 2
          ...   ...
      65   NEXT C2   100   IF T>=T1 THEN 160
          ...   ...
     100 NEXT C1   120   NEXT Q
                                          ...
(c)   10 FOR J=1 TO N   160 PRINT "T=";T
          ...   ...
      40   FOR K=1 TO M   200 NEXT P
          ...
      70   NEXT J   (f)   75 FOR X=A TO (A+B) STEP C
          ...   ...
     120 NEXT K   125 NEXT C

Programming Problems

4.42 The equation
$$x^5 + 3x^2 - 10 = 0$$
which was presented in Example 4.5, can be rearranged into the form
$$x = \sqrt{(10 - x^5)/3}$$

Rewrite the BASIC program presented in Example 4.5 to make use of the above form of the equation. Run the program, printing out the value of x calculated during each iteration. Compare the calculated results with those presented in Example 4.5.

4.43   Rewrite the program presented in Example 4.5 so that it makes use of a FOR-TO...NEXT loop rather than an IF-THEN...GO TO loop.

4.44   Rewrite the program presented in Example 4.9 so that the ON-GO TO statements are replaced by IF-THEN statements. What conveniences have been achieved by using the ON-GO TO statements?

4.45   Rewrite the program presented in Example 4.16 so that it makes use of an IF-THEN...GO TO loop rather than a FOR-TO...NEXT loop.

4.46   Prepare a detailed outline, a corresponding flowchart and a complete BASIC program for each of the problems presented below.

(a) Calculate the sum of the first 100 odd integers. Write the program two different ways:

   (i) Write a sequence of statements that will add the next integer to the sum each time the sequence is repeated. Let the decision to repeat the sequence or to terminate depend on the outcome of an IF-THEN statement.

   (ii) Use a FOR-TO...NEXT loop.

   What advantages and disadvantages characterize each method?

(b) Calculate the sum of the first N multiples of an integer K. (For example, if K=3 and N=10, then calculate the sum of $1 \times 3 + 2 \times 3 + \cdots + 10 \times 3$.) Make the program completely general by reading in values for N and K each time the program is run. Test the program by calculating the sum of the first 1000 multiples of the integer 3.

(c) Compute the value of K!, where K represents an integer whose value is read into the computer each time the program is run. Test the program by calculating the value of 10! (Note that K! is defined as $1 \times 2 \times 3 \times \cdots \times K$.)

(d) The sine of x can be calculated approximately by summing the first N terms of the infinite series

$$\sin x \ = \ x - \frac{x^3}{3!} + \frac{x^5}{5!} - \frac{x^7}{7!} + \cdots \quad (x \text{ in radians})$$

Write a complete BASIC program that will read in a value for x and then calculate its sine. Write the program two different ways:

   (i) Sum the first N terms, where N represents a positive integer that is read into the computer along with the numerical value for x.

   (ii) Continue adding successive terms in the series until the value of a term becomes smaller (in magnitude) than 10^{-5}.

   Test the program for $x = 1$, $x = 2$ and $x = -3$. In each case write out the number of terms used along with the final answer.

(e) Suppose you place a given sum of money into a savings account each year for 30 years. If the account earns 5 percent annually, payable at the end of each year, then how much must you save each year in order to accumulate $100,000 at the end of 30 years?

   Tabulate the total amount of money you will have accumulated at the end of each year.

   If the interest is compounded quarterly rather than annually, but the annual interest rate is kept the same, will the results be appreciably different?

   How practical would it be to solve this problem with a desk calculator and a table of logarithms?

(f) A class of students earned the following grades for the 6 examinations taken in a BASIC programming course.

Name	Exam Scores (percent)					
Adams	45	80	80	95	55	75
Brown	60	50	70	75	55	80
Davis	40	30	10	45	60	55
Fisher	0	5	5	0	10	5
Hamilton	90	85	100	95	90	90
Jones	95	90	80	95	85	80
Ludwig	35	50	55	65	45	70
Osborne	75	60	75	60	70	80
Prince	85	75	60	85	90	100
Richards	50	60	50	35	65	70
Smith	70	60	75	70	55	75
Thomas	10	25	35	20	30	10
Wolfe	25	40	65	75	85	95
Zorba	65	80	70	100	60	95

Write a BASIC program to determine an average score for each student, assuming that each of the first four exams contributes 15 percent to the final score and each of the last two exams contributes 20 percent. Include a FOR-TO...NEXT loop in the program.

(g) Rewrite the program for Problem 4.46(f), assuming each of the exams is weighted equally. Include a nest of 2 FOR-TO...NEXT loops in the program. Calculate the average score for each student with the inner loop, and use the outer loop to repeat the calculations for all of the students in the class.

(h) Write a BASIC program that will allow a typewriter terminal to be used as a desk calculator. Consider only the common arithmetic operations (addition, subtraction, multiplication and division).

(i) Write a BASIC program to calculate the roots of the quadratic equation

$$ax^2 + bx + c = 0$$

(See Examples 2.26 and 2.30.) Allow for the possibility that one of the constants has a value of zero, and that the quantity $b^2 - 4ac$ is less than or equal to zero.

Chapter 5

Some Additional Features of BASIC

This chapter presents some additional frequently used features of BASIC. We begin with a discussion of the built-in library functions, which simplify such common operations as calculating the absolute value of a number, log of a number, etc. Then we will consider the use of lists and tables, which allow us to manipulate collections of numerical quantities or strings as though they were single variables. Finally we present two additional statements for entering data, thus providing us with an alternative to the use of the INPUT statement.

5.1 Library Functions

The BASIC *library functions* (also called *standard functions* or *elementary functions*) provide a quick and easy way to evaluate many mathematical functions and to carry out certain logical operations. These library functions are prewritten routines that are included as an integral part of the language. Each function is accessed simply by stating its name, followed by whatever information must be supplied to the function, enclosed in parentheses. (A numeric quantity or a string that is passed to a function in this manner is called an *argument*.) Once the library function has been accessed the desired operation will be carried out automatically, without the need for detailed, explicit programming.

Example 5.1

Suppose we wanted to calculate the square root of the value represented by the variable X. We could write

     50 LET Y=SQR(X)

This would cause the variable Y to be assigned a value equal to the square root of X. The name of the square root function is SQR, and its argument, in this example, is the variable X.

Of course, we could have written

     50 LET Y=X↑.5

Thus the use of the square root function is not required, it is merely a convenience. (It should be pointed out, however, that calculating the square root of a number by means of the square root function requires less computer time than the corresponding exponentiation operation.)

Table 5.1 presents several of the commonly used library functions. A more extensive list, including the entries contained in Table 5.1, is shown in Appendix B.

Table 5.1   Commonly Used Library Functions

Function	Application	Description
ABS	10 LET Y=ABS(X)	Calculate the absolute value of x; $y = |x|$.
ATN	10 LET Y=ATN(X)	Calculate the arctangent of x; $y = \arctan(x)$.
COS	10 LET Y=COS(X)	Calculate the cosine of x; $y = \cos(x)$, x in radians.
COT	10 LET Y=COT(X)	Calculate the cotangent of x; $y = \cot(x)$, x in radians.
EXP	10 LET Y=EXP(X)	Raise e to the x power; $y = e^x$ †.
INT	10 LET Y=INT(X)	Assign to y the largest integer that algebraically does not exceed x.
LOG	10 LET Y=LOG(X)	Calculate the natural logarithm of x; $y = \log_e x$, $x > 0$.
SGN	10 LET Y=SGN(X)	Determine the sign of x ($y = +1$ if x is positive, $y = 0$ if $x = 0$, $y = -1$ if x is negative).
SIN	10 LET Y=SIN(X)	Calculate the sine of x; $y = \sin(x)$, x in radians.
SQR	10 LET Y=SQR(X)	Calculate the square root of x; $y = \sqrt{x}$, $x > 0$.
TAB	20 PRINT TAB(N);X	Causes printing head of typewriter terminal to be positioned at a given column. (Left column is considered column 0.)
TAN	10 LET Y=TAN(X)	Calculate the tangent of x; $y = \tan(x)$, x in radians.

†The symbol e represents the base of the natural (Naperian) system of logarithms. It is an irrational number whose approximate value is 2.718282.

The use of all of the functions in Table 5.1 should be readily apparent except for INT and TAB, which are discussed below. Notice that some of the functions (e.g., LOG, SQR) require a positive argument. If any such function is supplied a negative argument, the minus sign will be ignored and the calculation will be based on the absolute value of the argument. Usually, however, an error message will be printed when the function is evaluated, indicating that a negative argument has been supplied.

The INT function requires some additional explanation. This function causes an argument having a *positive* value to be *truncated* (i.e., the decimal portion of the number will be dropped). Thus the INT function will generate a positive integer whose magnitude is less than that of its argument. On the other hand, if the argument has a negative value the INT function will produce a negative integer whose magnitude is *greater* than that of its argument. This is illustrated in Example 5.2 below.

Example 5.2

Consider the statement

    10 LET Y=INT(X)

If X (the argument) represents the value 12.9, then Y will be assigned the value 12. On the other hand, if X represents −4.2, then Y will be assigned a value of −5.

The TAB function permits the programmer to specify the exact positioning of each output item listed in a PRINT statement. This allows greater flexibility in the spacing of output data than the methods described in Section 2.10. Each time the TAB function appears in an output list, the printed head of the typewriter terminal will move to the right until the specified column has been reached. (Note that the leftmost column is considered column 0.) If the printing head is already positioned beyond (i.e., to the right of) the indicated column, however, then the TAB function will be ignored.

Example 5.3

Suppose we wanted to print the values of A, B and C on one line, with the first value beginning in column number 9, the second in column 29 and the third in column 47. (Note that these are actually the 10th, 30th and 48th columns, respectively.) This is accomplished by writing

    100 PRINT TAB(9);A;TAB(29);B;TAB(47);C

On the other hand, consider the statement

150 PRINT "NAME AND ADDRESS";TAB(12);N$

In this case the TAB function will be ignored, since the print head will already be positioned at column number 16 after the string **NAME AND ADDRESS** has been printed. Hence the string represented by N$ will begin in column 16. If the argument of the TAB function were greater than 16, however, then the print head would be positioned as desired.

Use of a library function is not confined to a LET or a PRINT statement—a library function may appear wherever a variable might ordinarily be present. Moreover, the arguments need not be simple variables. Constants, subscripted variables, formulas—even references to other functions—can be used as valid function arguments. Truncation will be performed automatically if necessary for those functions that require integer-valued arguments (as, for example, the TAB function).

Example 5.4

Each of the following statements is a valid example of the use of a library function.

```
 40 LET X1=(−B+SQR(D))/(2*A)
 60 IF ABS(X−X1)<.00001 THEN 110
100 PRINT SIN(T), COS(T), TAN(T), LOG(T), EXP(T)
200 FOR J=0 TO INT(Y)
 75 LET A=LOG(SQR(ABS(P)))
```

The use of library functions is demonstrated in the following example. (Note that library functions were used in Figs. 4.2 and 4.10.)

Example 5.5 A Table of Functions

Suppose we wish to generate a table of values for $\sin(x)$, $\cos(x)$, $\tan(x)$, $\log(x)$ and e^x for 21 values of x ranging from 0 to π. This is easily accomplished with a FOR-TO loop, with the calculated data displayed in columnar form.

The Program Outline

The computation will proceed as follows.

1. Print the following six column headings.

X   SIN(X)   COS(X)   TAN(X)   LOG(X)   EXP(X)

2. Print the values of x, $\sin(x)$, $\cos(x)$, $\tan(x)$, $\log(x)$ and e^x for each value of x ranging from $x=0$ to $x=3.1416$, with a step size of 0.15708 (which is equal $3.1416 \div 20$). This will generate 21 lines of output.

3. Stop.

A corresponding flowchart is shown in Fig. 5.1.

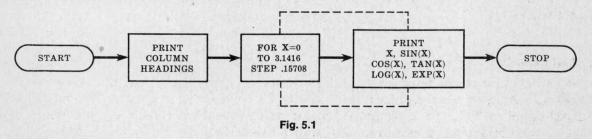

Fig. 5.1

The BASIC Program

A complete BASIC program, followed by the calculated output data, is shown in Fig. 5.2. The program is straightforward and requires no special explanation. It should be pointed out, however, that some care must be used in assigning arguments to the TAB functions so that the six columns of output are spaced evenly across the page. The program may have to be executed several times, with intermittent adjustments of the TAB arguments after each execution, before the columns are spaced correctly.

The output data clearly show the calculated values of $\sin(x)$, $\cos(x)$, $\tan(x)$, $\log(x)$ and e^x for each specified value of x. Notice that an error message is produced when we attempt to calculate the log of zero. This is followed by the number $-1.70141E+38$, which is the largest (in magnitude) negative number that the computer can accommodate. (Actually, the log of zero is defined to have a negative infinite value.) We could have avoided this situation by including an appropriate IF statement in the program.

```
10 REM GENERATION ØF A TABLE ØF MATHEMATICAL FUNCTIØNS
20 PRINT TAB(7);"X";TAB(15);"SIN(X)";TAB(27);"CØS(X)";
30 PRINT TAB(39);"TAN(X)";TAB(51);"LØG(X)";TAB(63);"EXP(X)"
40 PRINT
50 FØR X=0 TØ 3.1416 STEP .15708
60    PRINT TAB(3);X;TAB(13);SIN(X);TAB(25);CØS(X);
70    PRINT TAB(37);TAN(X);TAB(49);LØG(X);TAB(61);EXP(X)
80 NEXT X
90 END

> RUN
```

X	SIN(X)	CØS(X)	TAN(X)	LØG(X)	EXP(X)
0	0	1	0		
% LØG ØF ZERØ IN LINE 70					
	-1.70141E+38				1
0.15708	0.156435	0.987688	0.158385	-1.851	1.17009
0.31416	0.309018	0.951056	0.324921	-1.15785	1.36911
0.47124	0.453991	0.891006	0.509527	-0.752388	1.60198
0.62832	0.587786	0.809016	0.726545	-0.464706	1.87446
0.7854	0.707108	0.707105	1.	-0.241562	2.19328
0.94248	0.809018	0.587783	1.37639	-5.924C6E-2	2.56634
1.09956	0.891008	0.453988	1.96262	9.491C1E-2	3.00284
1.25664	0.951057	0.309014	3.C7771	0.228441	3.5136
1.41372	0.987689	0.156431	6.31389	0.346225	4.11122
1.5708	1	-3.65144E-6	-273864.	0.451585	4.81049
1.72788	0.987688	-0.156438	-6.31359	0.546895	5.62871
1.88496	0.951055	-0.309021	-3.C7764	0.633907	6.58609
2.04204	0.891004	-0.453995	-1.96259	0.713949	7.70631
2.19912	0.809014	-0.587789	-1.37637	0.788057	9.01707
2.3562	0.707103	-0.707111	-0.999989	0.85705	10.5508
2.51328	0.587781	-0.80902	-0.726534	0.921589	12.3454
2.67036	0.453985	-0.891009	-0.509518	0.982213	14.4452
2.82744	0.309011	-0.951059	-0.324912	1.03937	16.9C21
2.98452	0.156428	-0.987689	-0.158377	1.09344	19.777
3.1416	-7.25607E-6	-1	7.25607E-6	1.14473	23.1409

Fig. 5.2

Virtually all versions of BASIC include the library functions shown in Table 5.1 and Appendix B. Many versions of the language also include additional library functions, some of which may be unique to that particular version. Most of these are of a numeric nature, but some accept string arguments or return string values (or both). The reader should consult a reference manual to determine exactly what library functions are available at his particular installation.

5.2 Lists and Tables (Arrays)

When writing a complete program it is often convenient to refer to an entire collection of items at one time. Such a collection is usually referred to as an *array*. We may, for example, be concerned with a complete *list* of items (also known as a *one-dimensional array*), or with all of the entries in a *table* (a *two-dimensional array*). BASIC allows us to refer to the elements of lists and tables as though they were ordinary variables, thus making array manipulation as simple as possible.

The elements in a list or table can be either numerical quantities or strings. (Some versions of BASIC allow string lists but not string tables.) However, all of the elements in a given array must be of the same type (i.e., all numeric or all string). If an array contains numeric elements it must be named with a single letter, whereas a string array is referred to with a letter followed by dollar sign. Note that array names consisting of a letter followed by an integer, or a letter-integer-dollar sign, are not allowed.

Within a given program each array name must be unique, i.e., no two arrays can have the same name. On the other hand, an array and an ordinary variable can be assigned the same name. Such duplication of names within a program can be logically confusing, however, and is therefore not recommended.

Example 5.6

A program is to contain a list of names, and a table of numbers. The list will be called L$, and the table T.

It is also possible to include in the program an ordinary string variable called L$, and an ordinary numeric variable called T. These variables would be separate and distinct from the arrays L$ and T. It would probably be wiser, however, to name these variables differently (e.g., L1$ and T9), thus avoiding any possible confusion between the arrays and other program variables.

5.3   Subscripted Variables

The individual elements within an array are known as *subscripted variables*. Any such element can be referred to by stating the array name, followed by the value of the subscript, enclosed in parentheses. In the case of a table, 2 subscripts must be specified, separated by a comma. Thus P(3) is an element of the list P, and T(8,5) is an element of the table T. The subscripts must be integer-valued and cannot be negative.

Example 5.7

Ten names (strings) are to be placed in a single list. The list will be called L$, and the individual names will be referred to as L$(1), L$(2), ..., L$(10). Notice that the subscript takes on integer values ranging from 1 to 10.

Similarly, forty numbers are to be arranged in a table having 5 rows and 8 columns. We will refer to the table as T. The first subscript (representing the row number) will take on integer values ranging from 1 to 5, and the second subscript (representing the column number) will range from 1 to 8. Thus the number in the third row, fourth column will be referred to as T(3,4), etc.

A subscript need not necessarily be written as a constant. Variables, formulas and function names can also be used. However, the value that a subscript takes on must be either zero or a positive integer. If a formula or a function reference results in a noninteger value for a subscript, then that value will be truncated, thus resulting in an integer-valued subscript. Execution will be suppressed and an error message written if a negative value is generated for a subscript, or if too large a positive value is generated.

Example 5.8

All the subscripted variables shown below are written correctly.

P(3)	T(8,5)
P(K)	T(J1,J2)
P(C(J))	T(6,N)
P(2*A−B)	T(A1+B1, A2+B2)
P(SQR(X↑2+Y↑2))	T(ABS(X+Y), ABS(X−Y))

Consider the subscripted variable P(2*A−B). Suppose the formula 2*A−B has a value of 2.8. This value will be truncated, and the subscripted variable will be interpreted as P(2). If this formula has a value of −3.6, however, then an error message will be written and program execution will terminate.

Subscripted variables can be used within a program in the same manner as ordinary variables. This is illustrated in the following example.

Example 5.9   Word Unscrambling

An interesting problem involving the manipulation of subscripted variables is that of rearranging a group of letters to form all possible words. Suppose, for example, we are given four letters, such as OPST. We would like to form all possible combinations of these four letters and then write out each combination. Thus we can find all possible four-letter words that can be formed from the original four letters (viz., POST, POTS, TOPS, STOP, SPOT).

Computational Procedure

In order to do this, let us place the given letters in a list that we will call L\$. Each letter will be represented by a subscripted variable L\$(1), L\$(2), ... Hence our objective will be to write out all possible combinations of the subscripted variables.

Let us print out the given four letters in the order designated by the indices I1, I2, I3 and I4, where I1 is the subscript of the first letter to be printed, I2 refers to the second letter to be printed, and so on. For example, if I1=3, I2=2, I3=4 and I4=1, we would print the letters in the order

$$\text{L\$(3)} \qquad \text{L\$(2)} \qquad \text{L\$(4)} \qquad \text{L\$(1)}$$

We wish to write a BASIC program that will allow I1, I2, I3 and I4 to take on all possible values, with the restriction that each index have a unique numerical value. That is, no two indices will be allowed to represent the same number.

In addition to the INPUT and PRINT statements, the BASIC program will consist essentially of a nest of three FOR-TO loops. The outermost loop will assign a value to I1; the next loop will assign a value to I2, testing to make sure that I2 differs from I1. The innermost loop will establish a value for I3, again testing to see that I3 has a different value than I1 or I2. Finally, we can obtain a value for I4 by noting that the sum of the first four integers is 10. Therefore once I1, I2 and I3 have each been assigned a unique value, we can calculate I4 from the formula

$$I4 = 10 - (I1 + I2 + I3)$$

The Program Outline

We can outline the entire procedure as follows:

1. Read L\$(1), L\$(2), L\$(3) and L\$(4).

2. Do the following, for I1=1,2,3,4.

   (a) Assign a value to I1.

   (b) Do the following, letting I2=1,2,3,4.

      (i) Assign a value to I2.

      (ii) Test to see if I2 differs from I1. If not, increase I2 by one unit and test again.

      (iii) For each value of I1 and I2 do the following, letting I3=1,2,3,4.

         (1) Assign a value to I3.

         (2) Test to see that I3 differs from both I1 and I2. If not, increase I3 by one unit and test again.

         (3) Calculate a value for I4 from the formula I4=10−(I1+I2+I3).

         (4) Print out L\$(I1), L\$(I2), L\$(I3) and L\$(I4).

3. Stop.

A flowchart of the procedure is shown in Fig. 5.3.

The BASIC Program

The actual BASIC program appears in Fig. 5.4. Shown beneath the program is the output generated for the four letters OPST. We see that there are 24 different ways in which the four letters can be combined. It can be proven mathematically that this is the correct number of combinations. By visual inspection we can find the 5 recognizable words POST, POTS, SPOT, STOP and TOPS. These words have been circled in Fig. 5.4.

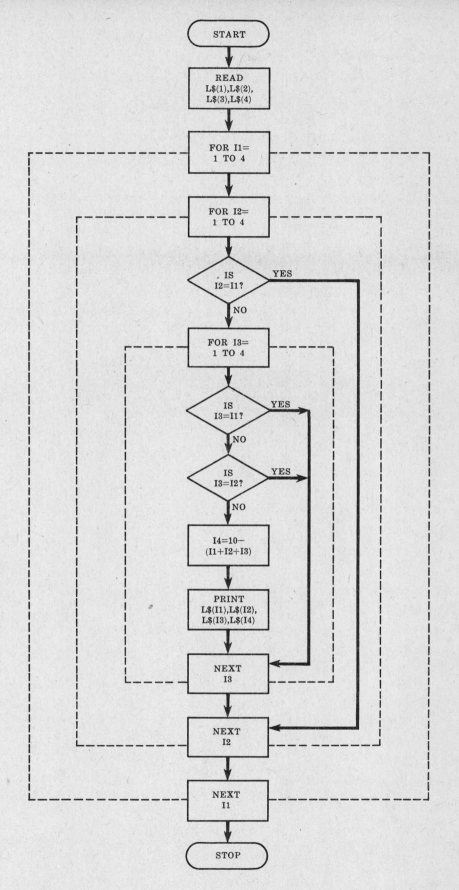

Fig. 5.3

```
10    REM FOUR-LETTER WORD UNSCRAMBLER
20    PRINT "TYPE ANY FOUR LETTERS:"
30    PRINT
40    INPUT L$(1),L$(2),L$(3),L$(4)
50    PRINT
60    FOR I1=1 TO 4
70       FOR I2=1 TO 4
80          IF I2=I1 THEN 150
90          FOR I3=1 TO 4
100            IF I3=I1 THEN 140
110            IF I3=I2 THEN 140
120            LET I4=10-(I1+I2+I3)
130            PRINT L$(I1);L$(I2);L$(I3);L$(I4)
140         NEXT I3
150      NEXT I2
160 NEXT I1
170 END

>RUN


TYPE ANY FOUR LETTERS:

?O,P,S,T

OPST
OPTS
OSPT
OSTP
OTPS
OTSP
POST
POTS
PSOT
PSTO
PTOS
PTSO
SOPT
SOTP
SPOT
SPTO
STOP
STPO
TOPS
TOSP
TPOS
TPSO
TSOP
TSPO
```

Fig. 5.4

5.4 Defining Arrays — The DIM Statement

BASIC automatically assigns 11 elements to every list and 121 elements (11 rows and 11 columns) to every table appearing in a program. Thus each subscript is allowed to range from 0 to 10. Of course we need not make use of all these array elements—a subscript can begin with some integer value greater than zero and end with an integer less than 10. (In Example 5.9, for instance, the subscript ranged only from 1 to 4.)

We can also make use of larger arrays if we wish. To do so, however, we must *define* the size of each array, i.e., we must specify the maximum number of elements in each array. This is accomplished by means of the *DIM (DIMENSION)* statement.

The DIM statement consists of a statement number, followed by the keyword DIM, followed by one or more array names, separated by commas. Each array name must be followed by one or two integer constants (one for a list, two for a table) enclosed in parentheses and, if two integers are shown, separated by a comma. These integers indicate the maximum value of each subscript that is permitted in an array.

Example 5.10

A program is to contain a numeric table called A, two numeric lists called B and C and a string list called F$. The table is to have 50 rows and 100 columns, B and C will have 100 elements and 50 elements respectively, and F$ will contain 65 elements. Hence the program may contain the following DIM statement.

        20 DIM A(50,100), B(100), C(50), F$(65)

This statement actually reserves 51 rows and 101 columns for A, 101 elements for B, 51 elements for C and 66 elements for F$. Thus the arrays are slightly larger than necessary. However, many programmers prefer to have a subscript begin with a value of 1 rather than 0, as though they were working with a subscripted algebraic variable. Under these circumstances it is easiest to write the DIM statement as shown above.

A DIM statement can appear anywhere in a BASIC program. However, it is good programming practice to place the DIM statement at the beginning of a program, where its presence will be readily apparent. This allows a programmer or user to determine maximum array sizes easily and quickly.

Lists having fewer than 11 elements and tables having fewer than 121 elements can also be included in a DIM statement, even though it may not be necessary to do so. This will cause fewer words of storage to be reserved in the computer's memory. Some care is required with tables, however, because one of the subscripts may exceed a value of 10 even though the total number of elements is less than 121. When this happens a DIM statement *must* be used. We will see such a situation in the next example.

Example 5.11

A program contains the following DIM statement.

        30 DIM P(6), Q(10), R(5,15)

This results in 7 words of storage being reserved for the 7 elements of P, 11 words for Q and 96 words (6 rows, 16 columns) for the table R.

The inclusion of P and Q in the DIM statement was really not necessary, since adequate storage would have been assigned automatically. Note, however, that by including P in the DIM statement we have saved 4 words of storage. On the other hand, the table R *must* be included in the DIM statement since the second subscript exceeds 10. This is true despite the fact that the total number of words required by R is less than 121.

We will see an example of a complete program requiring the presence of a DIM statement later in this chapter.

5.5   Entering Input Data — The READ and DATA Statements

Many BASIC programs require that a large number of data items be entered into the computer. This can be accomplished with the INPUT statement, though it may be somewhat cumbersome to do so. Usually it is more convenient to enter such data by means of the *READ* and *DATA statements*. These statements are also used to enter data when a program is run in the batch rather than the timesharing mode.

The READ statement specifies the variables whose values are to be entered into the computer. This statement consists of a statement number, followed by the keyword READ, followed by a list of input variables. The list can contain both ordinary and subscripted variables, representing numeric and/or string values. If the list contains two or more variables they must be separated by commas.

The purpose of the DATA statement is to assign appropriate values to the variables listed in the READ statement. The DATA statement is comprised of a statement number, followed by the keyword DATA, followed by a set of numbers and/or strings, separated by commas. Each number and/or string in a DATA statement must correspond to a variable of the same type in a READ statement.

Example 5.12

A BASIC program contains the statements

        30 READ K,N$,Z(1)
        . . .
        120 DATA 12,SEVENTEEN,−5

These statements cause the number 12 to be assigned to the variable K, the string SEVENTEEN to be assigned to N$, and −5 to be assigned to Z(1).

Each DATA statement need not correspond to a particular READ statement, although such one-to-one correspondence is permitted if desired (as we have seen in the last example). The important point is that *all* of the DATA statements in a program collectively form a *block* of data values. Each element in the data block must correspond to a variable in a READ statement. This correspondence must be with respect to both order and type.

Example 5.13

The following statements are included in a BASIC program.

        40 READ A,B,C
        50 READ P$,Q$
        60 READ F(1),F(2),F(3)
        . . .
        210 DATA 3,−2,11,AB
        220 DATA CD,−8,0,10

These statements cause the numbers 3, −2 and 11 to be assigned to A, B and C, the strings AB and CD to be assigned to P$ and Q$, and the numbers −8, 0, 10 to be assigned to the subscripted variables F(1), F(2) and F(3). Notice that the READ statements do not correspond to the DATA statements on a one-to-one basis, but the variables in the READ statements do correspond, in order and in type, to the elements in the data block.

The two DATA statements could just as well be combined, yielding the single statement

        210 DATA 3,−2,11,AB,CD,−8,0,10

The results would be the same as above.

It should be pointed out that data specified via READ-DATA statements are a part of a program, in contrast to data entered via INPUT statements. Therefore the data contained in a data block are stored whenever the program is stored, and are assigned to the appropriate set of variables whenever the program is executed. Hence such data are relatively permanent; they can be changed only by altering one or more DATA statements within the program.

The following rules must be observed when placing data items in a data block.

1. The data items must correspond in order and in type to the variables listed in the READ statements. There must be at least as many elements in the data block as there are variables in the READ statements. Extra data items will be ignored.

2. The data items within a DATA statement must be separated by commas. However, the last data item in a DATA statement should not be followed by a comma.

3. The data items must consist of numbers or strings. Variables and formulas are not permitted.

4. Strings containing commas or beginning with blank spaces must be enclosed in quotation marks. Other strings *may* be enclosed in quotation marks if desired.

DATA statements may appear anywhere in a BASIC program. However, it is good programming practice to place all DATA statements consecutively near the end of the program. Thus the location and composition of the data block will be readily apparent.

The following example illustrates the assignment of numeric data values to a set of subscripted variables and the manipulation of those subscripted variables. Use of the DIM statement is also demonstrated.

Example 5.14   Reordering a List of Numbers

Consider the well-known problem of rearranging a list of N numbers into a sequence of increasing magnitudes. The program is to be written in such a manner that unnecessary storage will not be used. Therefore the program will contain only one array, which will be rearranged one element at a time.

Computational Procedure

The procedure will be first to scan the entire list for the smallest number and interchange this number with the first number in the list. Next the remaining N−1 numbers are scanned for the smallest of these numbers, and this smallest number is interchanged with the second number. Then the last N−2 numbers are scanned for the smallest number, which is interchanged with the third number, and so on, until the entire list has been rearranged. This will require a total of N−1 passes through the list, though the list will decrease by one number for each subsequent scan.

In order to find the smallest number for each pass, we sequentially compare each number in the list with the starting number (the ith number). If the ith number is larger than, say, the jth number, then we interchange the two numbers; otherwise we leave the two numbers in their original positions. Once this procedure has been applied to the entire list, the first number in the list will be the smallest. We then repeat the entire procedure N−2 times, for a total of N−1 passes ($i = 1, 2, \ldots, N-1$).

The only remaining question is how the ith number and the jth number are interchanged. We first "set aside" the ith number for future reference; that is, we save the original value of the ith subscripted variable. Then we assign the value of the jth subscripted variable to the ith subscripted variable. Finally we assign the *original* value of the ith subscripted variable, which had been set aside, to the jth subscripted variable. The interchange is now complete.

The Program Outline

The entire computational procedure can be carried out with a double FOR-TO loop. To see how this is accomplished, consider the following outline:

1. Read in the size of the list (N).

2. Read in and then print out the list of N integer constants.

3. Perform the following calculations N−1 times, letting $i = 1, 2, \ldots, N-1$:
   Compare the ith number, which will be the starting number in the list, with each successive number (each jth number, where $j = i+1, i+2, \ldots, N$). Whenever the ith number is larger than the jth number, interchange the two numbers.

4. Print out the rearranged list of numbers.

5. Stop.

A flowchart of the procedure is shown in Fig. 5.5.

The BASIC Program

When writing the actual BASIC program let us refer to the list of integer constants as K. We will assume that K will never consist of more than 101 elements. Hence we will set the maximum permissible value of the subscript at 100.

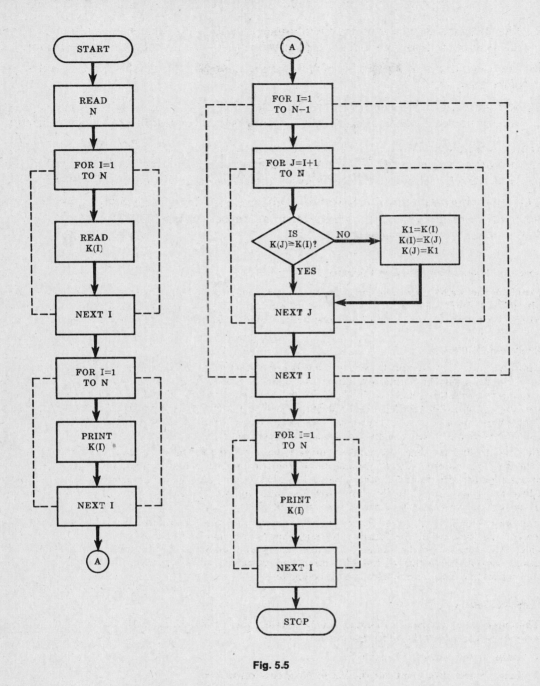

Fig. 5.5

The BASIC program is shown in Fig. 5.6. Notice the DIM statement near the start of the program (line 20), which establishes that K can contain as many as 101 elements. Observe also the use of FOR-TO loops in order to read in and print out the elements of K (e.g., see lines 40-60, 90-110 and 330-350).

The actual rearrangement is carried out with a double FOR-TO loops, as described above (lines 140-290). Three REM statements are included in the sequence. These statements help to clarify the logic of the double FOR-TO loop.

Finally, note that two **DATA** statements are included near the end of the program (lines 360 and 370), containing 21 data values. The first of these (the constant 20) is the value for N, which indicates that 20 elements of K will be utilized in this particular example. Following are the 20 values of K, in their original order (i.e., K(1)=595, K(2)=78, K(3)=1505, ..., K(20)=710).

At the bottom of Fig. 5.6 is the output generated by this particular example. We see the original list of numbers at the top of the output, followed by the list of rearranged numbers immediately thereafter.

```
10   REM PRØGRAM TØ REARRANGE A LIST ØF NUMBERS INTØ ASCENDING ØRDER
20   DIM K(100)
30   READ N
40   FØR I=1 TØ N
50      READ K(I)
60   NEXT I
70   PRINT "ØRIGINAL LIST ØF NUMBERS:"
80   PRINT
90   FØR I=1 TØ N
100     PRINT K(I);
110  NEXT I
120  PRINT
130
140  REM           REPEAT INTERCHANGE N-1 TIMES
150
160  FØR I=1 TØ N-1
170
180     REM       FIND SMALLEST NUMBER IN LIST AND INTERCHANGE
190
200     FØR J=I+1 TØ N
210        IF K(J)>=K(I) THEN 280
220
230        REM    INTERCHANGE K(J) AND K(I)
240
250        LET K1=K(I)
260        LET K(I)=K(J)
270        LET K(J)=K1
280     NEXT J
290  NEXT I
300  PRINT
310  PRINT "REØRDERED LIST ØF NUMBERS:"
320  PRINT
330  FØR I=1 TØ N
340     PRINT K(I);
350  NEXT I
360  DATA 20,595,78,1505,891,29,7,18,191,36,68,7051,509,212,46,726,1806
370  DATA 289,401,1488,710
380  END

>RUN


ØRIGINAL LIST ØF NUMBERS:

595   78   1505   891   29   7   18   191   36   68   7051   509   212   46   726
1806   289   401   1488   710

REØRDERED LIST ØF NUMBERS:

7   18   29   36   46   68   78   191   212   289   401   509   595   710   726
891   1488   1505   1806   7051
```

Fig. 5.6

The elements of a table are manipulated in much the same manner as the elements of a list. Double FOR-TO loops are frequently required for table input/output operations and for manipulation of the table elements. We will see an illustration of this in the next example.

Example 5.15   Table Manipulation

Consider the table of numbers shown in Table 5.2. Suppose we wish to sum all the elements in each row of the table, and all the elements in each column. Let us write a BASIC program which will allow us to carry out these elementary calculations.

Table 5.2

6	0	−12	4	17	21
−8	15	5	5	−18	0
11	3	1	−17	12	7
13	2	13	−9	24	4
−27	−3	0	14	8	−10

The Program Outline

The computation will proceed in accordance with the following outline.

1. Read the values for the number of rows (M) and the number of columns (N).

2. Read the elements of the table (T) on a row-by-row basis by proceeding as follows, for each value of I (the row counter) ranging from 1 to M.

   For a given value of I, let J (the column counter) range from 1 to N. Read a value of T(I,J) for each value of I and J.

3. Print the elements of T on a row-by-row basis. Hence for each value of I ranging from 1 to M, proceed as follows.

   For a given value of I, let J range from 1 to N. Print the value of T(I,J) for each value of I and J.

4. Calculate and print the sum of the elements in each row, and the sum of all individual row sums (i.e., the cumulative sum for all rows) as follows.

   (a) Set the initial value of the cumulative sum (S1) equal to zero.

   (b) Do the following for each value of I ranging from 1 to M.

      (i) Set the initial value of the row sum, S(I), equal to zero.

     (ii) For each value of J ranging from 1 to N, add T(I,J) to S(I), i.e., let

   $$S(I)=S(I)+T(I,J)$$

    (iii) Print the current value for I and the corresponding value for S(I).

    (iv) Add the value of S(I) to S1, i.e., let

   $$S1=S1+S(I)$$

   (c) Print the final value for S1 (i.e., the cumulative sum of all previously calculated row sums).

5. Calculate and print the sum of the elements in each column, and the sum of all individual column sums (i.e., the cumulative sum for all columns) as follows.

   (a) Set the initial value of the cumulative sum (S1) equal to zero.

   (b) Do the following for each value of J ranging from 1 to N.

      (i) Set the initial value of the column sum, S(J), equal to zero.

     (ii) For each value of I ranging from 1 to M, add T(I,J) to S(J), i.e., let

   $$S(J)=S(J)+T(I,J)$$

    (iii) Print the current value for J and the corresponding value for S(J).

    (iv) Add the value for S(J) to S1, i.e., let

   $$S1=S1+S(J)$$

   (c) Print the final value for S1 (i.e., the cumulative sum of all previously calculated column sums). Note that the cumulative column sum should equal the cumulative row sum; hence this value of S1 should equal the value printed in step 4. This serves as a check.

6. Stop.

Figure 5.7 contains a flowchart that corresponds to the above outline.

The BASIC Program

Figure 5.8 presents a complete BASIC program for this problem. Notice the nested FOR-TO loops that are used to read and print the elements of the table (see lines 70-110 and 170-220). Double FOR-TO loops are also used to form the row sums (lines 290-370) and the column sums (lines 460-540).

The DATA statements at the bottom of the program (lines 580 and 590) establish a data block having 32 elements. The first two numbers are the values for M and N, which indicate that this particular table will have 5 rows and 6 columns. The remaining 30 numbers are the values for the elements of T, on a row-by-row basis (thus requiring the second subscript, J, to increase most rapidly when reading the data).

We see that a DIM statement is not included in this program, since none of the subscripts take on values exceeding 10. If the array sizes were to be increased, then a DIM statement would, of course, be necessary. Finally, note that the program contains a number of REM statements and blank lines, which increase its readability and provide some indication of program logic.

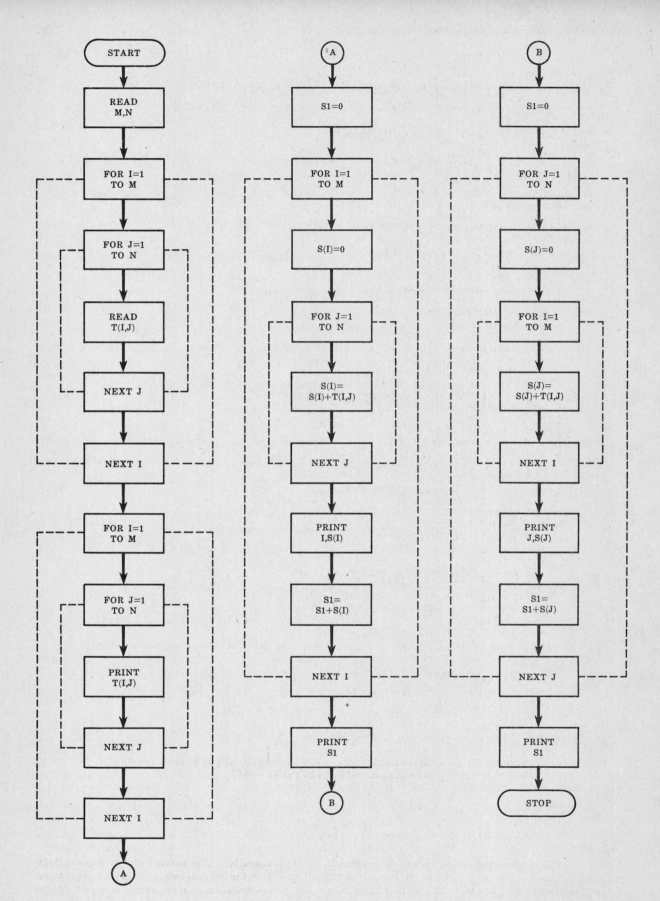

Fig. 5.7

```
10    REM PRØGRAM TØ SUM RØWS AND CØLUMNS ØF A TABLE
20
30    READ M,N
40
50    REM READ ELEMENTS ØF TABLE
60
70    FØR I=1 TØ M
80       FØR J=1 TØ N
90          READ T(I,J)
100      NEXT J
110   NEXT I
120
130   REM PRINT TABLE
140
150   PRINT "GIVEN TABLE:"
160   PRINT
170   FØR I=1 TØ M
180      FØR J=1 TØ N
190         PRINT T(I,J);
200      NEXT J
210   PRINT
220   NEXT I
230   PRINT
240
250   REM SUM ACRØSS EACH RØW
260
270   PRINT "SUM ØF CØLUMNS IN EACH RØW:"
280   PRINT
290   LET S1=0
300   FØR I=1 TØ M
310      LET S(I)=0
320      FØR J=1 TØ N
330         LET S(I)=S(I)+T(I,J)
340      NEXT J
350      PRINT "RØW ";I,"SUM=";S(I)
360      LET S1=S1+S(I)
370   NEXT I
380   PRINT
390   PRINT "SUM ØF RØW SUMS=";S1
400   PRINT
410
420   REM SUM DØWN EACH CØLUMN
430
440   PRINT "SUM ØF RØWS IN EACH CØLUMN:"
450   PRINT
460   LET S1=0
470   FØR J=1 TØ N
480      LET S(J)=0
490      FØR I=1 TØ M
500         LET S(J)=S(J)+T(I,J)
510      NEXT I
520      PRINT "CØLUMN ";J,"SUM=";S(J)
530      LET S1=S1+S(J)
540   NEXT J
550   PRINT
560   PRINT "SUM ØF CØLUMN SUMS=";S1
570
580   DATA 5,6,6,0,-12,4,17,21,-8,15,5,5,-18,0,11,3,1,-17,12,7
590   DATA 13,2,13,-9,24,4,-27,-3,0,14,8,-1C
600   END
```

Fig. 5.8

In Fig. 5.9 we see the output which is generated for this example. The given table is printed first, followed by the sum of the columns (elements) for each row and the cumulative sum of the row sums. Following these values are the individual column sums and the cumulative column sum. Notice that the cumulative row sum equals the cumulative column sum (81), as expected.

```
GIVEN TABLE:

  6   0  -12   4   17  21
 -8  15    5   5  -18   0
 11   3    1 -17   12   7
 13   2   13  -9   24   4
-27  -3    0  14    8 -10

SUM OF COLUMNS IN EACH ROW:

ROW   1              SUM= 36
ROW   2              SUM=-1
ROW   3              SUM= 17
ROW   4              SUM= 47
ROW   5              SUM=-18

SUM OF ROW SUMS= 81

SUM OF ROWS IN EACH COLUMN:

COLUMN   1           SUM=-5
COLUMN   2           SUM= 17
COLUMN   3           SUM= 7
COLUMN   4           SUM=-3
COLUMN   5           SUM= 43
COLUMN   6           SUM= 22

SUM OF COLUMN SUMS= 81
```

Fig. 5.9

5.6   Rereading Data — The RESTORE Statement

In the last section we saw that a correspondence is always maintained between the variables whose values are to be read (i.e., the variables listed in the READ statements) and the individual data items in a data block (the numbers and strings in the DATA statements). This is accomplished by means of an internal "pointer" which indicates the next data item to be read. In fact, two pointers are maintained if the data block contains both numeric and string data — one for the numeric constants, the other for the strings. Each time a data item is read the pointer is automatically advanced to the next data item of the same type.

There are certain kinds of problems that require some, perhaps all, of the data to be read more than once. To do this we must reset one or both pointers to the start of the data block. The *RESTORE statement* is used for this purpose.

The RESTORE statement consists of a statement number, followed by the keyword RESTORE. The appearance of this statement causes each pointer to be reset to the first data item of the proper type within the data block.

Example 5.16

A BASIC program contains the statements

```
30  READ A,B,C
    . . .
60  RESTORE
70  READ W,X,Y,Z
    . . .
200 DATA 1,3,5,7,9,11,13
```

Statement number 30 causes the variable A to be assigned a value of 1, B a value of 3 and C a value of 5. When statement number 60 is encountered the pointer is reset to the first number in the data block. Hence statement number 70 causes the variable W to be assigned a value of 1, X a value of 3, Y a value of 5 and Z a value of 7. If the RESTORE statement were not present then W would be assigned a value of 7, X a value of 9, and so on.

Notice that we have been concerned with only one pointer in this example since the data block contains only numeric constants.

The keyword RESTORE can be followed by an asterisk (∗) or dollar sign ($) if desired. If an asterisk is present then only the numeric pointer will be reset, whereas only the string pointer will be reset if the dollar sign is shown. Both an asterisk and a dollar sign are, however, not permitted.

Example 5.17

A BASIC program contains the statements

```
50  READ A,B,M$,N$
    ...
150 RESTORE*
160 READ C1,C2,F1$,F2$
    ...
250 DATA 2,4,RED,GREEN,6,8,BLUE,WHITE
```

Statement number 50 causes the variables A and B to be assigned the values 2 and 4, and the variables M$ and N$ will be assigned the strings RED and GREEN. The numeric pointer is reset by statement number 150. Hence statement 160 causes C1 and C2 to be assigned the values 2 and 4, whereas F1$ and F2$ will represent the strings BLUE and WHITE.

If statement number 150 were changed to

```
150 RESTORE$
```

then the string pointer would be reset rather than the numeric pointer. Therefore C1 and C2 would be assigned the values 6 and 8, but the strings RED and GREEN would be assigned to F1$ and F2$, respectively.

Now suppose that statement 150 were changed to

```
150 RESTORE
```

Then both pointers would be reset, resulting in C1=2, C2=4, F1$=RED and F2$=GREEN. Finally, if statement number 150 were deleted entirely, then statement 160 would result in C1=6, C2=8, F1$=BLUE and F2$=WHITE.

It should be clear that the values assigned to A, B, M$ and N$ will be unaffected by the subsequent RESTORE and READ statements in this example.

5.7 Closing Remarks

With this chapter we conclude our discussion of the "basic" features of BASIC. We have seen that use of the library functions allows the programmer to carry out certain programming operations (e.g., truncation, spacing of output data, etc.) as well as the more common mathematical operations. Collections of numbers and strings can be stored and manipulated by using lists and tables, and large quantities of data can be conveniently stored and assigned to program variables or array elements through the use of the READ and DATA statements. These features simplify the programming of a great many different problem situations.

Review Questions

5.1 What are library functions? What useful purpose do they serve?

5.2 What other names are sometimes used for library functions?

5.3 Name several of the more common library functions. State the purpose of each library function.

5.4 What is meant by an argument? Do all library functions require arguments?

5.5   How is a library function used in a BASIC program?

5.6   What happens if a negative value is supplied to a library function that requires a positive argument?

5.7   What is meant by truncation? Present an example illustrating truncation.

5.8   What is the purpose of the INT function? What happens when the INT function receives a positive argument? A negative argument?

5.9   What is the purpose of the TAB function? In which statement is it used?

5.10   Can a formula be used as a library function argument? Can a reference to another library function be used for this purpose?

5.11   What happens if a library function requiring an integer argument is supplied with an argument having a noninteger value?

5.12   What is meant by a list? A table?

5.13   What is meant by a one-dimensional array? A two-dimensional array? Compare your answer with the answer to the previous question.

5.14   What is meant by the elements of a list or table? What do these elements represent?

5.15   Can a single array contain both numbers and strings?

5.16   What is a subscripted variable? How do we refer to a particular subscripted variable?

5.17   Can a formula be used as a subscript? Can a reference to a library function be used for this purpose?

5.18   What restriction applies to the values that a subscript can take on?

5.19   What is the purpose of a DIM statement? When *must* this statement appear in a BASIC program?

5.20   Summarize the rules for writing a DIM statement.

5.21   Can a formula or a reference to a library function appear in a DIM statement?

5.22   Is there any purpose in specifying the size of a *small* array in a DIM statement? Explain.

5.23   What is the purpose of the READ and DATA statements?

5.24   Summarize the rules for writing a READ statement.

5.25   Summarize the rules for writing a DATA statement.

5.26   Does each READ statement require its own data statement? Explain.

5.27   What is meant by a data block? How is a data block formed?

5.28   Are data entered via an INPUT statement as permanent as data entered via READ-DATA statements? Explain.

5.29   Summarize the rules that must be observed when placing data items in a data block.

5.30   Where are DATA statements usually placed in a BASIC program?   Why?

5.31   How are list and table input/output operations usually carried out in BASIC?

5.32   Discuss the purpose and use of pointers in connection with a data block.

5.33   What is the purpose of the RESTORE statement?   Cite three different ways that this statement can be written.

Solved Problems

5.34   Write a BASIC statement that corresponds to each of the following algebraic equations.

(a) $z = \tan t$

        10 LET Z=TAN(T)

(b) $w = \log_e(v)$

        10 LET W=LOG(V)

(c) $y = ae^{bx} \sin cx$

        10 LET Y=A*EXP(B*X)*SIN(C*X)

(d) $x_1 = \dfrac{-b + \sqrt{b^2 - 4ac}}{2a}$

        10 LET X1=(−B+SQR(B↑2−4*A*C))/(2*A)

5.35   Write a BASIC statement for each of the following situations.

(a)   Determine the absolute value of the difference between the variables U and V. Assign this value to the variable W.

        10 LET W=ABS(U−V)

(b)   Determine the sign of x. If x is negative, go to statement 50; if x equals zero, go to statement 20; and if x is positive, go to statement 170.

        100 ON SGN(X)+2 GO TO 50,20,170

(c)   Determine the largest integer which algebraically does not exceed z, where $z = x^2 - y^2$. Assign this integer to the variable I.

        10 LET I=INT(X↑2−Y↑2)

(d)   In (c) above, if $x = 2.5$ and $y = 6.3$, what value will be assigned to the variable I?

        $x^2 - y^2 = -33.44$, hence $I = -34$.

(e)   Print the values of X\$, X, Y\$ and Y on one line. Let the string represented by X\$ begin in the 10th column, followed immediately by the value of X. Similarly, let Y\$ begin in the 46th column, followed immediately by Y.

        100 PRINT TAB(9);X\$;X;TAB(45);Y\$;Y

5.36   Each example below shows a reference to one or more subscripted variables. Describe the type of array referred to in each case.

(a)   10 DIM C1(100),N\$(100,3)

        C1 is a numeric list, N\$ is a string table.

(b)   50 LET P(I)=P(I)+Q(I,J)

   P is a numeric list, Q is a numeric table.

(c)   100 IF A$(5)=G$ THEN 220

   A$ is a string list.

(d)   150 ON X(K(I),J(I)) GO TO 100,20,180,20,250

   X is a numeric table, K and J are numeric lists.

(e)   200 PRINT X$(K),N1(K),N2(K)

   X$ is a string list, N1 and N2 are numeric lists.

5.37   Write one or more statements to carry out each of the following operations.

(a)   Sum the first 100 elements of the numeric list T.

```
10 LET S=0
20 FOR I=0 TO 99
      LET S=S+T(I)
40 NEXT I
```

(b)   Print the even elements of the numeric list T for values of the subscript ranging from 0 to 100, i.e., print T(0), T(2), T(4), ..., T(100).

```
10 FOR I=0 TO 100 STEP 2
20    PRINT T(I);
30 NEXT I
```

(c)   Calculate the sum of all elements of the numeric table P. Let M indicate the number of rows and N the number of columns.

```
10 LET S=0
20 FOR I=1 TO M
30    FOR J=1 TO N
40        LET S=S+P(I,J)
50    NEXT J
60 NEXT I
```

(d)   Print the elements in the third column of the string table K$. Display the output in columnar form, beginning in column number 12 (the column number here refers to the location on the output sheet).

```
10 FOR I=1 TO M
20    PRINT TAB(12);K$(I,3)
30 NEXT I
```

5.38   Write appropriate READ and DATA statements for each situation described below.

(a)   Assign the values $-1.6E-6$, -500, .4077, MAY, OCTOBER, 100, 110, 120, 130, 140 and 150 to the variables C1, C2, C3, X$, Y$, Z(1), Z(2), Z(3), Z(4), Z(5), and Z(6). List each subscripted variable separately in the READ statement.

```
10 READ C1,C2,C3,X$,Y$,Z(1),Z(2),Z(3),Z(4),Z(5),Z(6)
   . . .
200 DATA −1.6E−6,−500,.4077,MAY,OCTOBER,100,110,120,130,140,150
```

The READ and DATA statements can also be broken up if desired, e.g.,

```
10 READ C1,C2,C3,X$,Y$
20 READ Z(1),Z(2),Z(3),Z(4),Z(5),Z(6)
   . . .
200 DATA −1.6E−6,−500,.4077
210 DATA MAY,OCTOBER,100,110
220 DATA 120,130,140,150
```

(b) Assign the values given in part (a) above to their respective variables. Use a FOR-TO loop for the array elements.

```
10 READ C1,C2,C3,X$,Y$
20 FOR I=1 TO 6
30     READ Z(I)
40 NEXT I
   . . .
200 DATA −1.6E−6,−500,.4077,MAY,OCTOBER
210 DATA 100,110,120,130,140,150
```

(c) Assign the values given in part (a) above to their respective variables, as in part (b). At a later point in the program, reset the string pointer and assign the strings MAY and OCTOBER to the variables F$ and G$.

```
10 READ C1,C2,C3,X$,Y$
20 FOR I=1 TO 6
30     READ Z(I)
40 NEXT I
   . . .
100 RESTORE$
110 READ F$,G$
    . . .
200 DATA −1.6E−6,−500,.4077,MAY,OCTOBER
210 DATA 100,110,120,130,140,150
```

Supplementary Problems

5.39 Find out which library functions are available at your particular installation. (Refer to the BASIC reference manual published by the manufacturer of your computer.) Specify the purpose of each library function. Determine exactly how each function is referenced.

5.40 Write a BASIC statement that corresponds to each of the following algebraic equations.

(a) $y = \sqrt{\sin x - \cos x}$

(b) $p = qe^{-at}$

(c) $c = \log_e \sqrt{|a + b|} + \log_e \sqrt{|a - b|}$

(d) $w = ||u - v| - |u + v||$

(e) $z = \cos(x + \arctan y)$

5.41 Write a BASIC statement for each of the following situations.

(a) Determine the sign of the quantity $(ab - cd)/(f + g)$. Go to statement number 75 if the quantity is positive, to statement 260 if the quantity is zero, and to statement 135 if the quantity is negative.

(b) Print the following on one line of a typewriter terminal: "X=", followed by the value of the variable X; "Y=", followed by the value of Y; and "Z=", followed by the value of Z. Begin printing in columns 4, 28 and 52, respectively.

(c) Determine if the value of the variable N is even or odd, assuming that N has a positive integer value. (Hint: Compare the value of N/2 with the truncated value of N/2.)

(d) In part (c) above, what will happen if N has a negative integer value?

5.42   Each example below shows a reference to one or more subscripted variables. Describe the type of array referred to in each case.

(a)   75 LET N$(3)="ERROR-CHECK"

(b)   20 DIM A(12,25),A$(12,25),B(12),C$(25)

(c)   100 PRINT P$(I),P(I,J)

(d)   50 IF Z(J1,J2)<10 THEN 185

5.43   Shown below are several BASIC statements and sequences of statements containing subscripted variables. Some of the examples are written incorrectly. Identify all errors.

(a)   50 LET C(I,J)=(3*X↑2−2*Y↑3)/(17*Z)

(b)   75 LET P(K,5)=Q(K+1,J)+R(K,J+1)

(c)   20 INPUT M,N
      30 DIM A(M,N),X(N),Y(M)

(d)   10 DIM K(100),W(10,20),C1,C2,K(100)

(e)   150 LET S=S+T(K,−3)

(f)   200 LET X(K(I))=Y(K(I+1))+Z(K(I−1))

5.44   Write one or more statements to carry out each of the following operations.

(a)   Calculate the square root of the sum of the squares of the first 100 odd elements of the numeric list C, i.e., calculate $[X(1)^2+X(3)^2+X(5)^2+\cdots+X(199)^2]^{1/2}$.

(b)   Calculate the elements of the numeric table H which has 8 rows and 12 columns. Each element of H is determined by the formula

$$h_{ij} = \frac{1}{i+j-1}$$

(c)   A numeric list K has N elements. Print the value of each subscript and each corresponding element for those elements whose value does not exceed 15. Display the output in two columns, with the value of the subscript in the first column and the corresponding subscripted variable in the second column. Label each column. Start the first column of output in column number 8 (the column number here refers to the location on the output sheet), and the second column of output in column number 44.

(d)   A numeric table W has K rows and K columns. Calculate the product of the terms on the main diagonal of W, where the main diagonal runs from upper left to lower right, i.e., calculate W(1,1)*W(2,2)*W(3,3)*...*W(K,K).

(e)   Print the elements in the fourth column of the string table M$. Display the output in columnar form, beginning in column number 10 (the column number here refers to the location on the output sheet). Assume that M$ contains M rows.

(f)   Repeat problem (e) above, displaying the output in row form with one blank space between each element.

(g)   Print the elements in the fifth row of the string table M$. Display the output in row form with one blank space between each element. Assume that M$ contains N columns.

5.45   Write appropriate READ and DATA statements for each situation described below.

(a)   The following values are to be assigned to the list L$, the variables P,Q,R and H$, and the table T.

L$(1)=WHITE	P=2.25E+5	T(1,1)=1	T(2,1)=−2
L$(2)=YELLOW	Q=6.08E−9	T(1,2)=−3	T(2,2)=4
L$(3)=ORANGE	R=−1.29E+12	T(1,3)=5	T(2,3)=−6
L$(4)=RED	H$=RESTART	T(1,4)=−7	T(2,4)=8

List each subscripted variable separately in the READ statements.

(b)   Repeat part (a) above, using FOR-TO loops for the array elements.

(c)   Repeat part (a) above, using FOR-TO loops for the array elements, as in part (b). At a later point in the program, reset the numeric pointer and assign the values 2.25E+5, 6.08E−9 and −1.29E+12 to the variables P1, Q1 and R1.

(d) Repeat part (a) above, using FOR-TO loops for the array elements, as in part (b). At a later point in the program, reset the pointer and assign the strings WHITE, YELLOW, ORANGE and RED to the variables A1$, A2$, A3$ and A4$.

Programming Problems

5.46 Alter the program shown in Example 5.5 so that the logarithm is not calculated when x has a value of zero. Include a provision for printing 8 successive asterisks for the log of zero, thus indicating an overflow condition.

5.47 Write a BASIC program similar to the one in Example 5.5 that will generate a table of x, $\sin^2 x$, $\cos^2 x$, $\tan^2 x$, $\cotan^2 x$, $\sec^2 x$ and $\csc^2 x$. (Note that $\sec x = 1/\cos x$, and $\csc x = 1/\sin x$.) Generate 101 entries for evenly spaced values of x between 0 and π. (That is, let $x = 0, \pi/100, 2\pi/100, \ldots, 99\pi/100, \pi$.) Be sure that the output is adequately labeled.

5.48 Write a BASIC program which will produce a table of values of the equation

$$y = 2e^{-0.1t} \sin 0.5 t$$

where t varies between 0 and 60. Allow the size of the t increment to be entered as an input parameter.

5.49 Extend the word unscrambler program in Example 5.9 so that it prints out all possible 2-letter, 3-letter and 4-letter combinations of any given 4 letters. Select a set of 4 letters and execute the program. Identify all valid English words by inspecting the output visually. Can you determine, without running the program, how many different combinations of 2 or more letters will be generated?

5.50 Extend the program in Example 5.14 so that a list of numbers can be rearranged in any one of the following 4 ways.

(a) Smallest to largest, algebraically (that is, largest negative to largest positive values).

(b) Smallest to largest in magnitude (ignoring signs).

(c) Largest to smallest, algebraically.

(d) Largest to smallest in magnitude.

(Note that the elements of the list need not necessarily have positive values.)

Write the program in such a manner that only one rearrangement is carried out each time the program is executed. Include in the program a variable whose value is entered via an INPUT statement each time the program is executed. Let the particular rearrangement of the list of numbers be determined by the value assigned to this variable (e.g., if A=1 then rearrange from smallest to largest, algebraically; if A=2 rearrange from smallest to largest in magnitude; etc.).

Use the program to rearrange the numbers given in Table 5.3 Rearrange the numbers all four ways.

Table 5.3

43	−85	−4	65
−83	10	−71	−59
61	−51	−45	−32
14	49	19	23
−94	−34	−50	86

5.51 Write a BASIC program that will rearrange a list of words into alphabetical order. To do so, enter the words in a list, with each element representing one complete word. The list of words can then be alphabetized in the same manner that a list of numbers is rearranged from smallest to largest (see Example 5.14).

Use the program to rearrange the names given in Table 5.4.   Be careful with the first initials.

Table 5.4

Washington	Hayes
Adams, J.	Garfield
Jefferson	Arthur
Madison	Cleveland
Monroe	Harrison, B.
Adams, J. Q.	McKinley
Jackson	Roosevelt, T.
Van Buren	Taft
Harrison, W. H.	Wilson
Tyler	Harding
Polk	Coolidge
Taylor	Hoover
Fillmore	Roosevelt, F. D.
Pierce	Truman
Buchanan	Eisenhower
Lincoln	Kennedy
Johnson, A.	Johnson, L. B.
Grant	Nixon

5.52 Rewrite the BASIC program in Example 5.15 so that the *product* of the elements in each row and each column will be calculated.

5.53 Prepare a detailed outline, a corresponding flowchart and a complete BASIC program for each of the problems presented below.

(*a*) Suppose we are given a numeric table A having M rows and N columns, and a numeric list X having N elements.   We wish to generate a numeric list Y by carrying out the following operations.

$$Y(1)=A(1,1)*X(1)+A(1,2)*X(2)+\cdots+A(1,N)*X(N)$$
$$Y(2)=A(2,1)*X(1)+A(2,2)*X(2)+\cdots+A(2,N)*X(N)$$
$$\cdots$$
$$Y(M)=A(M,1)*X(1)+A(M,2)*X(2)+\cdots+A(M,N)*X(N)$$

Print out the input data (i.e., the values for the elements of A and X), followed by the computed values for the elements of Y.

Use the program to process the following set of data.

$$A = \begin{bmatrix} 1 & 2 & 3 & 4 & 5 & 6 & 7 & 8 \\ 2 & 3 & 4 & 5 & 6 & 7 & 8 & 9 \\ 3 & 4 & 5 & 6 & 7 & 8 & 9 & 10 \\ 4 & 5 & 6 & 7 & 8 & 9 & 10 & 11 \\ 5 & 6 & 7 & 8 & 9 & 10 & 11 & 12 \\ 6 & 7 & 8 & 9 & 10 & 11 & 12 & 13 \end{bmatrix}$$

$$X = \begin{bmatrix} 1 \\ -8 \\ 3 \\ -6 \\ 5 \\ -4 \\ 7 \\ -2 \end{bmatrix}$$

(b) Suppose that A is a numeric table having K rows and M columns, and that B is a numeric table having M rows and N columns. We wish to calculate the elements of the numeric table C, where each element of C is determined by

$$C(I,J)=A(I,1)*B(1,J)+A(I,2)*B(2,J)+\cdots+A(I,M)*B(M,J)$$

for $I = 1, 2, \ldots, K$ and $J = 1, 2, \ldots, N$. Print out the elements of A, B and C.

Use the program to process the following set of data.

$$A = \begin{bmatrix} 2 & -1/3 & 0 & 2/3 & 4 \\ 1/2 & 3/2 & 4 & -2 & 1 \\ 0 & 3 & -9/7 & 6/7 & 4/3 \end{bmatrix}$$

$$B = \begin{bmatrix} 6/5 & 0 & -2 & 1/3 \\ 5 & 7/2 & 3/4 & -3/2 \\ 0 & -1 & 1 & 0 \\ 9/2 & 3/7 & -3 & 3 \\ 4 & -1/2 & 0 & 3/4 \end{bmatrix}$$

(c) The *Legendre polynomials* can be calculated by means of the formulas

$$P_0 = 1$$
$$P_1 = x$$
$$\cdots$$
$$P_n = \left(\frac{2n-1}{n}\right)x P_{n-1} - \left(\frac{n-1}{n}\right)P_{n-2}$$

where $n = 2, 3, 4, \ldots$ and x is any number between -1 and $+1$.

Write a BASIC program that will generate a table of P_n vs. x for any specified value of n up to and including $n = 10$. Generate 201 values of P_n in each table, based upon evenly spaced values of x. (That is, let $x = -1.00, -0.99, -0.98, \ldots, -0.01, 0, 0.01, \ldots, 0.98, 0.99, 1.00$.) Output the results in a legible, columnar form.

(d) Write a BASIC program that will read in a set of temperatures, determine an average and then calculate the deviation of each temperature from the average.

The deviation is defined as

$$D(I)=T(I)-T1$$

where T1 represents the average temperature. Notice that a given deviation may be either positive or negative.

Test the program using the following set of temperatures: 28.2, 29.3, 33.7, 42.0, 58.4, 71.3, 84.1, 83.8, 74.5, 53.9, 41.6, 34.4.

(e) Consider a sequence of real numbers, x_i, $i = 1, 2, \ldots, M$. The mean is defined as

$$\bar{x} = \frac{x_1 + x_2 + \cdots + x_M}{M}$$

the deviation about the mean is

$$d_i = (x_i - \bar{x})$$

and the standard deviation is

$$\sigma = \left[\frac{d_1^2 + d_2^2 + \cdots + d_M^2}{M}\right]^{1/2}$$

Read in the first M elements of a 1-dimensional array. Calculate the sum of these elements, the mean, the deviations, the standard deviation, the algebraic maximum and the algebraic minimum.

Repeat the computation for K different arrays. Calculate the overall mean, the overall standard deviation, the absolute (largest) maximum and the absolute (algebraically smallest) minimum. Apply the program to the data given in Problem 4.46(f).

(f) Write a BASIC program to calculate the variance, $\bar{v}$, of a list of numbers in two ways, using the formulas

$$\bar{v} = \frac{1}{M}[(x_1 - \bar{x})^2 + (x_2 - \bar{x})^2 + \cdots + (x_M - \bar{x})^2]$$

and

$$\bar{v} = \frac{1}{M}(x_1^2 + x_2^2 + \cdots + x_M^2) - \bar{x}^2$$

In these formulas $\bar{x}$ is the mean (average) value, calculated as

$$\bar{x} = \frac{1}{M}(x_1 + x_2 + \cdots + x_M)$$

and M is the number of values in the list.

Mathematically the two formulas for $\bar{v}$ can be shown to be identical. When the given numbers have values that are very close together, however, then the value obtained for $\bar{v}$ using the second formula can be considerably in error. The reason for this is that we must calculate the difference between two values that are very nearly equal. Such calculated differences can be highly inaccurate. The first formula for the variance yields much more accurate results under these conditions.

Demonstrate that the above statements are true by calculating the variance of the data given in Table 5.5. (The correct value is $\bar{v} = 0.00339966$.)

Table 5.5

99.944	100.054	100.059	100.061
100.039	100.066	100.029	100.098
99.960	99.936	100.085	100.038
100.093	99.932	100.079	100.024
99.993	99.913	100.095	100.046

(*Note*: This example disproves the common misconception that a computer always yields answers that are absolutely correct.)

(g) Modify the program written for Problem 4.46(f) to do the following:

(i) After calculating an average score for each student, obtain a class average of the individual averages.

(ii) Calculate the difference between each student's average and the class average.

(h) Home mortgage costs are determined in such a manner that the borrower pays the same amount of money to the lending institution each month throughout the life of the mortgage. The fraction of the total monthly payment which is required as an interest payment on the outstanding balance of the loan varies, however, from month to month. Early in the life of the mortgage most of the monthly payment is required to pay interest, and only a small fraction of the total monthly payment is applied toward reducing the amount of the loan. Gradually, the outstanding balance becomes smaller, which causes the monthly interest payment to decrease, and the amount that is used to reduce the outstanding balance therefore increases. Hence the balance of the loan is reduced at an accelerated rate.

Typically the prospective home buyer knows how much money he must borrow and the time he will require for repayment. He then asks a lending institution how much his monthly payment will be at the prevailing interest rate. He should also be concerned with how much of each monthly payment is charged to interest, how much total interest he has paid since he first borrowed the money, and how much money he still owes the lending institution at the end of each month.

Write a BASIC program that can be used by a lending institution to provide a potential customer with this information. Assume that the amount of the loan, the annual interest rate and the duration of the loan are specified. The amount of the monthly payment is calculated by means of the formula

$$P = iA\left[\frac{(1+i)^n}{(1+i)^n - 1}\right]$$

where P = monthly payment, dollars

       A = total amount of the loan, dollars

       i = monthly interest rate expressed as a decimal, e.g., 1/2% would be written 0.005

       n = total number of monthly payments

The monthly interest payment can be calculated from the formula

$$I = iB$$

where I = monthly interest payment, dollars

       B = outstanding balance of the loan, dollars

The outstanding balance is simply equal to the original amount of the loan, less the sum of the previous payments toward principal. The monthly payment toward principal, i.e., the amount which is used to reduce the outstanding balance, is simply

$$T = P - I$$

where T = monthly payment toward principal.

Use the program to calculate the cost of a 25-year, \$20,000 mortgage at an annual rate of interest of 8 percent. Then repeat the calculations for an annual interest rate of 8.5 percent. How significant is the additional half percent in the interest rate over the entire life of the mortgage?

(*i*) The method used to calculate the cost of a home mortgage in Problem 5.53(*h*) above is known as a *constant payment* method, since each monthly payment is the same. Suppose instead that the monthly payments were computed by the method of simple interest. That is, suppose that each month the same amount is paid toward reducing the loan. Hence

$$T = A/n$$

In addition, interest is paid each month, the amount depending on the size of the outstanding balance; that is,

$$I = iB$$

Thus the monthly payment $P = T + I$ will decrease each month, as the outstanding balance diminishes.

Write a BASIC program to calculate the cost of a home mortgage using this method of repayment. Label the output clearly. Use the program to calculate the cost of a 25-year, \$20,000 loan at 8 percent annual interest. Compare the results with those obtained Problem 5.53(*h*).

(*j*) Suppose we are given a set of tabulated values for y vs. x, i.e.,

y_0	y_1	y_2	$\cdots$	y_n
x_0	x_1	x_2	$\cdots$	x_n

and we wish to obtain a value of y at some x that lies between two of the tabulated values. This problem is commonly solved by *interpolation*, i.e., by passing a polynomial $y(x)$ through the $n+1$ points such that $y(x_0) = y_0$, $y(x_1) = y_1$, ..., $y(x_n) = y_n$ and then evaluating y at the desired value of x.

A common way to carry out the interpolation is to use the *Lagrange form* of the interpolating polynomial. To do this we write

$$y(x) = f_0(x) \cdot y_0 + f_1(x) \cdot y_1 + \cdots + f_n(x) \cdot y_n$$

where $f_i(x)$ is a polynomial such that

$$f_i(x) = \frac{(x - x_0)(x - x_1) \cdots (x - x_{i-1})(x - x_{i+1}) \cdots (x - x_n)}{(x_i - x_0)(x_i - x_1) \cdots (x_i - x_{i-1})(x_i - x_{i+1}) \cdots (x_i - x_n)}$$

Notice that $f_i(x_i) = 1$ and $f_i(x_j) = 0$, where x_j is a tabulated value of x different from x_i. Therefore we are assured that $y(x_i) = y_i$.

Write a BASIC program to read in n pairs of data, where n does not exceed 10, and then obtain an interpolated value of y at one or more specified values of x. Use the program to obtain interpolated values of y at $x = 13.7$, $x = 37.2$, $x = 112$ and $x = 147$ from the data listed in Table 5.6. Determine how many tabulated pairs of data are required in each calculation in order to obtain a reasonably accurate interpolated value for y.

Table 5.6

y	0.21073	0.37764	0.45482	0.49011	0.50563	0.49245	0.47220	0.43433	0.33824	0.19390
x	0	10	20	30	40	50	60	80	120	180

(k) Example 4.5 describes the *method of successive substitutions* for solving an algebraic equation of the form $x = F(x)$ by means of an iterative technique employing the recursive formula $x_{i+1} = F(x_i)$.

Another method, usually more efficient, for solving equations of this type is *Newton-Raphson iteration* (sometimes called *Newton's method*). To use this method the algebraic equation must be written in the form $f(x) = 0$. The recursive formula

$$x_{i+1} = x_i - \frac{f(x_i)}{f'(x_i)}$$

is then employed, where $f'(x_i)$ represents the first derivative of $f(x)$ evaluated at x_i.

The iteration is carried out in the same manner as the method of successive substitutions. That is, a value of x_{i+1} is calculated from the recursive formula and compared with x_i. If the two values are not sufficiently close, then the value for x_{i+1} is substituted into the right-hand side of the recursive equation and the computation is repeated.

Write a BASIC program to solve a nonlinear algebraic equation by either of the above techniques. Determine which method will be used by assigning an appropriate numerical value to some input variable.

Use the program to solve the equation $x + \cos x = 1 + \sin x$ for some value of x bounded between $\pi/2$ and π. Solve using both techniques. Which method seems to be the best?

(l) Suppose we are given a number of discrete points (x_1, y_1), (x_2, y_2), ..., (x_n, y_n) which are read from a curve $y = f(x)$, where x is bounded between x_1 and x_n. We wish to approximate the area under the curve by breaking up the curve into a number of small rectangles and calculating the area of these rectangles. (This is known as the *trapezoidal rule*.) Use the formula

$$A = \tfrac{1}{2}(y_1 + y_2)(x_2 - x_1) + \tfrac{1}{2}(y_2 + y_3)(x_3 - x_2) + \cdots + \tfrac{1}{2}(y_{n-1} + y_n)(x_n - x_{n-1})$$

Notice that the average height of each rectangle is given by $\tfrac{1}{2}(y_i + y_{i+1})$ and that the width of each rectangle is equal to $(x_{i+1} - x_i)$, $i = 1, 2, ..., (n-1)$.

Use the program to calculate the area under the curve $y = x^3$ between the limits $x = 1$ and $x = 4$. Solve this problem first with 16 evenly spaced points, then with 61 points, and finally with 301 points. Note that the accuracy of the solution will improve as the number of points increases. (The exact answer to this problem is 63.75.)

(m) Problem 5.53(l) above describes a method known as the *trapezoidal rule* for calculating the area under a curve $y(x)$, where a set of tabulated values (y_1, x_1), (y_2, x_2), ..., (y_n, x_n) is used to describe the curve. If the tabulated values of x are equally spaced, then the equation given in Problem 5.53(l) can be simplified to read

$$A = \tfrac{1}{2}(y_1 + 2y_2 + 2y_3 + 2y_4 + \cdots + 2y_{n-1} + y_n) \, \Delta x$$

where Δx is the distance between successive values of x.

Another technique that applies when there is an even number of equally spaced intervals, i.e., an odd number of data points, is *Simpson's rule*. The computational equation for implementing Simpson's rule is

$$A = \tfrac{1}{3}(y_1 + 4y_2 + 2y_3 + 4y_4 + 2y_5 + \cdots + 4y_{n-1} + y_n) \, \Delta x$$

For a given value of Δx, Simpson's rule will yield a more accurate result than the trapezoidal rule.

Write a BASIC program for calculating the area under a curve using either of the above techniques, assuming an odd number of equally spaced data points. Determine which method will be used by assigning an appropriate numerical value to some input variable. Allow for as many as 101 sets of data, where the tabulated data points can either be read into the computer or calculated internally using an algebraic equation.

Use the program to compute the area under the curve

$$y = e^{-x^2}$$

where x ranges from 0 to 1. Calculate the area using each computational technique, and compare the results with the correct answer of A=0.7468241.

(n) A first-order differential equation with a known initial condition can be written as

$$\frac{dy}{dx} = f(x, y), \quad x \geq x_0$$

with $y(x_0) = y_0$, where y_0 represents a known numerical value. When solving a differential equation the objective is to obtain an equation, or a set of tabulated values, for y as a function of x.

A differential equation of this type can be solved by successively "stepping ahead" a small distance in the x direction. In other words, beginning with the known value $y(x_0)$, a value is calculated for $y(x_1)$, where $x_1 = x_0 + \Delta x$ and Δx is some prescribed small number (the step size). Then a value is obtained for $y(x_2)$, where $x_2 = x_1 + \Delta x$; then $y(x_3)$, where $x_3 = x_2 + \Delta x$; and so on, until a sufficient number of points have been calculated.

The easiest way to calculate a value for $y(x_{i+1})$, given a value for $y(x_i)$, is to use *Euler's method*:

$$y_{i+1} = y_i + f(x_i, y_i) \, \Delta x$$

where y_i represents $y(x_i)$, y_{i+1} represents $y(x_{i+1})$, and $f(x_i, y_i)$ represents dy/dx evaluated at (x_i, y_i). Euler's method is very easy to work with, but it results in a rather inaccurate approximation for the curve $y(x)$ unless Δx is chosen to be very small. Therefore a great many points may be required in order to calculate $y(x)$ over some reasonably large interval of x, $x_0 \leq x \leq x_n$.

A method that results in much more accurate values for y_{i+1} is the fourth order *Runge-Kutta method*

$$y_{i+1} = y_i + \tfrac{1}{6}(k_1 + 2k_2 + 3k_3 + k_4)$$

where
$$k_1 = f(x_i, y_i) \, \Delta x$$
$$k_2 = f(x_i + \Delta x/2, \, y_i + k_1/2) \, \Delta x$$
$$k_3 = f(x_i + \Delta x/2, \, y_i + k_2/2) \, \Delta x$$
$$k_4 = f(x_i + \Delta x, \, y_i + k_3) \, \Delta x$$

Thus for a given point (x_i, y_i), the procedure is to calculate $x_{i+1} = x_i + \Delta x$, then calculate values for k_1, k_2, k_3 and k_4, and finally obtain a value for y_{i+1}.

Write a BASIC program which will solve a first-order differential equation with a known initial condition using either of the above two techniques. Determine which method will be used by assigning an appropriate numerical value to an input variable. Specify the step size (Δx) and the total number of steps (n) as input parameters.

Use the program to solve the differential equation

$$\frac{dy}{dx} = x - y, \quad 0 \leq x \leq 2$$

where $y(0) = 1$. Obtain a solution using each of the above methods. Compare the results obtained with the correct solution, which is given by the equation $y = 2e^{-x} + x - 1$. Determine how small the step size must be for each method in order to obtain a solution which is accurate to three significant figures.

Part II

Advanced BASIC

Chapter 6

Functions and Subroutines

6.1 Defining a Function — The DEF Statement

To avoid repeated programming of the same calculations, the programmer will want to write his own functions, to be used along with the library functions. A single-line function is defined by means of the *DEF (DEFINE) statement*. This statement is comprised of a statement number, the keyword DEF and the function definition. The function definition itself consists of the function name, followed by an equal sign, followed by an appropriate constant, variable or formula. If the function requires arguments then they must appear immediately after the function name, enclosed in parentheses and separated by commas. Only nonsubscripted variables are permitted as arguments in a function definition.

Both numeric and string functions can be defined with the DEF statement. (A numeric function returns a numeric value, a string function returns a string value.) If the function is numeric then the function name must consist of three letters, the first two of which must be FN. Thus there can be as many as 26 separate numeric functions in a single program (FNA, FNB, FNC, . . .).

The name of a string function must consist of three letters followed by a dollar sign. Again the first two letters must be FN. As many as 26 separate string functions can be defined in a single program (FNA\$, FNB\$, FNC\$, . . .). A numeric and a string function having the same three letters (e.g., FNP and FNP\$) are separate entities and may therefore appear in the same program.

Example 6.1

Three typical single-line function definitions are shown below.

```
10 DEF FNA(X)=X↑3+2*X↑2−3*X+4
20 DEF FNC$="NAME AND ADDRESS:"
30 DEF FNR(A,B,C)=SQR(A↑2+B↑2−C↑2)
```

The first and third statements define the numeric functions FNA and FNR, and the second statement defines the string function FNC\$. Notice that the second function does not contain an argument. Also, note that the third function makes use of the library function SQR in the function definition.

A DEF statement can appear anywhere in a BASIC program. However, it is good programming practice to group together all function definitions and place them near the beginning or the end of a program. This contributes to an orderly and legible program structure.

It should be clear that the presence of a DEF statement serves only to *define* a function. In order to *evaluate* the function it is necessary to refer to the function name elsewhere in the program, just as we would do with a library function. We will see how this is accomplished in the next section.

6.2   Referencing a Function

A function is referenced (evaluated) by specifying the name of the function within a BASIC statement, as though the function name were an ordinary variable. The function name must be followed by an appropriate set of arguments, enclosed in parentheses and separated by commas.

When a function is evaluated the values of the arguments are specified by the function *reference,* not the function *definition.* For this reason the arguments appearing in a DEF statement are called *dummy arguments.* The names of the arguments in the function reference need not be the same as those in the function definition. However, the *number* of arguments must be the same, and the arguments must be of the correct *type* (i.e., numeric or string).

Example 6.2

Shown below is the skeletal structure of a BASIC program containing two references to a programmer-defined function.

        10 DEF FNA(X)=X↑3+2*X↑2−3*X+4
        . . .
        50 LET W=FNA(Y)+Z
        . . .
        90 IF FNA(C)>=C1 THEN 140

Statement number 50 causes the function FNA to be evaluated using the current value of the variable Y as an input parameter. (Hence the function will return the value of Y↑3+2*Y↑2−3*Y+4.) In statement 90 the same function is evaluated using the current value of C (thus returning the value of C↑3+2*C↑2−3*C+4).

Note that the function definition could have followed the function references rather than preceding them.

The arguments in a function reference must correspond to the dummy arguments on a one-to-one (argument-for-argument) basis when two or more arguments are required. Again the correspondence must be with respect to the number of arguments and the type of each argument, but not with respect to the names of the arguments.

Example 6.3

A BASIC program contains the following statements.

        80 LET A=FNR(C,X,Y)
        . . .
        250 DEF FNR(A,B,C)=SQR(A↑2+B↑2+C↑2)

The LET statement (line 80) will cause the function SQR(C↑2+X↑2+Y↑2) to be evaluated and the value assigned to the variable A.

Notice that the function reference (line 80) and the function definition (line 250) contain 3 numeric arguments each, but the names of the arguments do not correspond.

Recall from Section 6.1 that the arguments appearing in a function *definition* (the dummy arguments) must be nonsubscripted variables. We have much more freedom, however, in a function *reference.* Here the arguments can be written as constants, subscripted variables, formulas or references to other functions. It is the *value* of each argument that is actually used in the calculation.

Example 6.4

A BASIC program contains the statements

        30 DEF FNR(A,B,C)=SQR(A↑2+B↑2+C↑2)
        . . .
        170 LET X3=FNR(K(I),5*(P+Q),LOG(T))

Notice that the function definition contains only nonsubscripted variables as arguments. In the function reference, however, we see that the arguments are expressed as a subscripted variable, a formula and a reference to a library function. Execution of the program will cause the function

$$SQR(K(I)\uparrow 2+(5*(P+Q))\uparrow 2+LOG(T)\uparrow 2)$$

to be evaluated. The resulting value will then be assigned to the variable X3.

The variables used in a function definition need not be confined to the arguments. Other program variables (including subscripted variables) may also appear. When the function is evaluated the most recently assigned values of these variables will be used.

Example 6.5

The skeletal structure of a BASIC program is shown below.

```
30 DEF FNZ(X,Y)=(C1*X+C2*Y)/(C1+C2)
    ...
60 LET C1=10
70 LET C2=20
80 LET R=FNZ(P,Q)
```

Execution of statement number 80 will cause the function

$$(10*P+20*Q)/(10+20)$$

to be evaluated. Notice that the values of C1 and C2 are not supplied as arguments. The most recently assigned values for C1 and C2 (i.e. C1=10 and C2=20) are used when the function is evaluated.

In Example 6.6 below we see a more comprehensive illustration of the use of a programmer-defined function.

Example 6.6 Search for a Maximum

Suppose we wish to find the particular value of x which causes the function

$$y = x \cos x$$

to be maximized within the interval bounded by $x = 0$ on the left and $x = \pi$ on the right. We will require that the maximizing value of x be known quite accurately. We will also require that the search scheme be relatively efficient in the sense that the function $y = x \cos x$ should be evaluated as few times as possible.

An obvious way to solve this problem would be to generate a large number of closely spaced trial functions (that is, evaluate the function at $x = 0$, $x = 0.0001$, $x = 0.0002$, ..., $x = 3.1415$, and $x = 3.1416$) and determine the largest of these by visual inspection. This would not be very efficient, however, and it would require human intervention to obtain the final result. Instead let us use the following *elimination scheme*, which is a highly efficient computational procedure for all functions which have only one "peak" within the search interval.

Computational Procedure

Suppose we place two search points at the center of the interval, located a very small distance from each other, as shown in Fig. 6.1, where

X1 = left end of the search interval
X2 = left-hand interior search point
X3 = right-hand interior search point
X4 = right end of the search interval
D = distance between X2 and X3.

If X1, X4 and D are known, then the interior points can be calculated as

X2=X1+.5*(X4−X1−D)
X3=X1+.5*(X4−X1+D)=X2+D

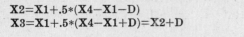
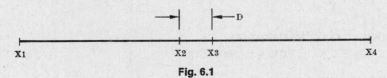

Fig. 6.1

Let us evaluate the function $y = x \cos x$ at X2 and at X3, and let us call these values Y2 and Y3, respectively.   Suppose Y2 turns out to be greater than Y3.   Then we know that the maximum that we are seeking will lie somewhere between X1 and X3.   Hence we retain only that portion of the search interval which ranges from $x = $ X1 to $x = $ X3 (we will now refer to the old point X3 as X4, since it is now the right end of the new search interval), and generate two *new* search points X2 and X3.   These points will be located at the center of the new search interval, a distance D apart, as shown in Fig. 6.2.

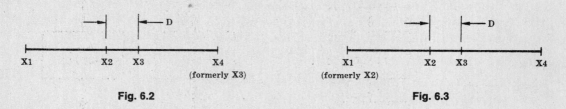

Fig. 6.2   **Fig. 6.3**

On the other hand, suppose now that in our *original* search interval the value of Y3 turned out to be greater than Y2.   This would indicate that our new search interval should lie between X2 and X4.   Hence we rename the point which was originally called X2 to be X1 and we generate two *new* search points, X2 and X3, at the center of the new search interval, as shown in Fig. 6.3.

We continue to generate a new pair of search points at the center of each new interval, compare the respective values of y, and eliminate a portion of the search interval until the search interval becomes smaller than 3*D.   Once this happens we cannot distinguish the interior points from the boundaries.   Hence the search is ended.

Each time we make a comparison between Y2 and Y3 we eliminate that portion of the search interval which contains the smaller value of y.   If both interior values of y should happen to be identical (which can happen, though it is unusual), then the search procedure stops, and the maximum is assumed to occur at the center of the two search points.

Once the search has ended, either because the search interval has become sufficiently small or because the two interior points yield identical values of y, we can calculate the approximate location of the maximum as

X5=.5*(X2+X3)

The corresponding maximum value of the function can then be obtained as X5*COS(X5).

The Program Outline

1. Define the function $y = x \cos x$.

2. Read the initial values of X1 and X4, and a value for D.

3. Set I=1 (where I is an iteration counter).

4. Calculate a pair of interior points.

5. Write out the values of x at the ends of the interval and at the interior points, and write out the corresponding values for y.

6. Compare Y2 and Y3:

    (*a*) If Y2 is greater than Y3, let X3 be called X4, thus defining a new search interval, and proceed to step 7.

    (*b*) If Y3 is greater than Y2, let X2 be called X1, thus defining a new search interval, and proceed to step 7.

    (*c*) If Y2 equals Y3, then proceed to step 9 below.

7. Test to see if I=100.   If so, write an appropriate message and stop.   Otherwise, increment the iteration counter and continue.

8. Test to see if (X4—X1)>3*D.   If so, return to step 4 above.   Otherwise, proceed below.

9. Calculate   X5=.5*(X2+X3)
                       Y5=X5*COS(X5)

    then write out the final results and stop.

A flowchart of the procedure is given in Fig. 6.4.

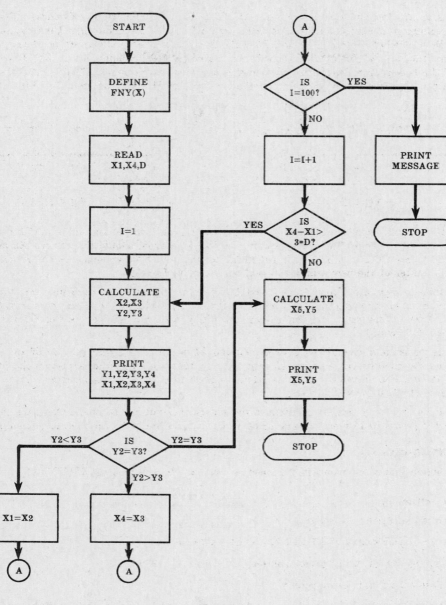

Fig. 6.4

The BASIC Program

The actual BASIC program appears in Fig. 6.5. For simplicity we have included a function definition to evaluate the quantity $y = x \cos x$. (Note that a reference to the library function COS is contained within the function definition.) We see that the function is referenced in lines 170, 180, 200 and 440. A different value for the argument (i.e., a different value of x) is supplied in each function reference.

Figure 6.6 shows the output generated by the program for the case X1=0, X4=3.14159 and D=0.0001. We see that the maximum value of y is approximately 0.5611, occurring at $x = 0.8604$. Notice that this result has been obtained to a high degree of accuracy with only 14 pairs of search points!

The procedure given in this example can also be used to *minimize* a function of x. In fact, the same program can be used, given some very minor modification. Such a minimization procedure can provide us with a highly effective technique for calculating the roots of a nonlinear algebraic equation. For example, suppose we want to find the particular value of x which causes some function $f(x)$ to equal zero. A typical function of this nature might be $f(x) = x - \sin x + \cos x - 1$. If we let $y(x) = f(x)^2$, then the function $y(x)$ will always be positive except for those values of x which are roots of the given function, i.e., for which $y(x)$ will equal zero. Thus any value of x which causes $y(x)$ to be minimized will also be a root of the equation $f(x) = 0$.

```
 10   REM SEARCH FØR A MAXIMUM ØF THE FUNCTIØN Y=X*CØS(X)
 20   DEF FNY(X)=X*CØS(X)
 30   PRINT "LEFT END ØF INTERVAL (X1) =";
 40   INPUT X1
 50   PRINT
 60   PRINT "RIGHT END ØF INTERVAL (X4) =";
 70   INPUT X4
 80   PRINT
 90   PRINT "MINIMUM SEPARATIØN BETWEEN INTERIØR PØINTS (D) =";
100   INPUT D
110   LET I=1
120
130   REM CALCULATE INTERIØR PØINTS
140
150   LET X2=X1+.5*(X4-X1-D)
160   LET X3=X2+D
170   LET Y2=FNY(X2)
180   LET Y3=FNY(X3)
190   PRINT
200   PRINT "Y1=";FNY(X1),"Y2=";Y2,"Y3=";Y3,"Y4=";FNY(X4)
210   PRINT "X1=";X1,"X2=";X2,"X3=";X3,"X4=";X4
220   IF Y2<Y3 THEN 300
230   IF Y2=Y3 THEN 400
240
250   REM Y2 GREATER THAN Y3 - RETAIN LEFT INTERVAL
260
270   LET X4=X3
280   GØ TØ 340
290
300   REM Y3 GREATER THAN Y2 - RETAIN RIGHT INTERVAL
310
320   LET X1=X2
330
340   REM TEST FØR END ØF SEARCH
350
360   IF I=100 THEN 470
370   LET I=I+1
380   IF (X4-X1)>3*D THEN 130
390
400   REM CØMPUTE FINAL SØLUTIØN
410
420   LET X5=.5*(X2+X3)
430   PRINT
440   PRINT ,"XMAX=";X5,"YMAX=";FNY(X5)
450   STØP
460
470   REM TERMINATE CØMPUTATIØN BECAUSE ØF MAXIMUM ITERATIØN CØUNT
480
490   PRINT "MAXIMUM NUMBER ØF ITERATIØNS EXCEEDED - CØMPUTATIØN ENDS"
500   END
```

Fig. 6.5

6.3   Multiline Functions

There are many calculations that cannot be carried out using a single statement.   This is especially true of computations that involve lengthy arithmetic formulas or conditional branching operations.   The multiline function format is well suited for calculations of this type.

A multiline function, like a single-line function, can have any number of dummy input arguments but returns only one value.   The first statement must be a DEF statement. Unlike a single-line function, however, the function definition is not included in the DEF statement.   The last statement must be a *FNEND (FUNCTION END) statement,* which consists simply of a statement number followed by the keyword FNEND.

Between the DEF and FNEND statements there can be any number of statements which define the function.   One of these statements must assign a value to the function name.   Usually this is accomplished with a LET statement in which the function name appears to the left of the equal sign.   The same naming convention is used as with single-line functions.

```
        LEFT END ØF INTERVAL (X1) = ?0

        RIGHT END ØF INTERVAL (X4) = ?3.14159

        MINIMUM SEPARATIØN BETWEEN INTERIØR PØINTS (D) = ?.0001

        Y1= 0          Y2= 8.06277E-5              Y3=-7.64780E-5
        Y4=-3.14159
        X1= 0          X2= 1.57075    X3= 1.57085      X4=  3.14159

        Y1= 0          Y2= 0.555356   Y3= 0.555372   Y4=-7.64780E-5
        X1= 0          X2= 0.785372   X3= 0.785473   X4= 1.57085

        Y1= 0.555356   Y2= 0.450865   Y3= 0.450795   Y4=-7.64780E-5
        X1= 0.785372   X2= 1.17806    X3= 1.17816    X4= 1.57085

        Y1= 0.555356   Y2= 0.545438   Y3= 0.545412   Y4= 0.450795
        X1= 0.785372   X2= 0.981716   X3= 0.981816   X4= 1.17816

        Y1= 0.555356   Y2= 0.560534   Y3= 0.560529   Y4= 0.545412
        X1= 0.785372   X2= 0.883544   X3= 0.883644   X4= 0.981816

        Y1= 0.555356   Y2= 0.560405   Y3= 0.56041    Y4= 0.560529
        X1= 0.785372   X2= 0.834458   X3= 0.834558   X4= 0.883644

        Y1= 0.560405   Y2= 0.561094   Y3= 0.561095   Y4= 0.560529
        X1= 0.834458   X2= 0.859001   X3= 0.859101   X4= 0.883644

        Y1= 0.561094   Y2= 0.560972   Y3= 0.560969   Y4= 0.560529
        X1= 0.859001   X2= 0.871273   X3= 0.871373   X4= 0.883644

        Y1= 0.561094   Y2= 0.561072   Y3= 0.561071   Y4= 0.560969
        X1= 0.859001   X2= 0.865137   X3= 0.865237   X4= 0.871373

        Y1= 0.561094   Y2= 0.561093   Y3= 0.561093   Y4= 0.561071
        X1= 0.859001   X2= 0.862069   X3= 0.862169   X4= 0.865237

        Y1= 0.561094   Y2= 0.561096   Y3= 0.561096   Y4= 0.561093
        X1= 0.859001   X2= 0.860535   X3= 0.860635   X4= 0.862169

        Y1= 0.561094   Y2= 0.561096   Y3= 0.561096   Y4= 0.561096
        X1= 0.859001   X2= 0.859768   X3= 0.359868   X4= 0.860635

        Y1= 0.561096   Y2= 0.561096   Y3= 0.561096   Y4= 0.561096
        X1= 0.859768   X2= 0.860152   X3= 0.360252   X4= 0.860635

        Y1= 0.561096   Y2= 0.561096   Y3= 0.561096   Y4= C.561096
        X1= 0.860152   X2= 0.860343   X3= 0.860443   X4= C.860635

            XMAX= 0.860393                   YMAX= 0.561096
```

Fig. 6.6

Example 6.7

The skeletal structure of a multiline function is shown below.

```
200 DEF FNA(X,Y,Z)
    ...
250 LET FNA=...
260 FNEND
```

This function is called FNA, and it makes use of the dummy input arguments X, Y and Z. The value returned by the function is computed in statement number 250.

The grammatical rules that apply to multiline functions are the same as those for single-line functions (e.g., a function definition can appear anywhere in a program; a function is referenced by specifying its name followed by a list of arguments, enclosed in parentheses and separated by commas; etc.). In addition, control cannot be transferred between a statement within a function and a point exterior to the function.

Example 6.8

Shown below is a part of a BASIC program containing a multiline function definition and a reference to that function. The purpose of the function is to determine the smallest of a pair of numbers.

```
20 DEF FNM(A,B)
30 LET FNM=A
40 IF A<=B THEN 60
50 LET FNM=B
60 FNEND
   ...
150 PRINT FNM(FNM(C1,C2),FNM(C2,C3))
```

Notice that the function FNM is nested within itself in statement number 150. This statement causes the smallest of the three quantities represented by C1, C2 and C3 to be printed.

Variables other than those specified as arguments may appear in a multiline function, just as in a single-line function. This includes subscripted as well as nonsubscripted variables. The currently assigned values of these variables will be used each time the function is evaluated.

Example 6.9

A BASIC program contains the following multiline function definition.

```
100 DEF FNY(X)
110 IF X>300 THEN 140
120 LET FNY=A+B*X+C*X↑2
130 GO TO 150
140 LET FNY=D+E*X+F*X↑2
150 FNEND
```

Notice that the value of X is supplied via an argument when the function is referenced. However, the values of A, B, C, D, E and F are not supplied as arguments. Thus the most recently assigned values for these variables will be used whenever the function is evaluated.

It should be understood that a function having arguments of a given type can result in a value which is of a different type (e.g., a function having string arguments can be used to determine a numeric value). Furthermore, the arguments themselves need not be of the same type (i.e., both numeric and string arguments can be present). This is true for both multiline and single-line functions. Remember, however, that the arguments in a function reference must correspond in number and in type with the dummy arguments in the function definition.

Example 6.10

Presented below is the skeletal structure of a multiline function which requires both a numeric and a string argument. The function itself returns a string value (hence the dollar sign in the function name).

```
100 DEF FNW$(C,N$)
    ...
140 LET FNW$=...
150 FNEND
```

When referencing this function it will be necessary to supply a numeric and a string argument, in that order. The names of the arguments need not, of course, be the same as the names of the dummy arguments. Hence an appropriate function reference might be

```
250 LET N$=FNW$(X,T$)
```

Examples 6.15 and 6.20 illustrate the use of multiline functions in complete BASIC programs.

6.4   Encoding and Decoding Data — The CHANGE Statement

When a string is represented within a computer the characters that make up the string are stored not as characters but as an encoded sequence of numbers.   Each digit, letter and special character is represented by its own unique number.

There are several different numerical coding schemes which are used at various installations.   Perhaps the most common of these is the 7-bit ASCII Code[†], in which the letter A is represented by the number 65, B by the number 66, and so on.   Table 6.1 shows the ASCII equivalents of the more common characters.

Table 6.1   The 7-bit ASCII Character Code

Character	Code	Character	Code
A	65	0	48
B	66	1	49
C	67	2	50
D	68	3	51
E	69	4	52
F	70	5	53
G	71	6	54
H	72	7	55
I	73	8	56
J	74	9	57
K	75	+	43
L	76	—	45
M	77	/	47
N	78	*	42
O	79	↑	94
P	80	(	40
Q	81	)	41
R	82	<	60
S	83	>	62
T	84	=	61
U	85	?	63
V	86	$	36
W	87	"	34
X	88	,	44
Y	89	.	46
Z	90	;	59
		Carriage Return	13
		Line Feed	10
		Space	32

[†]American Standard Code for Information Interchange, a widely used code proposed by the American National Standards Institute.

The conversions from characters to numbers, and vice versa, are carried out automatically within the computer. Usually the programmer is not even aware of the fact that such conversion takes place. Sometimes, however, it is desirable to work with the numerical equivalent of the characters in a string. This allows each character to be manipulated individually. The *CHANGE statement* allows us to carry out this conversion.

There are two different ways that the CHANGE statement can be written. The first of these consists of a statement number, the keyword CHANGE, a string variable, the keyword TO, and a numeric list, in that order. This statement causes each character in a string to be converted to its numerical equivalent and stored in a numeric list. The first element in the list (for which the subscript has a value of zero) will indicate the number of encoded characters contained in the list.

Example 6.11

A BASIC program contains the statement

    100 CHANGE N$ TO N

where N is the name of a numeric list. Suppose that N$ represents the string MONDAY, and that the ASCII code shown in Table 6.1 is applicable. Then execution of the CHANGE statement will cause the elements of N to be assigned the following values.

    N(0)= 6 (indicating 6 characters in the string)
    N(1)=77 (the numerical equivalent of the letter M)
    N(2)=79 (the numerical equivalent of the letter O)
    N(3)=78 (the numerical equivalent of the letter N)
    N(4)=68 (the numerical equivalent of the letter D)
    N(5)=65 (the numerical equivalent of the letter A)
    N(6)=89 (the numerical equivalent of the letter Y)

It is now possible to access the numerical equivalent of any character in the given string simply by referring to the appropriate subscripted variable.

The position of the string variable and the numeric list can be interchanged in the CHANGE statement. That is, the statement can be written as a statement number, followed by the keyword CHANGE, a numeric list, the keyword TO and a string variable. In this form the statement causes the elements of the numeric list to be converted into a string of characters. The character conversion begins with the second element of the list (for which the subscript has a value of one); the first element in the list (subscript equal to zero) will indicate the number of characters in the string, as before.

Example 6.12

A BASIC program contains the statement

    225 CHANGE L TO A$

where L is the name of a numeric list. Suppose that the elements of L have the following values, which represent 7-bit ASCII characters.

    L(0)=11   L(6)=32
    L(1)=83   L(7)=67
    L(2)=65   L(8)=76
    L(3)=78   L(9)=65
    L(4)=84   L(10)=85
    L(5)=65   L(11)=83

When the CHANGE statement is executed each element of L, beginning with L(1), will be converted to its corresponding character and the resulting string will be assigned to A$. Hence A$ will represent the string SANTA CLAUS.

In Example 6.15 we will see a complete BASIC program that makes use of the CHANGE statement.

6.5 The ASC and CHR$ Functions

Closely associated with the CHANGE statement are the library functions ASC and CHR$. The first of these, ASC, converts any single character to its ASCII equivalent. This function will therefore accept only a single character as an argument.

Example 6.13

Consider the statement

    50 LET C=ASC(P)

This statement will cause a value of 80 to be assigned to the variable C, since 80 is the ASCII equivalent of the letter P.

Similarly, the statement

    70 IF L(I)=ASC( ) THEN 110

will result in a transfer of control to statement number 110 if the subscripted variable L(I) represents the value 32, since 32 is the ASCII representation for a blank space.

The purpose of the library function CHR$ is just the opposite of ASC. That is, CHR$ is used to convert the ASCII representation of a single character into that character. In this case the value of the argument must be a recognized ASCII integer quantity. Noninteger values will automatically be truncated.

Example 6.14

Consider the statement

    75 LET A$=CHR$(X)

If the variable X has a value of 42, then A$ will represent the character *, since 42 is the ASCII representation for an asterisk.

In a similar vein, the statement

    310 PRINT CHR$(L(I));

will cause the letter P to be printed if L(I) has a value of 80.

The ASC and CHR$ functions, as well as the CHANGE statement, are included in the following programming example.

Example 6.15 A Piglatin Generator

Piglatin is an encoded form of English that is often used by children as a game. A piglatin word is formed from an English word by transposing the first sound (usually the first letter) to the end of the word, and then adding the letter "a". Thus the word "cat" becomes "atca", "BASIC" becomes "ASICBA", "piglatin" becomes "iglatinpa" (or "igpa atinla", if spelled as two separate words), and so on.

We wish to write a BASIC program which will accept a line of English text and then print out the text in piglatin.

Computational Procedure

We will assume that each textual message can be typed on one line of a 72-character typewriter terminal, with a space between successive words. The computational procedure will then be straightforward, consisting of a means of extracting each word from the textual message, rearranging the word, adding the letter "a" and then printing the rearranged word. In principle it is quite simple to extract each word from the line of text, since the blank spaces allow us to distinguish one word from another.

The detailed computation is somewhat tricky, however, since the characters in the line of text can be manipulated individually only if they are first changed to their ASCII-encoded numerical equivalents. Before printing each rearranged word it will be necessary to change the ASCII numbers back into characters. The CHANGE statement and the CHR$ function will be used for this purpose.

The extraction of the ASCII quantities representing a single word from the entire list of ASCII numbers must be carried out carefully. Two "pointers" (numeric variables) will be used for this purpose. The first pointer will indicate the location of the ASCII equivalent of the first letter in the word, and the second pointer will indicate where the ASCII equivalent of the last letter can be found. These pointers will have to be reset after each word has been rearranged.

We will use a multiline function in order to extract each word, i.e., to position the pointers. There will be no problem in positioning the first pointer, since we know that the first word will start in location 1, and each successive word will begin 2 places beyond the end of the previous word. In order to position the second pointer, however, we will have to examine each ASCII-encoded character beyond the first pointer until we find a blank space. The second pointer will then be positioned one place before the blank space.

The Program Outline

In order to write a detailed outline of the computational procedure let us first define the following symbols.

$N\$$ = the given line of text (a string)

L = a numeric list containing the ASCII equivalents of the characters in the line of text (note that L will consist of 72 individual encoded quantities)

$P1$ = the location in L of the ASCII equivalent of the first letter of a particular word (a number between 1 and 72)

$P2$ = the location in L of the ASCII equivalent of the last letter of a particular word (a number between 1 and 72, but not less than the value of $P1$)

Consider the multiline function FNP, which will return a value for $P2$, given a value for $P1$. The computation will proceed as follows.

1. For each value of the subscript I beginning with $I=P1+1$, test to see if the subscripted variable $L(I)$ contains the ASCII equivalent of a blank space.

   (a) If some $L(I)$ represents a blank space (indicating the end of a word), let $P2=I-1$.

   (b) If all of the $L(I)$ represent something other than a blank space, set $P2=72$ (the end of a line).

2. Return the value of $P2$ to the function reference point. Figure 6.7 shows a flowchart of the above procedure.

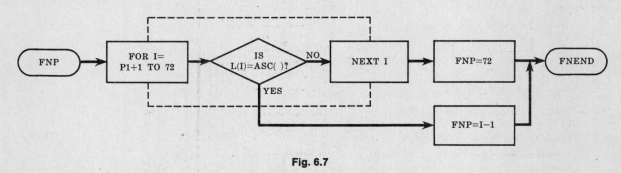

Fig. 6.7

The remainder of the program will proceed in the following manner.

1. Read $N\$$.

2. Test to see if $N\$$ represents the word END. If so, terminate the computation; otherwise, proceed with step 3 below.

3. Assign to each element in L the ASCII equivalent of a blank space (thus "erasing" whatever may have been stored in L before).

4. Change $N\$$ to L.

5. Let $P1=1$.

6. Reference the function FNP to establish a value for $P2$.

7. Rearrange and print the characters in the word as follows.

   (a) If the word contains only one letter, then $P2$ will coincide with $P1$. Hence proceed directly to step 7(c) below.

   (b) Print the characters represented by $L(P1+1)$ through $L(P2)$ consecutively.

   (c) Print the character represented by $L(P1)$, followed immediately by the letter "a" and a blank space.

8. Establish the beginning of the next word as follows.

   (*a*) Let P1=P2+2.

   (*b*) If the new value of P1 exceeds 72, then the line of text has been exceeded. Therefore go back to step 1 and read a new line of text.

   (*c*) If L(P1) represents a blank space (even though P1 does not exceed 72), then the end of the textual message has been reached. Therefore go back to step 1 and read a new line of text.

   (*d*) Go back to step 6 and establish a new value for P2.

Note that this strategy will continue to read successive lines of text until the word END has been encountered (see steps 1 and 2 above).

A flowchart corresponding to the above steps is shown in Fig. 6.8.

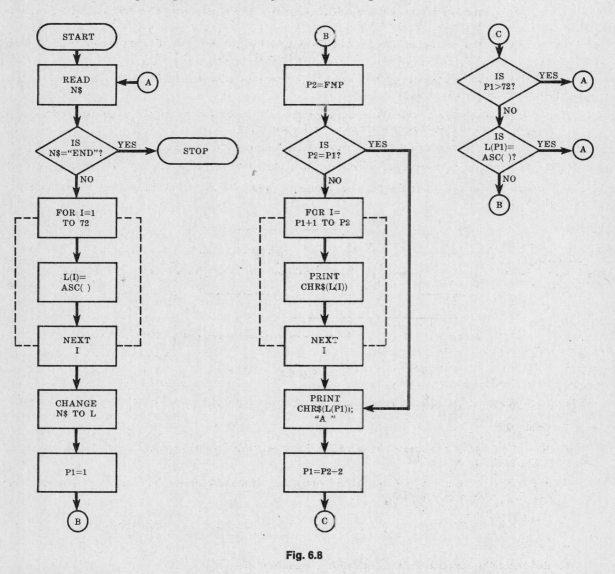

Fig. 6.8

The BASIC Program

Figure 6.9 contains the actual BASIC program for this problem. Notice the use of the ASC library function in lines 70, 210 and 390, and the CHR$ function in lines 310 and 330. These functions are used to convert single characters to and from their ASCII equivalents.

The computation of P2 for a given value of P1 is programmed as a multiline function in lines 40-120. It should be pointed out that this particular program could just as easily have been written without the use of a programmer-defined function. The purpose of the function, in this case, is to structure a relatively self-contained part of the computational strategy as an equally self-contained program element. Hence the advantage of the function is *organizational* rather than *computational*. In many other programs, however, the presence of a programmer-defined function will eliminate the need for repeated programming of the same set of calculations.

```
10    REM            PIGLATIN GENERATØR
20    DIM L(72)
30
40    DEF FNP(P1)
50    REM            THIS FUNCTIØN FINDS THE END ØF A SINGLE WØRD
60    FØR I=P1+1 TØ 72
70        IF L(I)=ASC( ) THEN 110
80    NEXT I
90    LET FNP=72
100   GØ TØ 120
110   LET FNP=I-1
120   FNEND
130
140   REM            READ A LINE ØF TEXT
150
160   PRINT
170   PRINT
180   INPUT N$
190   IF N$="END" THEN 410
200   FØR I=1 TØ 72
210       LET L(I)=ASC( )
220   NEXT I
230   CHANGE N$ TØ L
240   LET P1=1
250   LET P2=FNP(P1)
260
270   REM            PRINT WØRD IN PIGLATIN
280
290   IF P2=P1 THEN 330
300   FØR I=P1+1 TØ P2
310       PRINT CHR$(L(I));
320   NEXT I
330   PRINT CHR$(L(P1));"A ";
340
350   REM            FIND NEXT WØRD
360
370   LET P1=P2+2
380   IF P1>72 THEN 140         'END ØF LINE
390   IF L(P1)=ASC( ) THEN 140  'END ØF TEXT
400   GØ TØ 250
410   END
```

Fig. 6.9

In Fig. 6.10 we see the output generated by the program for three typical lines of text. Each single-line input message is followed immediately by the corresponding line of piglatin. Execution of the program is terminated after the word END is entered from the typewriter terminal.

```
?THIS IS A PIGLATIN GENERATØR
HISTA SIA AA IGLATINPA ENERATØRGA

?WHAT SØRT ØF GARBLED MESSAGE IS THIS ANYHØW
HATWA ØRTSA FØA ARBLEDGA ESSAGEMA SIA HISTA NYHØWAA

?NØW IS THE TIME FØR ALL GØØD MEN TØ CØME TØ THE AID ØF THEIR CØUNTRY
ØWNA SIA HETA IMETA ØRFA LLAA ØØDGA ENMA ØTA ØMECA ØTA HETA IDAA FØA HEI
RTA ØUNTRYCA

?END
```

Fig. 6.10

6.6 Generating Random Numbers — The RND Function

Many interesting computer applications are based upon the generation of random numbers. In BASIC it is very easy to generate a random number by means of the RND library function. This function returns a different random number, with a value between zero and one, each time the function is referenced. An argument is not required.

Example 6.16

A BASIC program contains the statements

```
20 DIM X(100)
   . . .
50 FOR I=1 TO 100
60     LET X(I)=RND
70 NEXT I
```

These statements will cause 100 random numbers to be generated and stored in the list X. Each random number will be a decimal quantity whose value lies between zero and one.

Example 6.17

Suppose we wish to generate a random number having a value between 3 and 7. This can be accomplished by writing

```
100 LET X=3+(7−3)*RND
```

or simply

```
100 LET X=3+4*RND
```

Example 6.18

The statement shown below will generate an integer-valued random number between 1 and 6. Each digit will occur with equal likelihood.

```
100 LET X=1+INT(6*RND)
```

In interpreting this statement it should be understood that the RND function can return a function very close to 1, but not exactly 1. Thus if RND returns a value of 0.99999999, then 6*RND will yield a value of 5.9999994, and INT(6*RND) will result in a value of 5. Hence X will be assigned a value of 6.

We will see a complete BASIC program that makes use of the RND function in Example 6.20.

6.7   The RANDOMIZE Statement

The numbers obtained from the RND function are not truly random, since they are generated by using a fixed computational procedure. However, such numbers *appear* to be random and they have the same statistical properties as numbers which are truly random. Therefore these numbers are often referred to as *pseudo-random* numbers.

Every time a program containing the RND function is executed the same sequence of pseudo-random numbers will be generated. This reproducibility of the random number sequence is very helpful when debugging a program. On the other hand, it is often desirable to generate a different sequence of pseudo-random numbers each time a debugged program is executed. This can be accomplished by means of the *RANDOMIZE statement*.

The RANDOMIZE statement consists of simply a line number followed by the keyword RANDOMIZE. Its purpose is to provide a different starting point for the random number generator. Therefore the RANDOMIZE statement must precede the first reference to the RND function in a program.

Example 6.19

A BASIC program contains the statements

```
20 DIM X(100)
30 RANDOMIZE
   . . .
50 FOR I=1 TO 100
60     LET X(I)=RND
70 NEXT I
```

These statements will cause a sequence of 100 pseudo-random numbers to be generated and stored in the list X, just as in Example 6.16. Unlike Example 6.16 however, a different sequence of random numbers will be generated each time the program is executed.

Example 6.20   A Game of Chance (Shooting Craps)

In this example we will simulate a game of "craps" on a computer. Craps is a popular dice game in which a player throws a pair of dice one or more times until he either wins or loses. The game can be computerized by substituting the generation of random numbers for the actual throwing of the dice.

Rules of the Game

There are 2 ways a player can win in craps. He can throw the dice once and obtain a score of either 7 or 11, or he can obtain a 4, 5, 6, 8, 9 or 10 on the first throw, and then come up with the same score on a subsequent throw before obtaining a score of 7. Conversely, there are 2 ways a player can lose. Either he can throw the dice once and obtain a score of 2, 3 or 12, or he can obtain a 4, 5, 6, 8, 9 or 10 on the first throw, and then obtain a score of 7 on a subsequent throw before coming up with the same score as he had on the first throw.

Computational Procedure

Let us computerize the game in a conversational manner, so that one throw of the dice will be simulated each time the player depresses the carriage return on the typewriter terminal. A message will then appear indicating the outcome of each throw. The game will continue until the player types the word END. In addition, we will include a provision for printing the rules of the game if the player enters the word RULES.

In order to simulate one throw of the dice we will generate two random numbers, each having an integer value between 1 and 6. The sum of these two numbers will represent the score obtained by throwing the dice. It is convenient to use a programmer-defined function for this purpose, since each reference to the function will simulate a different throw of the dice.

The main part of the program will examine the score obtained from each throw and determine if the player has won or lost the game, or whether another throw is required. An appropriate message, along with the simulated score, will be printed in each case. Also included will be a block of PRINT statements which will cause the rules to be printed in response to the player typing RULES.

The Program Outline

1. Initialize the random number generator.

2. Read a value for the string variable N$.

    (a) Stop the execution if N$=END.

    (b) If N$=RULES print the rules of the game and then repeat this step (i.e., read a new value for N$.

    (c) If N$ represents some string other than the words END or RULES, then proceed to step 3 below. (Note that any single character can be assigned to N$ for this purpose. A carriage return may be most convenient, since the carriage return bar is particularly conspicuous on a typewriter terminal.)

3. Simulate one throw of the dice, calling the resulting score K.

    (a) A value of K = 2, 3 or 12 indicates a loss. Hence print an appropriate message and return to step 2.

    (b) A value of K = 7 or 11 indicates a win. Hence print an appropriate message and return to step 2.

    (c) A value of K = 4, 5, 6, 8, 9 or 10 will require additional throws of the dice. Hence print an appropriate message and proceed with step 4 below.

4. Let K1=K. (This will allow subsequent values of K to be compared with the original value, which will now be called K1.)

5. Read a new value for N$ and then simulate another throw of the dice, thus generating a new value for K. (Note that the dice will not be thrown until the player signals to do so by entering some character, such as a carriage return, for N$).

6. Compare K with K1.

    (*a*) A value of K=K1 indicates a win.   Hence print an appropriate message and return to step 2.

    (*b*) A value of K=7 indicates a loss.   Hence print an appropriate message and return to step 2.

    (*c*) If K does not equal either K1 or 7, then return to step 5 and generate a new value for K.

A flowchart of the procedure is shown in Fig. 6.11.

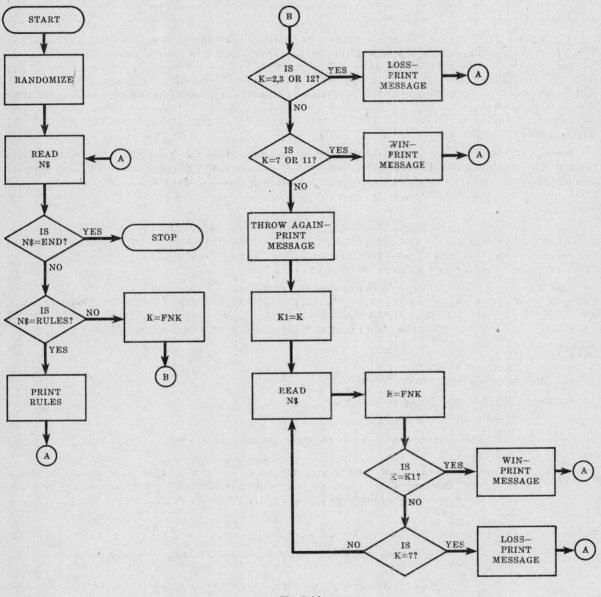

Fig. 6.11

The simulation of one throw of the dice will be carried out in a programmer-defined function as follows.

    1. Let K2=1+INT(6*RND).
        (See Example 6.18 for an explanation of this statement.)

    2. Let K3=1+INT(6*RND).

    3. Let K=K2+K3.

4. Return the current value for K to the function reference point.

A corresponding flowchart is shown in Fig. 6.12. Note that the calculated value of K is called FNK within the function.

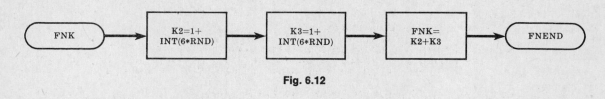

Fig. 6.12

The BASIC Program

Figure 6.13 contains a complete BASIC program for carrying out the computation. Notice that lines 500 through 550 define the multiline function FNK, which simulates the throw of a pair of dice. This function is referenced at two different points within the program — namely, lines 90 and 180.

Within the programmer-defined function FNK we see two references to the library function RND. Also, notice that statement number 20 is a RANDOMIZE statement, which is used to initialize the random number generator each time the program is executed. It is significant that the RANDOMIZE statement precedes the first reference to the RND function (through reference to function FNK).

```
10   REM            SIMULATIØN ØF A GAME ØF CRAPS
20   RANDØMIZE
30   INPUT N$
40   IF N$="END" THEN 600
50   IF N$="RULES" THEN 300
60
70   REM            SIMULATE ØNE PLAY ØF CRAPS
80
90   LET K=FNK
100  ØN (K-1) GØ TØ 110,110,150,150,150,130,150,150,150,130,110
110  PRINT K; "- - YØU LØSE ØN THE FIRST THRØW"
120  GØ TØ 250
130  PRINT K; "- - YØU WIN ØN THE FIRST THRØW"
140  GØ TØ 250
150  LET K1=K
160  PRINT K; "- - THRØW THE DICE AGAIN"
170  INPUT N$
180  LET K=FNK
190  IF K=K1 THEN 220
200  IF K=7 THEN 240
210  GØ TØ 160
220  PRINT K; "- - YØU WIN BY MATCHING YØUR FIRST SCØRE"
230  GØ TØ 250
240  PRINT K; "- - YØU LØSE BY FAILING TØ MATCH YØUR FIRST SCØRE"
250  PRINT
260  GØ TØ 30
270
300  REM          PRINT RULES ØF CRAPS
310
320  PRINT,"RULES ØF CRAPS"
330  PRINT
340  PRINT "TØ WIN: ØBTAIN A 7 ØR 11 ØN THE FIRST THRØW"
350  PRINT "    ØR: ØBTAIN A 4,5,6,8,9 ØR 10 ØN THE FIRST THRØW"
360  PRINT,"AND MATCH YØUR ØRIGINAL SCØRE BEFØRE THRØWING A 7"
370  PRINT
380  PRINT "TØ LØSE: ØBTAIN A 2,3 ØR 12 ØN THE FIRST THRØW"
390  PRINT "     ØR: ØBTAIN A 4,5,6,8,9 ØR 10 ØN THE FIRST THRØW"
400  PRINT,"AND THRØW A 7 BEFØRE MATCHING YØUR ØRIGINAL SCØRE"
410  PRINT
420  GØ TØ 30
500  DEF FNK
510  REM          THIS FUNCTIØN SIMULATES ØNE THRØW ØF A PAIR ØF DICE
520  LET K2=1+INT(6*RND)
530  LET K3=1+INT(6*RND)
540  LET FNK=K2+K3
550  FNEND
600  END
```

Fig. 6.13

In Fig. 6.14 we see a representative listing of output data. First we see the rules printed out, in response to the player typing in the word RULES. Following this we see 5 typical plays (3 wins and 2 losses). Finally, the player has typed the word END, causing the program execution to terminate.

```
?RULES
                    RULES ØF CRAPS

TØ WIN: ØBTAIN A 7 ØR 11 ØN THE FIRST THRØW
    ØR: ØBTAIN A 4,5,6,8,9 ØR 10 ØN THE FIRST THRØW
              AND MATCH YØUR ØRIGINAL SCØRE BEFØRE THRØWING A 7

TØ LØSE: ØBTAIN A 2,3 ØR 12 ØN THE FIRST THRØW
     ØR: ØBTAIN A 4,5,6,8,9 ØR 10 ØN THE FIRST THRØW
               AND THRØW A 7 BEFØRE MATCHING YØUR ØRIGINAL SCØRE

?
11 - - YØU WIN ØN THE FIRST THRØW

?
5 - - THRØW THE DICE AGAIN
?
7 - - YØU LØSE BY FAILING TØ MATCH YØUR FIRST SCØRE

?
3 - - YØU LØSE ØN THE FIRST THRØW

?
7 - - YØU WIN ØN THE FIRST THRØW

?
4 - - THRØW THE DICE AGAIN
?
8 - - THRØW THE DICE AGAIN
?
9 - - THRØW THE DICE AGAIN
?
11 - - THRØW THE DICE AGAIN
?
6 - - THRØW THE DICE AGAIN
?
5 - - THRØW THE DICE AGAIN
?
4 - - YØU WIN BY MATCHING YØUR FIRST SCØRE

?END
```

Fig. 6.14

6.8   Defining a Subroutine

Sometimes it is more convenient to structure a sequence of statements as a *subroutine* rather than a function. Subroutines are similar to functions in the sense that they can be referenced from other places in a program. Unlike a function, however, a subroutine is not given a name, and it can be used to determine more than one numeric and/or string quantity. Furthermore, arguments are not used. Hence a subroutine can exchange information with the rest of the program in a very general manner.

A subroutine need not begin with any special statement. Thus a subroutine may begin with a REM statement, a LET statement, a FOR-TO statement, an INPUT statement, etc. The last statement, however, must be a *RETURN statement*, which consists simply of a statement number followed by the keyword RETURN. This statement causes control to be transferred back to the statement following the point of reference. (It should be understood that control *cannot* be transferred by some other type of branching statement, such as GO TO, IF-THEN or ON-GO TO.)

Example 6.21

A typical subroutine is shown below.

```
300 REM SUBROUTINE TO CALCULATE CRITICAL CONSTANTS
310 LET C1=(A+B+C)/3
320 LET C2=SQR(A↑2+B↑2+C↑2)
330 LET C3=SQR(A*B*C)
340 RETURN
```

Notice that the subroutine begins with a REM statement and ends with a RETURN statement. The variables A, B and C must be assigned numerical values before the subroutine is first referenced.

A subroutine may contain several RETURN statements if desired. This is often necessary if the subroutine contains a conditional branch or a multiple branch. When the subroutine is executed, the first RETURN statement to be encountered will cause control to be transferred from the subroutine.

Example 6.22

The skeletal structure of a subroutine containing multiple RETURN statements is shown below.

```
500 REM SAMPLE SUBROUTINE WITH MULTIPLE RETURNS
510 ON N 520,580,650
520 LET X=...
    . . .
570 RETURN
580 LET Y=...
    . . .
640 RETURN
650 LET Z=...
    . . .
690 RETURN
```

This subroutine contains a multiple branch, with control being transferred to statement 520, 580 or 650 (all of which are contained within the subroutine), depending on the value of N. Control will then be transferred back to the statement following the subroutine reference when any one of the RETURN statements is encountered.

6.9 Referencing a Subroutine — The GOSUB Statement

A subroutine is referenced by means of the *GOSUB statement*. This statement consists of a statement number, the keyword GOSUB, and the number of the first statement in the subroutine. Execution of this statement will cause a transfer of control to the subroutine. Control will then be transferred back to the statement following GOSUB when a RETURN statement is encountered within the subroutine.

Example 6.23

A BASIC program contains the following statements.

```
120 GOSUB 300
130 PRINT "Z=";Z
    . . .
300 LET X=A+B  ⎤
    . . .       ⎬  Subroutine
380 RETURN     ⎦
```

When statement number 120 (GOSUB) is encountered during program execution, control will be transferred to statement number 300 and the subroutine will be executed. Upon reaching statement number 380 (RETURN), control will be transferred back to statement number 130, which is the first statement after GOSUB.

A program may contain more than one reference to the same subroutine. Control will always be returned from the subroutine to the statement following the particular GOSUB statement that referenced the subroutine.

Example 6.24

A BASIC program contains the following statements.

```
120 GOSUB 300
130 PRINT "Z=";Z
    . . .
180 GOSUB 300
190 IF Z<10 THEN 250
    . . .
300 LET X=A+B  ⎫
    . . .      ⎬  Subroutine
380 RETURN     ⎭
```

Statements 300 through 380 define a subroutine, as in Example 6.23. If the subroutine is referenced by statement number 120, then control will be returned to statement 130 following execution of the subroutine. Similarly, if the subroutine is referenced by statement 180, then control will return to statement 190 after the subroutine has been executed.

It is possible for one subroutine to contain a reference to another subroutine. Subroutines that are structured in this manner are said to be *nested*. (Recall that we have encountered this term in Chapter 4, when we discussed nested FOR-TO loops.)

Example 6.25

The following statements are contained in a BASIC program.

```
 50 GOSUB 200
    . . .
200 LET C=A+B  ⎫
    . . .      ⎪
240 GOSUB 300  ⎬  First subroutine
    . . .      ⎪
270 RETURN     ⎭
    . . .
300 LET P=Q+R  ⎫
    . . .      ⎬  Second subroutine
350 RETURN     ⎭
```

This program contains two subroutines. The first subroutine consists of statements 200 through 270, and the second is made up of statements 300 through 350. Notice that the second subroutine is referenced from a point within the first subroutine (line 240); hence the subroutines are nested.

When statement number 350 is encountered during program execution, control is transferred back to the statement following line 240. Hence control is transferred from the second subroutine to the first. Similarly, statement number 270 will return control to the statement following line 50, thus transferring control from the first subroutine to the initial reference point.

Nested subroutines must maintain a strict hierarchical ordering. That is, if subroutine A references subroutine B, then subroutine B cannot reference subroutine A. On the other hand, subroutine B can be referenced from the main part of the program as well as from subroutine A.

Examples 6.26 and 6.28 illustrate the use of subroutines in complete BASIC programs.

Example 6.26 A Monthly Payroll

In this example we will determine the amount of federal, state and local income tax to be withheld, given an employee's gross salary, marital status and number of exemptions. A more complete payroll computation will not be attempted, since the program structure can become quite complicated.

Table 6.2 indicates the amount of federal income tax to be withheld on a monthly basis for both single and married employees.

Table 6.2   Federal Income Tax Withholding Rates

MONTHLY Payroll Period				
(a) SINGLE person—including head of household:		(b) MARRIED person—		
If the amount of wages is:	The amount of income tax to be withheld shall be:	If the amount of wages is:	The amount of income tax to be withheld shall be:	
Not over $88	0	Not over $88	0	

Over—	But not over—		of excess over—	Over—	But not over—		of excess over—
$88	−$133	14%	−$88	$88	−$183	14%	−$88
$133	−$217	$6.30 plus 17%	−$133	$183	−$333	$13.30 plus 17%	−$183
$217	−$433	$20.58 plus 20%	−$217	$333	−$708	$38.80 plus 16%	−$333
$433	−$583	$63.78 plus 18%	−$433	$708	−$1167	$98.80 plus 19%	−$708
$583	−$917	$90.78 plus 21%	−$583	$1167	−$1667	$186.01 plus 21%	−$1167
$917	—	$160.92 plus 24%	−$917	$1667	—	$291.01 plus 25%	−$1667

In order to use this table it is necessary to calculate an adjusted monthly gross income, which is equal to the gross monthly income less $54.20 for each exemption. The particular tax rate that is applicable will depend on which tax bracket the adjusted gross income falls into. Notice that there are 2 different sets of tax brackets — one for single employees and one for married persons.

The state tax will be calculated as 1 percent of all gross income up to $600 a month, $1\frac{1}{2}$ percent of any additional income up to $2000 a month, and 2 percent of any excess over $2000. The local tax will be levied at a rate of 1 percent of the first $800 of gross income. Monthly earnings in excess of $800 will not be taxed at the local level.

Computational Procedure

Let us calculate the adjusted monthly gross income, the state tax and the local tax in a subroutine, and federal tax within another subroutine. This allows us to segregate the program into separate computational packages. The subroutines will be nested, with the federal tax subroutine being referenced by the other subroutine. The remainder of the program will simply read in the required data (i.e., name, employee number, gross monthly salary, marital status and number of exemptions); reference the subroutines; compute the net monthly salary and print out the desired results (namely, the amount of federal, state and local tax to be withheld and the net monthly salary) for each employee.

Within the federal tax subroutine we will refer to the numbers in the left-hand columns of the tax table, which determine the various income brackets, as elements of the array C. We will define C to be a two-dimensional 6×2 array. If the second subscript (J) is equal to 1 we will refer to the data for single persons, whereas J=2 will indicate the data for married persons. Hence C(1,1)=88, C(2,1)=133, ..., C(6,1)=917, C(1,2)=88, C(2,2)=183, ..., C(6,2)=1667.

In a similar manner let T be a two-dimensional, 6×2 array which contains the amount of the base tax in each income bracket, and let R be a two-dimensional, 6×2 array which represents the tax rate (expressed as a decimal) for each income bracket. Thus T(1,1)=0, T(2,1)=6.30, ..., T(6,1)=160.92, T(1,2)=0, T(2,2)=13.30, ..., T(6,2)=291.01; and R(1,1)=0.14, R(2,1)=0.17, ..., R(6,1)=0.24, R(1,2)=0.14, R(2,2)=0.17, ..., R(6,2)=0.25.

The Program Outline

Let us define the following symbols.

N$	= employee's name	P2	= adjusted gross monthly salary
M$	= marital status (M for married, S for single)	P3	= net monthly salary
N	= employee number	T1	= state tax withheld
E	= number of exemptions	T2	= local tax withheld
P1	= gross monthly salary	T3	= federal tax withheld

The computation will be carried out as indicated below.

1. Assign numerical values to the 6×2 arrays C, R and T by means of READ and DATA statements. (A nest of double FOR-TO loops will be required for each array, as discussed in Chapter 5.)

2. Read an appropriate string value for N$.

   (a) If N$=END then terminate the computation.

   (b) Otherwise proceed with step 3 below.

3. Read an appropriate string or numeric value for N, P1, M$ and E.

4. Compute numeric values for T1, T2 and T3 by referencing the appropriate subroutines.

5. Calculate a value for P3 using the formula

$$P3=P1-(T1+T2+T3)$$

6. Print the current values for T3, T1, T2 and P3.

7. Return to step 2 and begin to process data for the next employee.

The subroutine that is referenced directly in step 4 above will proceed as follows.

1. Examine the value of P1.

   (a) If P1 does not exceed $600, then calculate a value for T1 (state tax) as

$$T1=0.01*P1$$

   and proceed to step 2 below.

   (b) If P1 exceeds $600 but does not exceed $2000, then calculate a value for T1 using the formula

$$T1=6+0.015*(P1-600)$$

   and proceed to step 2 below.

   (c) If P1 exceeds $2000, then evaluate T1 as

$$T1=27+0.02*(P1-2000)$$

   and proceed with step 2 below.

2. Again examine the value of P1.

   (a) If P1 does not exceed $800, then calculate a value for T2 (local tax) as

$$T2=0.01*P1$$

   and proceed to step 3 below.

   (b) If P1 exceeds $800, then set T2=8 and proceed with step 3 below.

3. Calculate a value for P2 (adjusted gross monthly salary) using the formula

$$P2=P1-54.20*E$$

   (a) If P2 is less than or equal to zero, then set T3 (federal tax) equal to zero and return to the main part of the program.

   (b) If P2 has a positive value then reference the subroutine that will determine a value for T3, and then return to the main part of the program.

The subroutine that computes a value for T3 (federal tax) will proceed in the following manner.

1. Determine whether the employee is single or married by examining the string M$.

   (a) If M$=S, assign a value of 1 to the subscript J and proceed to step 2 below.

   (b) If M$=M, then let J=2 and proceed with step 2 below.

2. Assign an initial value of zero to T3.

3. Compare P2 with C(I,J) for all values of I ranging from 1 to 6.

   (a) If P2 does not exceed C(1,J), then retain the value of T3=0 and return to the reference point.

   (b) If P2 exceeds C(1,J), then proceed through the loop until a value of C(I,J) is found that exceeds P2. If such a value is formed then calculate a value for T3 as

$$T3=T(I-1,J)+R(I-1,J)*(P2-C(I-1,J))$$

   and return to the reference point.

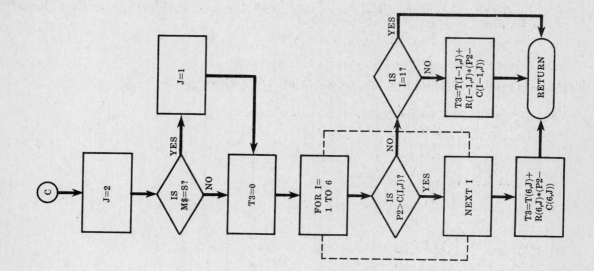

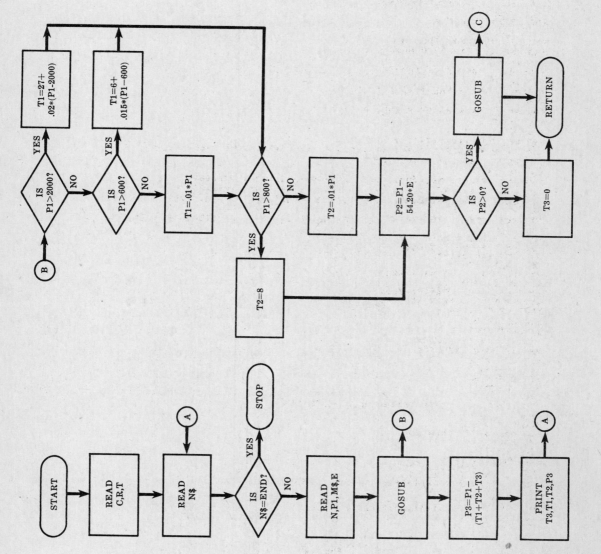

Fig. 6.15

(c) If P2 exceeds C(I,J) at the end of the loop (i.e., when I=6), then calculate a value for T3 using the formula

$$T3=T(6,J)+R(6,J)*(P2-C(6,J))$$

and return to the reference point.

Figure 6.15 contains a detailed flowchart corresponding to the above outline.

```
10   REM           CØMPUTATIØN ØF A MØNTHLY PAYRØLL
20   DIM C(6,2),R(6,2),T(6,2)
30   FØR J=1 TØ 2
40      FØR I=1 TØ 6
50         READ C(I,J)
60      NEXT I
70   NEXT J
80   FØR J=1 TØ 2
90      FØR I=1 TØ 6
100        READ R(I,J)
110     NEXT I
120  NEXT J
130  FØR J=1 TØ 2
140     FØR I=1 TØ 6
150        READ T(I,J)
160     NEXT I
170  NEXT J
180  PRINT,"MØNTHLY PAYRØLL"
190  PRINT
200  PRINT "NAME";
210  INPUT N$
220  IF N$="END" THEN 800
230  PRINT "EMPLØYEE NUMBER";
240  INPUT N
250  PRINT "GRØSS SALARY";
260  INPUT P1
270  PRINT "MARITAL STATUS (M ØR S)";
280  INPUT M$
290  PRINT "NUMBER ØF EXEMPTIØNS";
300  INPUT E
310  GØSUB 400
320  LET P3=P1-(T1+T2+T3)
330  PRINT "FEDERAL TAX=$";T3,"STATE TAX=$";T1,"LØCAL TAX=$";T2
340  PRINT "NET SALARY=$";P3
350  GØ TØ 190
360  DATA 88,133,217,433,583,917,88,183,333,708,1167,1567
370  DATA .14,.17,.20,.18,.21,.24,.14,.17,.16,.19,.21,.25
380  DATA 0,6.3,20.58,63.78,90.78,160.92,0,13.3,38.8,93.8,186.01,291.01
390
400  REM CØMPUTATIØN ØF STATE TAX, LØCAL TAX AND ADJUSTED GRØSS SALARY
410
420  IF P1>2000 THEN 480
430  IF P1>600 THEN 460
440  LET T1=.01*P1
450  GØ TØ 490
460  LET T1=6+.015*(P1-600)
470  GØ TØ 490
480  LET T1=27+.02*(P1-2000)
490  IF P1>800 THEN 520
500  LET T2=.01*P1
510  GØ TØ 530
520  LET T2=8
530  LET P2=P1-54.20*E
540  IF P2>0 THEN 570
550  LET T3=0
560  RETURN
570  GØSUB 600
580  RETURN
590
600  REM           CØMPUTATIØN ØF FEDERAL TAX
610
620  LET J=2
630  IF M$="M" THEN 650
640  LET J=1
650  LET T3=0
660  FØR I=1 TØ 6
670     IF P2>C(I,J) THEN 710
680     IF I=1 THEN 730
690     LET T3=T(I-1,J)+R(I-1,J)*(P2-C(I-1,J))
700     GØ TØ 730
710  NEXT I
720  LET T3=T(I,J)+R(I,J)*(P2-C(I,J))
730  RETURN
800  END
```

Fig. 6.16

The BASIC Program

A complete BASIC program is shown in Fig. 6.16. Notice that the first subroutine, which computes the adjusted gross income and the state and local tax, is comprised of statements 400 through 580. Two separate RETURN statements are included (lines 560 and 580). The subroutine is referenced by statement number 310, in the main part of the program.

Statements 600 through 730 make up the second subroutine, which is used to calculate the federal tax. We see that this subroutine contains only one RETURN statement (line 730), and is referenced by statement number 570 in the first subroutine. (Hence the subroutines are nested.) Note that a FOR-TO loop (lines 660 through 710) is included within this second subroutine.

It is also interesting to observe that this program contains both READ and INPUT statements. The READ statements are used to assign values to the arrays C, R and T at the start of the program execution, whereas the INPUT statements are used to enter the information required for each employee.

The reader should understand that this program could just as easily have been written without making use of subroutines. Hence the purpose of the subroutines, in this example, is to organize the program into several well-defined, self-contained "packages." We have seen a similar situation with regard to programmer-defined functions in Example 6.15. There are some situations, however, in which the programming effort is simplified significantly through the use of subroutines. This is especially true of programs that contain several references to the same subroutine.

Finally, Fig. 6.17 shows a typical set of output for seven different employees. Notice that all of the data (both input and output data) for each employee are shown in a well-organized and neatly labeled block.

```
                              MØNTHLY PAYRØLL

             NAME ?ANDREWS, J J
             EMPLØYEE NUMBER ?2717
             GRØSS SALARY ?870.00
             MARITAL STATUS (M ØR S) ?M
             NUMBER ØF EXEMPTIØNS ?2
             FEDERAL TAX=$ 108.984          STATE TAX=$ 10.05          LØCAL TAX=$ 8
             NET SALARY=$ 742.966

             NAME ?CØHEN, A M
             EMPLØYEE NUMBER ?5375
             GRØSS SALARY ?1250.00
             MARITAL STATUS (M ØR S) ?M
             NUMBER ØF EXEMPTIØNS ?3
             FEDERAL TAX=$ 170.886          STATE TAX=$ 15.75          LØCAL TAX=$ 8
             NET SALARY=$ 1055.36

             NAME ?DIPASQUALE, G V
             EMPLØYEE NUMBER ?4660
             GRØSS SALARY ?2075.00
             MARITAL STATUS (M ØR S) ?S
             NUMBER ØF EXEMPTIØNS ?1
             FEDERAL TAX=$ 425.832          STATE TAX=$ 28.5           LØCAL TAX=$ 8
             NET SALARY=$ 1612.67

             NAME ?HØLLAND, C J
             EMPLØYEE NUMBER ?0892
             GRØSS SALARY ?520.00
             MARITAL STATUS (M ØR S) ?S
             NUMBER ØF EXEMPTIØNS ?2
             FEDERAL TAX=$ 59.5             STATE TAX=$ 5.2            LØCAL TAX=$
             5.2
             NET SALARY=$ 450.1

             NAME ?JØNES, D M
             EMPLØYEE NUMBER ?6839
             GRØSS SALARY ?1120.00
             MARITAL STATUS (M ØR S) ?M
             NUMBER ØF EXEMPTIØNS ?2
             FEDERAL TAX=$ 156.484          STATE TAX=$ 13.8           LØCAL TAX=$ 8
             NET SALARY=$ 941.716

             NAME ?KØWALSKI, S
             EMPLØYEE NUMBER ?8462
             GRØSS SALARY ?1100.00
             MARITAL STATUS (M ØR S) ?M
             NUMBER ØF EXEMPTIØNS ?3
             FEDERAL TAX=$ 142.386          STATE TAX=$ 13.5           LØCAL TAX=$ 8
             NET SALARY=$ 936.114

             NAME ?LØWE, H G
             EMPLØYEE NUMBER ?9587
             GRØSS SALARY ?1075.00
             MARITAL STATUS (M ØR S) ?M
             NUMBER ØF EXEMPTIØNS ?5
             FEDERAL TAX=$ 117.04           STATE TAX=$ 13.125         LØCAL TAX=$ 8
             NET SALARY=$ 936.835

             NAME ?END
```

Fig. 6.17

6.10 Graphical Output

Many computer programs generate a list of numeric output data that is eventually plotted on graph paper. In such cases it is often very effective to have the computer generate the graph directly on a typewriter terminal, in addition to the regular numerical output data. This allows the user to see the general appearance of the graph, and then refer to the more precise tabulation of the data if necessary.

It is very easy to produce a graph on a typewriter terminal. To do so we must make use of a FOR-TO loop which includes a PRINT statement containing the TAB function. A graph produced in this manner will run vertically down the printed page, with the actual curve being represented by a number of closely spaced discrete points, as shown in Fig. 6.18.

The detailed mechanics of producing the graph are best described by means of an example.

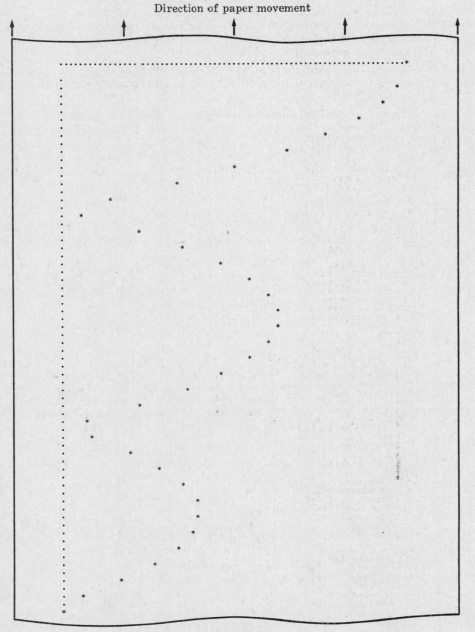

Direction of paper movement

Fig. 6.18

Example 6.27

A BASIC program has generated two numeric lists, Y and T, which describe the position of a projectile at various times. (The elements of Y represent the height of the projectile, and the elements of T represent the corresponding times.) We wish to produce a graph of Y against T, thus indicating the trajectory of the projectile, on a standard 72-character typewriter terminal. In order to generate the graph as clearly as possible we will double space the points on the curve, i.e., we will place a blank line between each asterisk, as shown in Fig. 6.18.

Since the graph will be positioned vertically along the page, the Y axis will be generated by a single line of dots (periods). The T axis will run perpendicular to the printed line (i.e., down the page). Hence one dot of the T axis will be printed by each line of output.

Let us first print out the Y axis, showing the position of the projectile at the top of the axis (at time zero). To do this we print a dot (period) in each of the first 71 positions, and then place an asterisk in the 72nd position. Hence we can write

```
580 FOR J=0 TO 70
590     PRINT TAB(J);".";
600 NEXT J
610 PRINT TAB(71);"*"
620 PRINT "."
```

Statements 580 through 610 will produce the Y axis, as described above. A subsequent line, containing only a dot in the first column (to represent a part of the T axis), will be generated by statement 620. This line is required in order to obtain the desired double spacing.

Next we will want to print the position of the projectile at different times. Let us generate two lines of output for each time. The first of these will contain a dot (representing the T axis) in the first column, and an asterisk (representing the position of the projectile) at some appropriate position along the line. The second line will be a spacer, containing only a dot in the first position. To accomplish this we can write

```
630 FOR I=2 TO I1
640     LET J=INT(71*Y(I)/Y(1))
650     IF J=0 THEN 680
660     PRINT ".";TAB(J);"*"
670     GO TO 690
680     PRINT "*"
690     PRINT "."
700 NEXT I
```

where I1 is an integer variable that indicates the last point to be plotted (the last time). Notice that the first line of output is produced by statements 640 through 680, and the second line is generated by statement 690.

The statement

```
640     LET J=INT(71*Y(I)/Y(1))
```

may require some additional clarification. First, note that Y(1) is the original height of the projectile. If we assume that this represents the *maximum* height of the projectile, then Y(I), the height of the projectile at the Ith time, will be some number bounded between zero and Y(1). We are seeking a value for J, an integer which is bounded between 0 and 71. The value for J will indicate the position of the asterisk on the graph, i.e., J=0 corresponds to Y(I)=0 and J=71 corresponds to Y(I)=Y(1). Hence by direct proportion,

$$\frac{J}{71} = \frac{Y(I)}{Y(1)} \qquad \text{or} \qquad J=71*Y(I)/Y(1)$$

Since J can take on only integer values, we write

```
J=INT(71*Y(I)/Y(1))
```

In Example 6.28 we will see a complete BASIC program that generates both numerical and graphical outputs.

Example 6.28   Simulation of a Bouncing Ball

In this example we would like to calculate the movement of a rubber ball as it bounces up and down under the force of gravity, while at the same time traveling in the horizontal direction with a constant velocity. We will assume that the initial vertical displacement (that is, the original height above the ground) is specified (H), along with the horizontal velocity (V) and the number of times the ball bounces

(N). Also known will be the bounce coefficient (C), which is the ratio of the vertical velocity just after impact to the vertical velocity just before impact.

Computational Procedure

In order to calculate the position of the ball at various times, we will first select a small increment of time (D), and then make use of the following laws of physics, which apply within each time increment:

$$T(I+1)=T(I)+D$$
$$X(I+1)=X(I)+V*D$$
$$Z(I+1)=Z(I)-G*D$$
$$Y(I+1)=Y(I)+.5*(Z(I)+Z(I+1))*D$$

where X refers to the horizontal displacement (originally zero at the start of the problem), Z is the vertical velocity (also zero at the start of the problem), Y is the height above the ground and G is the acceleration due to gravity (32.2 ft/sec^2). The subscripts I and I+1 refer to the values of the different variables at the start and end of the time increment, respectively.

If a bounce occurs during the time increment, the computational formulas must be modified somewhat. A bounce condition is signified by a negative value for Y(I+1), which is physically impossible. When this condition occurs we recalculate Z(I+1) and Y(I+1) as follows. First calculate the time required for the ball to hit the ground, starting from its position at the start of the Ith time increment. If we call this time D1, then, from simple proportionality,

$$\frac{D1}{D} = \frac{Y(I)-0}{Y(I)-Y(I+1)}$$

which can be written in BASIC as

$$D1=D*Y(I)/(Y(I)-Y(I+1))$$

We can compute the vertical velocity immediately *before* impact as

$$Z=Z(I)-G*D1$$

so that the vertical velocity immediately *after* impact will be

$$Z1=-C*(Z(I)-G*D1)$$

Now the vertical velocity at the end of the time increment will be

$$Z(I+1)=Z1-G*(D-D1)$$

and the vertical displacement at the end of the time increment can be written as

$$Y(I+1)=.5*(Z1+Z(I+1))*(D-D1)$$

The Program Outline

We now have enough information at our disposal to write an outline of a complete BASIC program. Specifically,

1. Read H, V, N, C and D.

   (a) If H=0, then terminate the computation.

   (b) If H is assigned some positive value, then proceed below.

2. Initialize all parameters:

I=1 (I is the increment counter)	X(1)=0
B=0 (B is the bounce counter)	Z(1)=0
T(1)=0	Y(1)=H

3. Compute the horizontal and vertical displacement and the vertical velocity for each time increment, using the formulas given above.

4. If the ball hits the ground during the time increment, test to see whether this is a bounce condition or a program termination.

   (a) Bounce condition (B<N) – recalculate the vertical velocity and the vertical displacement to account for the bounce, increment the bounce counter (i.e., B=B+1), and then continue to the next time increment.

   (b) Terminal condition (B=N) – obtain the final time and the horizontal displacement when the ball hits the ground.

5. Print the final values for X and T, followed by a complete tabulation of T, X, Y and Z.

6. Plot Y against T, using the method discussed in Example 6.27.

7. Return to step 1.

An overall flowchart of the computation is shown in Fig. 6.19. Notice that the computation of T(I+1), X(I+1), Z(I+1) and Y(I+1) is shown within the structure of a subroutine.

The reader who has studied numerical calculus should recognize that we are integrating the second-order differential equation $d^2y/dt^2 = -g$ in this example. The integration technique is known as a *modified Euler method*.

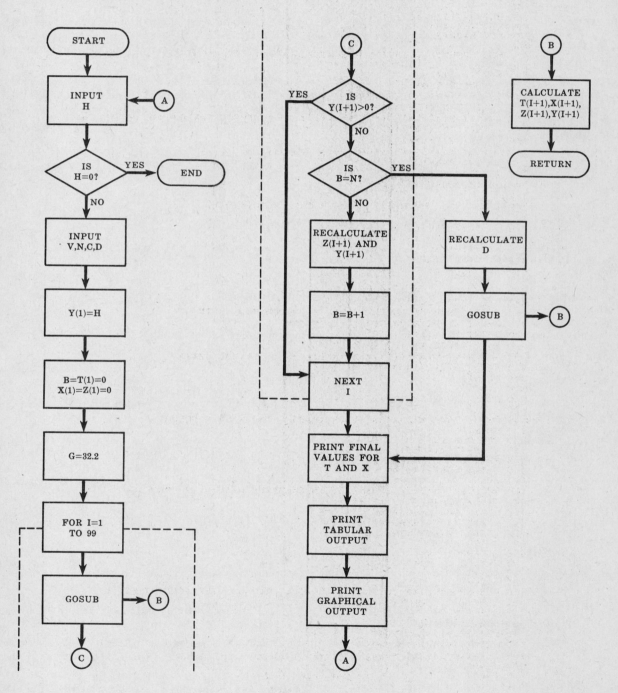

Fig. 6.19

```
10   REM           SIMULATIØN ØF A BØUNCING BALL
20   DIM X(100),Y(100),Z(100),T(100)
30   PRINT "INITIAL HEIGHT ØF BALL (FT)";
40   INPUT H
50   IF H=0 THEN 810
60   PRINT "INITIAL HØRIZØNTAL VELØCITY (FT/SEC)";
70   INPUT V
80   PRINT "NUMBER ØF BØUNCES";
90   INPUT N
100  PRINT "BØUNCE CØEFFICIENT";
110  INPUT C
120  PRINT "LENGTH ØF TIME INCREMENT (SEC)";
130  INPUT D
140  PRINT
150
160  REM           INITIALIZE PARAMETERS
170
180  LET B=T(1)=X(1)=Z(1)=0
190  LET Y(1)=H
200  LET G=32.2
210
220  REM CØMPUTE VELØCITY AND DISPLACEMENT FØR EACH TIME INCREMENT
230
240  FØR I=1 TØ 99
250     GØSUB 730
260     IF Y(I+1)>0 THEN 330
270     IF B=N THEN 360
280     LET D1=D*Y(I)/(Y(I)-Y(I+1))      'CØRRECT FØR BØUNCE CØNDITIØN
290     LET Z1=-C*(Z(I)-G*D1)
300     LET Z(I+1)=Z1-G*(D-D1)
310     LET Y(I+1)=.5*(Z1+Z(I+1))*(D-D1)
320     LET B=B+1
330  NEXT I
340  GØ TØ 400
350
360  REM           BALL HITS GRØUND FØR LAST TIME
370
380  LET D=D*Y(I)/(Y(I)-Y(I+1))
390  GØSUB 730
400  LET I1=I+1
410  LET T1=T(I1)
420  LET X1=X(I1)
430
440  REM           PRINT NUMERICAL ØUTPUT
450
460  PRINT "HØRIZØNTAL DISTANCE TRAVELED=";X1;"FT"
470  PRINT "TIME REQUIRED=";T1;"SECS"
480  PRINT
490  FØR I=1 TØ I1
500     PRINT "T=";T(I),"X=";X(I),"Y=";Y(I),"Z=";Z(I)
510  NEXT I
520  PRINT
530
540  REM           PRINT GRAPHICAL ØUTPUT
550
560  PRINT "GRAPHICAL SØLUTIØN TØ BØUNCING BALL PRØBLEM"
570  PRINT
580  FØR J=0 TØ 70
590     PRINT TAB(J);".";
600  NEXT J
610  PRINT TAB(71);"*"
620  PRINT "."
630  FØR I=2 TØ I1      'GENERATE SUCCESSIVE PØINTS ØF CURVE
640     LET J=INT(71*Y(I)/Y(1))
650     IF J=0 THEN 680
660     PRINT ".";TAB(J);"*"
670     GØ TØ 690
680     PRINT "*"
690     PRINT "."
700  NEXT I
710  GØ TØ 30
720
730  REM SUBRØUTINE TØ CALCULATE VELØCITY AND DISPLACEMENT AT END
740  REM           ØF TIME INCREMENT
750
760  LET T(I+1)=T(I)+D
770  LET X(I+1)=X(I)+V*D
780  LET Z(I+1)=Z(I)-G*D
790  LET Y(I+1)=Y(I)+.5*(Z(I+1)+Z(I))*D
800  RETURN
810  END
```

Fig. 6.20

The BASIC Program

Figure 6.20 shows a complete BASIC program for carrying out the computation. The program allows for as many as 100 consecutive time increments; thus the length of the time increment (D) should be chosen sufficiently large so that the number of time increments does not exceed this figure. (On the other hand, D cannot be assigned too large a value or else the given formulas for calculating T(I+1), X(I+1), Y(I+1) and Z(I+1) will not apply. As a rule of thumb, each bounce should be represented by 8 to 20 points.)

The subroutine which is used to evaluate T(I+1), X(I+1), Z(I+1) and Y(I+1) is comprised of statements 730-800. It should be understood that the subroutine structure is not at all essential for carrying out these calculations. Use of a subroutine is desirable, however, since this block of statements is referenced from two different places within the program (namely statements 250 and 390).

The generation of the tabular output data is carried out in a straightforward manner by means of a FOR-TO loop (statements 490 through 510). Although the method used to generate the graph (statements 560 through 700) is less obvious, we see that this portion of the program is identical to the material discussed in Example 6.27. Hence the logic used should be readily apparent.

Figure 6.21(a) contains the numerical output which is generated for the following input data.

$$H = 2.00 \text{ ft}, \quad V = 1.20 \text{ ft/sec}, \quad N = 3, \quad C = 0.80, \quad D = 0.05 \text{ sec}$$

We see that a distance of 2.06 feet is required for the ball to experience three complete bounces. The corresponding time is 1.72 seconds.

```
INITIAL HEIGHT ØF BALL (FT) ?2.00
INITIAL HØRIZØNTAL VELØCITY (FT/SEC) ?1.20
NUMBER ØF BØUNCES ?3
BØUNCE CØEFFICIENT ?0.80
LENGTH ØF TIME INCREMENT (SEC) ?0.05

HØRIZØNTAL DISTANCE TRAVELED= 2.06344 FT
TIME REQUIRED= 1.71953 SECS

T= 0         X= 0            Y= 2           Z= 0
T= 0.05      X= 6.00000E-2   Y= 1.95975     Z=-1.61
T= 0.1       X= 0.12         Y= 1.839       Z=-3.22
T= 0.15      X= 0.18         Y= 1.63775     Z=-4.83
T= 0.2       X= 0.24         Y= 1.356       Z=-6.44
T= 0.25      X= 0.3          Y= 0.99375     Z=-8.05
T= 0.3       X= 0.36         Y= 0.551       Z=-9.66
T= 0.35      X= 0.42         Y= 2.77500E-2  Z=-11.27
T= 0.4       X= 0.48         Y= 0.396269    Z= 7.5392
T= 0.45      X= 0.54         Y= 0.732979    Z= 5.9292
T= 0.5       X= 0.6          Y= 0.989189    Z= 4.3192
T= 0.55      X= 0.66         Y= 1.1649      Z= 2.7092
T= 0.6       X= 0.72         Y= 1.26011     Z= 1.0992
T= 0.65      X= 0.78         Y= 1.27482     Z=-0.5108
T= 0.7       X= 0.84         Y= 1.20903     Z=-2.1208
T= 0.75      X= 0.9          Y= 1.06274     Z=-3.7308
T= 0.8       X= 0.96         Y= 0.835949    Z=-5.3408
T= 0.85      X= 1.02         Y= 0.528659    Z=-6.9508
T= 0.9       X= 1.08         Y= 0.140869    Z=-8.5608
T= 0.95      X= 1.14         Y= 0.233292    Z= 6.1104
T= 1.        X= 1.2          Y= 0.498562    Z= 4.5004
T= 1.05      X= 1.26         Y= 0.683332    Z= 2.8904
T= 1.1       X= 1.32         Y= 0.787602    Z= 1.2804
T= 1.15      X= 1.38         Y= 0.811372    Z=-0.329597
T= 1.2       X= 1.44         Y= 0.754642    Z=-1.9396
T= 1.25      X= 1.5          Y= 0.617413    Z=-3.5496
T= 1.3       X= 1.56         Y= 0.399683    Z=-5.1596
T= 1.35      X= 1.62         Y= 0.101453    Z=-6.7696
T= 1.4       X= 1.68         Y= 0.189303    Z= 4.58198
T= 1.45      X= 1.74         Y= 0.378152    Z= 2.97198
T= 1.5       X= 1.8          Y= 0.486501    Z= 1.36198
T= 1.55      X= 1.86         Y= 0.514351    Z=-0.248016
T= 1.6       X= 1.92         Y= 0.4617      Z=-1.85802
T= 1.65      X= 1.98         Y= 0.328549    Z=-3.46802
T= 1.7       X= 2.04         Y= 0.114898    Z=-5.07802
T= 1.71953   X= 2.06344      Y= 9.58086E-3  Z=-5.7069
```

Fig. 6.21(a)

In Fig. 6.21(b) we see a computer-prepared graph showing the position of the ball at various times. The individual bounces can be seen very clearly in this figure.

Finally, the bottom of Fig. 6.21(b) shows a request for a new set of input data. The computation is terminated by supplying a zero value for H.

GRAPHICAL SØLUTIØN TØ BØUNCING BALL PRØBLEM

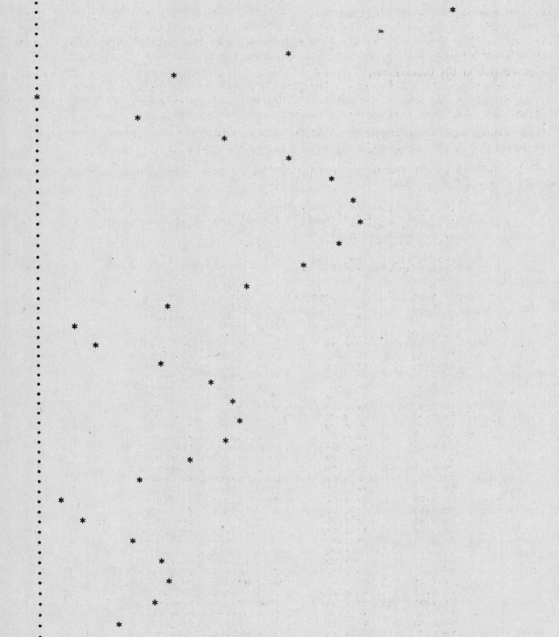

INITIAL HEIGHT ØF BALL (FT) ?0

Fig. 6.21(b)

Review Questions

6.1   What are the differences between a function and a subroutine?

6.2   Are functions and/or subroutines ever *required* in a BASIC program?   What are the advantages in their use?

6.3   In what way can functions and subroutines be helpful in improving the organization of a BASIC program?

6.4   Summarize the rules for naming functions.   How are numeric functions distinguished from string functions?

6.5   What is the purpose of the DEF statement?   How is it written?

6.6   What are the rules that govern the use of arguments in a function?   Can a function make use of variables that are not specified as arguments?

6.7   What is the difference between a function definition and a function reference?   How is a function referenced?

6.8   What are dummy arguments?   What correspondence must exist between a set of arguments in a function reference and the associated dummy arguments?

6.9   Can an argument consist of something other than a nonsubscripted variable (e.g., a constant, subscripted variable or formula)?   Is this also true of a dummy argument?

6.10   How is a DEF statement written for a multiline function?

6.11   Cite two places where the function name must appear in a multiline function.

6.12   What is the purpose of the FNEND statement?   How is it written?

6.13   Can control be transferred out of a multiline function by means of a GO TO statement?   A RETURN statement?

6.14   Must the value returned by a function be of the same type as the function's arguments?

6.15   Is it necessary that all of the arguments in a function must be of the same type?

6.16   How are characters stored within a computer?

6.17   What is the 7-bit ASCII code?

6.18   What is the purpose of the CHANGE statement?   Cite two different ways that it can be written.

6.19   What is purpose of the ASC function?   How is it used?

6.20   What is the purpose of the CHR$ function?   How is it used?

6.21   What is the purpose of the RND function?   How is it used?   Does this function require an argument?

6.22   What is meant by pseudo-random numbers?   How do pseudo-random numbers differ from numbers that are truly random?

6.23   What is the purpose of the RANDOMIZE statement?   How is it written?

6.24 Summarize the rules for defining a subroutine. Must a subroutine begin with any particular statement?

6.25 Can arguments be included in a subroutine?

6.26 Can a subroutine end with an FNEND statement? A RETURN statement? An END statement?

6.27 What is the purpose of the RETURN statement? How is it written? What happens when a RETURN statement is encountered during program execution?

6.28 Can a subroutine contain more than one RETURN statement? Explain.

6.29 What is the purpose of a GOSUB statement? How is it written? Can a program which has only one subroutine contain more than one GOSUB statement?

6.30 Can a FOR-TO loop be included in a subroutine or a multiline function?

6.31 Can control be transferred out of a subroutine by means of a GO TO statement? An IF-THEN statement?

6.32 Describe the hierarchical ordering that must be observed when subroutines are nested.

6.33 What advantage is there in the graphical display of output data?

6.34 Which library functions are used to produce graphical output? In what type of programming structure are these functions usually included?

Solved Problems

6.35 Write a BASIC function for each of the situations described below.

(a) Evaluate the algebraic formula $z = \dfrac{(u/v) + (x/y)}{2}$

    10 DEF FNZ(U,V,X,Y)=(U/V+X/Y)/2

(b) If X represents a positive decimal quantity, obtain a rounded value for X with two digits to the right of the decimal point.

    20 DEF FNY(X)=.01*INT(100*(X+.005))

(c) Evaluate the algebraic formula $p = \begin{cases} \log(t^2 - a) & \text{for } t^2 > a \\ \log(t^2) & \text{for } t^2 \leq a \end{cases}$

```
30 DEF FNP(T,A)
40 IF T<=A THEN 70
50 LET FNP=LOG(T↑2-A)
60 GO TO 80
70 LET FNP=LOG(T↑2)
80 FNEND
```

(d) Calculate the sum of the first N elements of the numeric list L, i.e., compute the sum L(1)+L(2)+ · · · +L(N).

```
100 DEF FNS(N)
110 LET S=0
120 FOR I=1 TO N
130     LET S=S+L(I)
140 NEXT I
150 LET FNS=S
160 FNEND
```

(e) Suppose that M$ and N$ each represent a single letter. Construct a single string containing the two letters, arranged in alphabetical order.

```
200 DEF FNN$(M$,N$)
210 LET L(0)=2
220 IF M$>N$ THEN 260
230 LET L(1)=ASC(M$)
240 LET L(2)=ASC(N$)
250 GO TO 280
260 LET L(1)=ASC(N$)
270 LET L(2)=ASC(M$)
280 CHANGE L TO L$
290 LET FNN$=L$
300 FNEND
```

(f) Calculate the average of two random numbers, each having a value between A and B.

```
100 DEF FNR(A,B)
110 LET R1=A+(B−A)*RND
120 LET R2=A+(B−A)*RND
130 LET FNR=(R1+R2)/2
140 FNEND
```

This function can also be written as simply

```
100 DEF FNR=A+(B−A)*(RND+RND)/2
```

6.36 Each of the situations described below requires a reference to one of the functions defined in Problem 6.35. Write an appropriate BASIC statement, or a sequence of statements, in each case.

(a) Print a value for f, where

$$f = \frac{(a/b) + (c/d)}{2}$$

[See Problem 6.35(a).]

```
100 PRINT FNZ(A,B,C,D)
```

(b) Suppose T represents some positive quantity whose value may exceed 1. Calculate a value for T1, where T1 has the same value as T except that the decimal portion of T1 is rounded to two digits. [See Problem 6.35(b).]

```
110 LET T1=INT(T)+FNY(T−INT(T))
```

(c) Let P1 represent the quantity

$$\log[(a + b)^2 − c] \quad \text{if } (a + b)^2 > c$$

and

$$\log[(a + b)^2] \quad \text{if } (a + b)^2 \leqq c$$

[See Problem 6.35(c).]

```
30 LET P1=FNP((A+B),C)
```

(d) A numeric list L contains 101 elements. Beginning with L(1), determine how many consecutive elements can be added without the sum exceeding a value of 25. [See Problem 6.35(d).]

```
40 FOR J=1 TO 100
50    IF FNS(J)>25 THEN 80
60 NEXT J
70 LET J=101
80 PRINT "N=";J-1
```

(e) The variables M and N each represent the ASCII equivalent of a single letter (character). Form a string consisting of the two letters, in alphabetical order. [See Problem 6.35(e).]

```
80 LET L$=FNN$(CHR$(M),CHR$(N))
```

(f) Determine the average of two random numbers, each having a value between 1 and 10. Transfer control to statement number 250 if this average value exceeds 5. [See Problem 6.35(f).]

```
100 IF FNR(1,10)>5 THEN 250
```

6.37 Each of the following problems contains a function definition and/or function reference which is incorrectly written. Identify all errors.

(a) 10 DEF FNW(A,B,C↑2,3)=((A+B)*C↑2)/3

   Constants and formulas cannot be used as dummy arguments.

(b) 10 DEF FNC(T1,T2,N)=((T1−T2)/T2)↑N

   . . .

   60 LET V=C*FNC(2*A,F$)

   The arguments in the function reference do not agree in number or in type with the dummy arguments in the function definition.

(c) 10 DEF FN4(X(1),X(2),X(3))=X(1)+2*X(2)−3*X(3)

   This statement contains two errors:

   (i) The function is named incorrectly.

   (ii) Subscripted variables cannot appear as dummy arguments.

(d) 10 DEF FNG(A,B,C)
     20 LET P=A+B*X+C*X↑2
     30 LET Q=B+C*X
     40 LET G=P+Q*X+C*X↑2
     50 FNEND

   The function name (FNG) is not assigned a value within the function.

(e) 100 DEF FNC(X,Y,Z)
     110 IF X+Y>Z THEN 140
     120 LET FNC=LOG(Z−(X+Y))
     130 RETURN
     140 LET FNC=LOG(Z)
     150 FNEND

   Control cannot be transferred out of a function by means of a RETURN statement.

6.38 The following groups of statements represent portions of BASIC programs that contain one or more subroutines. Each example is written correctly.

(a)   10 DIM L(100)
. . .

    60 GOSUB 200
. . .

120 GOSUB 200
. . .

160 GOSUB 200
. . .

190 STOP
200 LET S=0
210 FOR I=1 TO N
220   LET S=S+L(I)   Subroutine
230 NEXT I
240 RETURN
250 END

Notice that the subroutine is referenced from three different points within the program.

(b)   50 GOSUB 120
. . .

120 IF A>B THEN 150
130 LET C=SQR((B−A)↑N)
140 RETURN   Subroutine
150 LET C=SQR(((A+B)/(A−B))↑N)
160 RETURN

The subroutine in this example contains two RETURN statements.

(c)   10 DEF FNZ(X,Y)=X↑2+Y↑2
. . .

    70 GOSUB 180
. . .

180 REM SAMPLE SUBROUTINE
. . .
210 LET W=FNZ(A,B+C)   Subroutine
. . .
250 RETURN

Notice that the subroutine references the programmer-defined function FNZ.

(d)   75 GOSUB 300
. . .

125 GOSUB 200
. . .

200 LET Z=C1*X+C2*Y
. . .
250 GOSUB 300   First subroutine
. . .
290 RETURN
300 LET W=(U+V)/Z
. . .   Second subroutine
370 RETURN
380 END

This example makes use of nested subroutines. Notice that the second subroutine is referenced by both the first subroutine and the main part of the program.

6.39 The following groups of statements represent portions of BASIC programs that contain subroutines.   Each example contains one or more errors.   Identify all errors.

(*a*)   45 GOSUB 165
         . . .
     165 LET C=C1+C2+C3
         . . .
     190 GO TO 60   } Subroutine
         . . .
     225 RETURN
     230 FNEND
     235 END

This example contains two errors:

(i) Control cannot be transferred out of a subroutine by means of a GO TO statement.

(ii) A subroutine cannot end with an FNEND statement.

(*b*)   60 GOSUB 200
         . . .
     120 IF X<Y THEN 225
         . . .
     200 REM START OF SUBROUTINE   } Subroutine
         . . .
     300 RETURN

Control cannot be transferred into a subroutine by an IF-THEN statement.

(*c*)   30 GOSUB 100
         . . .
     100 REM SUBROUTINE A
         . . .
     120 GOSUB 200   } Subroutine A
         . . .
     160 RETURN
     200 REM SUBROUTINE B
         . . .
     225 GOSUB 100   } Subroutine B
         . . .
     245 RETURN

The subroutines are not nested properly.   (Subroutine A references subroutine B, which in turn references subroutine A.)

6.40 Write a portion of a program to generate a graph of the function $y = \sin t$.   Generate 130 points, doubly spaced, with the t axis running down the center of the printed page. Let the time increment be 0.1 second.

```
10 FOR J=0 TO 70
20    IF J=35 THEN 50
30    PRINT TAB(J);".";
40    GO TO 60
50    PRINT TAB(J);"*";
60 NEXT J
70 PRINT
```

(*Continued on next page.*)

```
 80  PRINT TAB(35);"."
 90  LET T=0
100  FOR I=2 TO 130
110      LET T=T+.1
120      LET J=35+INT(35*SIN(T))
130      IF J>35 THEN 190
140      IF J=35 THEN 170
150      PRINT TAB(J);"*";TAB(35);"."
160      GO TO 200
170      PRINT TAB(J);"*"
180      GO TO 200
190      PRINT TAB(35);".";TAB(J);"*"
200      PRINT TAB(35);"."
210  NEXT I
220  END
```

Supplementary Problems

6.41   Write a BASIC function to evaluate each of the algebraic formulas shown below.

(a) $y = ax^b$

(b) $q = c_0 + c_1 r + c_2 r^2 + c_3 r^3 + c_4 r^4$

(c) $i = (j + k)^{j+k}$

(d) $r = \begin{cases} \sqrt{b^2 - 4ac} & \text{if } b^2 > 4ac \\ \sqrt{4ac - b^2} & \text{if } b^2 < 4ac \end{cases}$

6.42   Write a BASIC function for each of the situations described below.

(a) If Z represents some positive quantity whose value may exceed 1, obtain a rounded, integer value.

(b) Calculate the product of the first N elements of the numeric list T, i.e., compute the product $T(1)*T(2)*\ldots*T(N)$.

(c) Generate 5 random numbers, each having a value between A and B, where A and B represent positive quantities and B>A.   Return the value of the largest number.

(d) Examine the sign of the number represented by some variable X.   If X is negative, return the string NEGATIVE; if X is positive, return the string POSITIVE; and if X has a value of zero, return the string ZERO.

(e) Suppose N$ represents a multiletter word.   Examine each of the letters and return the letter that comes first in the alphabet.

6.43   Each of the situations described below requires a reference to a function defined in Problem 6.41 or 6.42.   Write an appropriate BASIC statement, or a sequence of statements, in each case.

(a) Evaluate $t = (c_1 + c_2)(x + y)^3$ [see Problem 6.41(a)].

(b) Evaluate $q = c_0 + c_1 \log (x) + c_2 \log (x)^2 + c_3 \log (x)^3 + c_4 \log (x)^4$ [see Problem 6.41(b)].

(c) Print the value of $f = (a - b + c)^{a-b+c}$ [see Problem 6.41(c)].

(d) Calculate the difference between a given number, represented by the variable X, and its closest integer. Express this difference as a positive quantity. [See Problem 6.42(a).]

(e) A numeric list T contains 61 elements. Beginning with T(1), determine how many consecutive elements must be multiplied together in order that the product will exceed 1000. Assume that all of the quantities are positive. [See Problem 6.42(b).]

(f) Generate 20 sets of 5 random numbers, each having a value between 2 and 5. Print the largest random number obtained in each set of 5. [See Problem 6.42(c).]

6.44 Each of the following problems show a part of a BASIC program involving a function or a subroutine. At least one error is present in every case. Identify all errors.

(a)   10 DEF FNK(J,K)=(C1*J+C2*K)/(J+K)
       ...
      60 LET T=FNK(A,B,C)

(b)   10 DEF FNC(X,Y)
      20 IF X<Y THEN 50
      30 LET C=SQR((X−Y)/2)
      40 RETURN
      50 LET C=SQR(X/(X+Y))
      60 RETURN
      70 FNEND

(c)   50 GOSUB 200
       ...
      80 GO TO 230
       ...
     200 REM SUBROUTINE A ⎤
       ...   ⎥
     230 LET Z=X+Y   ⎬ Subroutine
       ...   ⎥
     250 RETURN   ⎥
     260 FNEND   ⎦

(d)   10 DEF FNZ1(A↑2,B↑2)
       ...
      50 LET FNZ1=(A↑2−B↑2)/(A↑2+B↑2)
      60 FNEND

(e)   10 DEF FNK(J,K)=(C1*J+C2*K)/(J+K)
       ...
      80 PRINT J,K,FNK

(f) 100 GOSUB 200
       ...
     200 REM SUBROUTINE A ⎤
       ...   ⎥
     240 IF D<.01 THEN 150 ⎬ Subroutine
       ...   ⎥
     270 RETURN   ⎦

(g)   10 DEF FNX(A,B,C)
       ...
      50 GOSUB 300
       ...
      80 FNEND
       ...
     300 REM FIRST SUBROUTINE ⎤
       ...   ⎥
     330 LET Y=FNX(U,V,W)   ⎬ Subroutine
       ...   ⎥
     350 RETURN   ⎦

Programming Problems

6.45   Modify the program shown in Example 6.6 to *minimize* a given function. Use the program to obtain the roots of the following equations, using the method described at the end of Example 6.6.

(a) $x + \cos x = 1 + \sin x,\ \pi/2 < x < \pi$

(b) $x^5 + 3x^2 = 10,\ 0 \le x \le 3$ (see Example 4.5)

6.46   Modify the program shown in Example 6.15 so that the function FNP is replaced by a subroutine.

6.47   Modify the program shown in Example 6.20 so that a sequence of craps games will be simulated automatically, in a nonconversational manner. Include a counter that will determine the total number of wins, and an input variable whose value will specify how many games will be simulated.

Use the program to simulate some large number of games (e.g., 1000). Estimate the probability of coming out ahead when playing craps. (This value, expressed as a decimal, is equal to the number of wins divided by the total number of games played. If the probability exceeds .500, it favors the player; otherwise it favors the "house.")

6.48   Modify the program shown in Example 6.26 to process a weekly payroll. Use a function rather than a subroutine to calculate the amount of federal tax withheld.

The amount of federal income tax to be withheld on a weekly basis is shown in Table 6.3. These figures are based upon an adjusted weekly gross income, equal to the weekly gross income less $35.58 for each exemption.

Table 6.3   Federal Income Tax Withholding Rates

WEEKLY Payroll Period					
(a) SINGLE person – including head of household:			(b) MARRIED person—		
If the amount of wages is:		*The amount of income tax to be withheld shall be:*	*If the amount of wages is:*		*The amount of income tax to be withheld shall be:*
Not over $20		0	Not over $20		0
Over—	*But not over—*		*Over—*	*But not over—*	
					of excess over—
					of excess over—
$20	–$31	14% –$20	$20	–$42	14% –$20
$31	–$50	$1.54 plus 17% –$31	$42	–$77	$3.08 plus 17% –$42
$50	–$100	$4.77 plus 20% –$50	$77	–$163	$9.03 plus 16% –$77
$100	–$135	$14.77 plus 18% –$100	$163	–$269	$22.79 plus 19% –$163
$135	–$212	$21.07 plus 21% –$135	$269	–$385	$42.93 plus 21% –$269
$212	–	$37.24 plus 24% –$212	$385	–	$67.29 plus 25% –$385

The state tax will be calculated as 1 percent of all gross income up to $150 a week, $1\frac{1}{2}$ percent of any additional income up to $500, and 2 percent of any excess over $500. The local tax will be computed as 1 percent of the first $200 of gross income. Weekly earnings in excess of $200 will not be taxed at the local level.

6.49   Modify the bouncing ball program in Example 6.28 to solve the following problem. A target is located a distance L feet from the origin (L is an input parameter). Determine by trial-and-error what horizontal velocity the ball should have so that it hits the target after the second bounce. Assume the target is a small circle that rests on the ground. Show the location of the target on the output graph.

6.50   Write a BASIC program that will generate a graph of each of the following functions.

(a) $y = 2\sqrt{x}$, for values of x varying from 0 to 10.

(b) $y = x^3$, for values of x varying from -1 to $+1$.

(c) $y = 2e^{-0.1t}\sin 0.5t$, for values of t varying from 0 to 60.   (See Problem 5.48.)

In each case plot enough points so that the curve can be seen clearly.

6.51   Write a BASIC program that will generate a picture of the American flag. Use an asterisk to denote each star. Represent each stripe by several lines of repeated R's or W's, depending on the color of the stripe.

6.52   Prepare a detailed outline, a corresponding flowchart and a complete BASIC program for each of the problems presented below. Include functions and subroutines wherever it is practicable to do so.

(a)   Calculate the average of a set of N numbers. Carry out the calculations within a programmer-defined function. Use the program to process the data given in Problem 5.53(d).

(b)   Extend the program in Problem 6.52(a) to calculate the deviation of each number from the average. Use the program to process the data given in Problem 5.53(d). Can a programmer-defined function be used for this purpose?

(c)   Calculate the area under a curve, using the methods described in Problems 5.53(l) and 5.53(m). Use the program to calculate the area under the curve $y = x^3$ between the limits $x = 1$ and $x = 4$.

(d)   Another way to calculate the area under a curve is to employ the *Monte Carlo* method, which makes use of randomly generated numbers. Suppose that the curve $y = f(x)$ is positive for any value of x between the specified lower and upper limits $x = a$ and $x = b$. Let the largest value of y be y^*.   The Monte Carlo method proceeds as follows:

   (i)   Begin with a counter set equal to zero.

   (ii)   Generate a random number, r_x, whose value lies between a and b.

   (iii)   Evaluate $y(r_x)$.

   (iv)   Generate a second random number, r_y, whose value lies between 0 and y^*.

   (v)   Compare r_y with $y(r_x)$. If r_y is less than or equal to $y(r_x)$, then this point will fall under or on the given curve. Hence the counter is incremented by 1.

   (vi)   Steps (ii) through (v) are repeated a large number of times. Each time will be called a *cycle*.

   (vii)   When a specified number of cycles has been completed the fraction of points which fell on or under the curve, F, is computed as the value of the counter divided by the total number of cycles. The area under the curve is then obtained as $A = Fy^*(b - a)$.

   Write a BASIC program to implement this strategy. Use the program to find the area under the curve $y = e^{-x^2}$ between the limits $x = 0$ and $x = 1$. Determine how many cycles are required to obtain an answer which is accurate to three significant figures. Compare the computer time required for this problem with the time required for Problem 5.53(m).

(e)   Calculate an average score for each student in a class, and then calculate a class average of the individual averages. [See Problems 4.46(f) and 5.53(g).] Determine the *median* of the individual averages (a value which is equalled or exceeded by half of the individual averages). Use a function to calculate the averages, and a different function to compute the median. Apply the program to the data given in Problem 4.46(f). Can subroutines be used rather than functions?

(f)   A normally distributed random variate x, with mean μ and standard deviation σ, can be generated from the formula

$$x = \mu + \sigma \frac{\sum_{i=1}^{N} r_i - N/2}{\sqrt{N/12}}$$

where r_i is a uniformly distributed random number whose value lies between 0 and 1. A value of $N = 12$ is frequently selected when using this formula. The underlying basis for the formula is the *central limit theorem,* which states that a set of mean values of uniformly distributed random variates will be normally distributed.

   Write a BASIC program that will generate a specified number of normally distributed random variates with a given mean and a given standard deviation. Let the number of random variates, the mean and the standard deviation be input parameters.

   Use the program to generate a histogram of a normal distribution with $\mu = 2.5$ and $\sigma = 1.5$.

(g) Write a BASIC program that will allow a person to play a game of tic-tac-toe against the computer. Write the program in such a manner that the computer can be either the first or the second player. If the computer is to be the first player, let the first move be generated randomly. Write out the complete status of the game after each move. Have the computer acknowledge a win by either party when it occurs.

(h) Write a BASIC program which will simulate a game of blackjack between 2 players. Note that the computer will not be a participant in this game, but will simply deal the cards to each player and provide each player with one or more "hits" (additional cards) when requested.

The cards are dealt in order, first one card to each player, then a second card to each player. Additional hits may then be requested.

The object of the game is to obtain 21 points, or as many points as possible without exceeding 21 points, on each hand. A player is automatically disqualified if his hand exceeds 21 points. Face cards count 10 points, and an ace can count either 1 point or 11 points. Thus a player can obtain 21 points with his first two cards (blackjack!) if he is dealt an ace and either a ten or a picture card. If the player has a low score with his first two cards he may ask for one or more hits.

A random number generator should be used to simulate the dealing of the cards. Be sure to include a provision that the same card is not dealt more than once.

(i) Write a BASIC program that will encode or decode a line of text (a string). To encode a line of text proceed as follows.

1. Convert each character (including blank spaces) to its ASCII equivalent.

2. Generate a positive random integer. Add this integer to the ASCII equivalent of each character. (The same integer will be used for the entire line of text.)

3. Suppose that N1 represents the lowest permissible value in the ASCII code, and N2 represents the highest permissible value. If the number obtained in step 2 above (i.e., the original ASCII equivalent plus the random integer) exceeds N2, then subtract the largest possible multiple of N2 from this number, and add the remainder to (N1 −1). Hence the encoded number will always fall between N1 and N2, and will therefore always represent some character.

4. Print the characters that correspond to the encoded ASCII values.

The procedure is reversed when decoding a line of text. Be certain, however, that the same random number is used in decoding as was used in encoding.

Chapter 7

Vectors and Matrices

In Chapter 5 we learned that all of the elements in an array can be referred to collectively by specifying a common array name. When carrying out array manipulations, however, it was necessary to work individually with each element of the array (i.e., each subscripted variable). Usually this was accomplished by means of a FOR-TO loop.

Most versions of BASIC contain a collection of special statements, known as *matrix statements,* for carrying out the more common array operations. Usually a single matrix statement will be used for a given operation. Thus it is possible to perform an operation on all of the elements in an array without making use of a FOR-TO loop. We will see how this is accomplished in this chapter.

7.1 Vector and Matrix Operations

"Vector" and "matrix" are mathematical terms that refer to a list and a table, respectively. Thus a vector is a one-dimensional array, and a matrix is a two-dimensional array. Since a vector is actually a special kind of matrix, most of the general rules that apply to matrices are also valid for vectors.

As before, we will use subscripted variables to represent the individual array elements. In the case of a matrix we will let the first subscript represent the row and the second subscript will indicate the column. Thus $A(3,2)$ will represent the element in the third row, second column of the matrix A. Moreover, we will refer to a matrix having m rows and n columns as an $m \times n$ matrix. (Remember that the size of a vector or matrix must be specified by a DIM statement if the value of a subscript exceeds 10.)

The most common vector and matrix operations are addition, subtraction, scalar multiplication and vector multiplication. A special BASIC statement is available for each of these operations. The language also contains a matrix assignment statement. Each of these statements is discussed separately below.

Assignment

The matrix assignment statement is of the form

        10 MAT C=A

This statement causes each element of A to be assigned to the corresponding element of C.

Example 7.1

Suppose that A represents the following 2×3 matrix.

$$A = \begin{bmatrix} 3 & 5 & -9 \\ 2 & -6 & 7 \end{bmatrix}$$

The matrix statement

    10 MAT C=A

will cause C to be a 2×3 matrix whose elements are

$$C = \begin{bmatrix} 3 & 5 & -9 \\ 2 & -6 & 7 \end{bmatrix}$$

Subscripted variables are used to refer to the individual matrix elements. Hence C(1,1)=3, C(1,2)=5, C(1,3)=−9, C(2,1)=2, C(2,2)=−6 and C(2,3)=7.

Addition

Matrix addition is carried out by a statement of the form

    10 MAT C=A+B

The result of this statement is that each element of C is assigned the sum of the corresponding elements of A and B, i.e., C(I,J)=A(I,J)+B(I,J). The matrices A and B must have the same number of rows and the same number of columns.

Example 7.2

Suppose that A and B are 2×3 matrices whose elements have the following values.

$$A = \begin{bmatrix} 3 & 5 & -9 \\ 2 & -6 & 7 \end{bmatrix} \qquad B = \begin{bmatrix} 2 & 2 & 0 \\ -4 & 5 & 1 \end{bmatrix}$$

The matrix statement

    10 MAT C=A+B

will cause C to be a 2×3 matrix whose elements are as follows.

$$C = \begin{bmatrix} (3+2) & (5+2) & (-9+0) \\ (2-4) & (-6+5) & (7+1) \end{bmatrix} = \begin{bmatrix} 5 & 7 & -9 \\ -2 & -1 & 8 \end{bmatrix}$$

A matrix can be updated with a matrix addition statement, e.g., a statement of the form

    10 MAT A=A+B

is permissible. However multiple sums, such as

    10 MAT D=A+B+C

are not allowed.

Subtraction

The matrix subtraction statement is very similar to the matrix addition statement except that the plus sign is replaced by a minus sign. Thus the statement

    10 MAT C=A−B

will cause each element of C to be assigned the difference of the corresponding values of A and B, i.e., C(I,J)=A(I,J)−B(I,J). The matrices A and B must have the same number of rows and the same number of columns.

Example 7.3

Suppose that A and B are 2×3 matrices having the same elements as in Example 7.2. The matrix statement

    10 MAT C=A−B

will cause the following values to be assigned to C.

$$C = \begin{bmatrix} (3-2) & (5-2) & (-9-0) \\ (2+4) & (-6-5) & (7-1) \end{bmatrix} = \begin{bmatrix} 1 & 3 & -9 \\ 6 & -11 & 6 \end{bmatrix}$$

As with the matrix addition statement, a matrix can be updated via matrix subtraction. Thus a statement such as

    10 MAT A=A−B

is permissible. On the other hand, statements such as

    10 MAT D=A−B−C

and

    10 MAT D=A+B−C

are not allowed.

Scalar Multiplication

In scalar multiplication all of the elements in a matrix are multiplied by a given constant. This is accomplished in BASIC with a statement of the form

    10 MAT C=(K)*A

where A and C are matrices and K is an ordinary variable. Each element of C will be obtained as C(I,J)=(K)*A(I,J)

Example 7.4

Suppose that A is the same 2×3 matrix given in Examples 7.1 and 7.2, and that K is a variable whose value is 3.5. The statement

    10 MAT C=(K)*A

will cause the elements of C to have the following values.

$$C = (3.5)* \begin{bmatrix} 3 & 5 & -9 \\ 2 & -6 & 7 \end{bmatrix} = \begin{bmatrix} 10.5 & 17.5 & -31.5 \\ 7 & -21 & 24.5 \end{bmatrix}$$

The term contained in parentheses need not be a single variable. Constants, subscripted variables, formulas and function references may also appear. The point is, this term must represent a single numerical quantity. The scalar term must always be enclosed in parentheses.

Example 7.5

Shown below are several examples of valid scalar multiplication statements.

    10 MAT C=(100)*A
    10 MAT C=(2*X+Y)*A
    10 MAT C=(SQR(P↑2+Q↑2))*A

In these examples A and C are matrices, X, Y, P and Q are ordinary numeric variables, and SQR represents the square root library function.

A vector can be updated with the scalar multiplication statement. Thus the statement

    10 MAT A=(10)*A

is permissible.   As with matrix addition and subtraction, however, statements such as

        10 MAT C=(10)*A*B

and

        10 MAT C=(10)*A+B

are not allowed.

Matrix Multiplication

Two matrices can be multiplied if the number of columns in the first matrix is the same as the number of rows in the second matrix.   The result will be a matrix having the same number of rows as the first matrix and the same number of columns as the second.   Thus if A is a $k \times m$ matrix and B is an $m \times n$ matrix, then the matrix operation C=A*B will generate a new matrix, C, having k rows and n columns.   Each element of C will be obtained as

$$C(I,J)=A(I,1)*B(1,J)+A(I,2)*B(2,J)+\cdots+A(I,K)*B(K,J)$$

Matrix multiplication can be carried out in BASIC by means of a statement of the form

        10 MAT C=A*B

where A, B and C are matrices, and A has the same number of columns as B has rows.

Example 7.6

Suppose that we are given the following 2 matrices.

$$A = \begin{bmatrix} 1 & 2 & 3 & 4 \\ 5 & 6 & 7 & 8 \end{bmatrix} \qquad B = \begin{bmatrix} 9 & 5 & 1 \\ 8 & 4 & 0 \\ 7 & 3 & 9 \\ 6 & 2 & 8 \end{bmatrix}$$

The matrix statement

        10 MAT C=A*B

will result in the 2×3 matrix

$$C = \begin{bmatrix} 70 & 30 & 60 \\ 190 & 86 & 132 \end{bmatrix}$$

where the individual elements were obtained as follows.

        C(1,1)=(1×9)+(2×8)+(3×7)+(4×6)=70
        C(1,2)=(1×5)+(2×4)+(3×3)+(4×2)=30
        C(1,3)=(1×1)+(2×0)+(3×9)+(4×8)=60
        C(2,1)=(5×9)+(6×8)+(7×7)+(8×6)=190
        C(2,2)=(5×5)+(6×4)+(7×3)+(8×2)=86
        C(2,3)=(5×1)+(6×0)+(7×9)+(8×8)=132

Unlike the matrix statements presented earlier, a matrix *cannot* be updated by means of the matrix multiplication statement.   Nor can more than two matrices appear in a matrix product.   Thus statements of the form

        10 MAT A=A*C

and

        10 MAT D=A*B*C

are not allowed.   It is possible, however, to multiply a matrix by itself, i.e., to write

        10 MAT C=A*A

provided A is a *square* matrix (i.e., A must have the same number of rows and columns).

7.2 Vector and Matrix Input/Output

Matrix input/output operations are carried out in much the same manner as ordinary input/output operations. BASIC provides us with three matrix I/O statements— *MAT READ*, *MAT PRINT* and *MAT INPUT*. Each is discussed individually below.

MAT READ

The purpose of the MAT READ statement is to enter values for the elements of a vector or a matrix. This statement is used in conjunction with one or more DATA statements (see Section 5.5). A typical MAT READ statement might appear as

        10 MAT READ A

where A represents a vector or a matrix whose dimensions have been specified.

Execution of the MAT READ statement causes a set of values contained in a data block to be assigned to the appropriate elements of the vector or matrix. The assignment always begins with the subscript (or subscripts) equal to 1, i.e., the zeroth elements are ignored. In the case of a matrix, the data will be assigned on a row-by-row basis.

Example 7.7

A portion of a BASIC program is shown below.

        10 DIM A(5,3)
        ...
        40 MAT READ A
        ...
        200 DATA 1,3,5,7,9,11,13,15,17,19,21,23,25,27,29

Execution of this program will cause the following values to be assigned to the elements of A.

A(1,1)=1	A(1,2)=3	A(1,3)=5
A(2,1)=7	A(2,2)=9	A(2,3)=11
A(3,1)=13	A(3,2)=15	A(3,3)=17
A(4,1)=19	A(4,2)=21	A(4,3)=23
A(5,1)=25	A(5,2)=27	A(5,3)=29

Observe that the data are assigned row-by-row.

Notice that A actually contains 24 elements, since the subscripts range from 0 to 5 and 0 to 3, respectively. Only 15 elements of A are assigned values, however, because the zeroth elements are ignored.

If the DIM statement were not present then A would automatically consist of 121 elements (each subscript ranging from 0 to 10). Therefore 100 values would be required in the data block. An error would result if only 15 values were supplied, as in the above DATA statement.

A single MAT READ statement can contain several vectors and matrices if desired. The successive vectors and matrices must be separated by commas. All elements of the first vector/matrix will be read in before any elements of the second vector/matrix, and so on. As before, the elements of each matrix will be assigned row-by-row.

Example 7.8

A portion of a BASIC program is presented below.

        10 DIM X(2,2),Y(5),Z(2,3)
        50 MAT READ X,Y,Z
        150 DATA 1,2,3,4,5,6,7,8,9,10,11,12,13,14,15

When the program is executed the following values will be assigned to the elements of X, Y and Z.

X(1,1)=1	Y(1)=5	Z(1,1)=10
X(1,2)=2	Y(2)=6	Z(1,2)=11
X(2,1)=3	Y(3)=7	Z(1,3)=12
X(2,2)=4	Y(4)=8	Z(2,1)=13
	Y(5)=9	Z(2,2)=14
		Z(2,3)=15

Thus we see that the first 4 values in the data block are assigned to X, the next five values are assigned to Y and the last 6 values to Z.   Each matrix is assigned values by rows.

MAT PRINT

The MAT PRINT statement is used to print the elements of a vector or a matrix. A typical MAT PRINT statement can be written as

        10 MAT PRINT A

where A represents either a vector or a matrix.   The elements of A will be printed in columnar form if A is a vector, and in a tabular, row-by-row form if A is a matrix.   As with the MAT READ statement, the zeroth elements will be ignored.

The elements of each row of a matrix will be widely separated, with a maximum of 5 elements on each printed line.   Hence several lines may be required for each row.   A blank line will appear between successive rows, thus distinguishing one row from another.

Example 7.9

Consider the following BASIC program.

        10 DIM X(3,8),Y(6)
        20 MAT READ X,Y
        30 MAT PRINT X
        40 MAT PRINT Y
        50 DATA 1,2,3,4,5,6,7,8,9,10,11,12,13,14,15
        60 DATA 16,17,18,19,20,21,22,23,24,25,26,27,28,29,30
        70 END

Execution of this program will produce the following output.

```
 1              2              3              4              5
 6              7              8


 9             10             11             12             13
14             15             16


17             18             19             20             21
22             23             24


25
26
27
28
29
30
```

Notice that each row of X requires 2 lines, since only 5 elements can be printed in each line.   A blank line separates each successive row.   Also, notice that Y is printed in columnar form since it is a vector.

The spacing between successive array elements can be altered by placing a comma or a semicolon after the array name in the MAT PRINT statement.   Vectors are handled somewhat differently than matrices.   The rules governing the spacing of array elements are given below.

1. Vectors

    (a) If a vector name is followed by a comma, then the elements are printed in row form rather than columnar form.   Wide spacing (not more than 5 elements per line) will be used.

    (b) If a vector name is followed by a semicolon, then the elements are printed in row form with minimum spacing between them.

2. Matrices

Following a matrix name with a comma will have no effect on the spacing of the output. If the matrix name is followed by a semicolon, however, then the matrix will be printed row-by-row, with minimum spacing between the elements. Successive rows will still be separated by a blank line.

Example 7.10

Let us again consider the BASIC program presented in Example 7.9. If the MAT PRINT statements are changed to

```
30 MAT PRINT X,
40 MAT PRINT Y,
```

then the following output will be generated when the program is executed.

```
1        2        3        4        5
6        7        8

9        10       11       12       13
14       15       16

17       18       19       20       21
22       23       24


25       26       27       28       29
30
```

We see that the matrix X is printed in the same manner as before, but the vector Y now appears in row form.

On the other hand, suppose we replace the commas in the MAT PRINT statement with semicolons, i.e., let us write

```
30 MAT PRINT X;
40 MAT PRINT Y;
```

The output will now appear as follows.

```
1  2  3  4  5  6  7  8

9  10  11  12  13  14  15  16

17  18  19  20  21  22  23  24


25  26  27  28  29  30
```

The elements within each row are now spaced much more closely.

Several vectors and matrices can appear in the same MAT PRINT statement if desired. The successive entries must be separated by commas or semicolons. The appearance of the output for each vector or matrix will be determined by the type of punctuation mark following that vector or matrix.

Example 7.11

The two MAT PRINT statements in Example 7.9 can be replaced by the single statement

```
30 MAT PRINT X,Y
```

When the program is executed the output will be spaced as shown in Example 7.9.

On the other hand, suppose that this MAT PRINT statement is changed to

```
30 MAT PRINT X,Y,
```

(note the addition of the last comma). Execution of the program will now generate a set of widely spaced output, with the vector elements displayed in row form as shown at the beginning of Example 7.10.

If the commas are replaced with semicolons, i.e.,

>   30 MAT PRINT X;Y;

then the output will be closely spaced, as in the second part of Example 7.10.

Finally, it should be pointed out that the MAT PRINT statement can contain only vector and matrix names. Formulas, function references, etc., are not permitted. Thus a statement of the form

>   100 MAT PRINT A+B,C*D,(K)*X

would not be allowed.

MAT INPUT

The MAT INPUT statement is used to enter vector elements directly from a typewriter terminal. A typical MAT INPUT statement might appear as

>   10 MAT INPUT A

where A represents a vector name. Most versions of BASIC allow only one vector to appear in a MAT INPUT statement.

When the MAT INPUT statement is executed a question mark (?) appears at the start of a new line on the typewriter terminal, indicating a request for data. Further execution of the program will temporarily be halted while the user types in the required vector elements, separated by commas. The first data value will be assigned to A(1), the second to A(2), and so on (where A is the vector name). The zeroth vector element will be ignored.

After the last element has been typed the user must depress the RETURN key, thus causing the data to be transmitted to the computer. Execution of the program will then be resumed.

It is important to note that *any number* of data values can be entered (provided, of course, that the number of data values does not exceed the maximum permissible number of vector elements, as specified by a DIM statement). Hence it is possible to enter only a *partial set* of vector elements via the MAT INPUT statement. This feature accounts for the frequent use of the MAT INPUT statement in many BASIC programs.

Example 7.12

A BASIC program contains the following 2 statements.

>   10 DIM A(100)
>   . . .
>   50 MAT INPUT A

When statement number 50 is encountered during program execution, a question mark will be printed at the start of a new line on the typewriter terminal. Further execution of the program will temporarily be suspended.

Suppose that the following line of data is entered on the typewriter terminal in response to the question mark.

>   ?12,-3,17,10,62,-87,49,5,39,9,-7,-22

When the RETURN key is depressed the data will be transmitted to the computer, causing the following values to be assigned to the vector A.

A(1)=12	A(5)=62	A(9)=39
A(2)=-3	A(6)=-87	A(10)=9
A(3)=17	A(7)=49	A(11)=-7
A(4)=10	A(8)=5	A(12)=-22

Notice that the vector element A(0) and the elements A(13) through A(100) are not affected.

Sometimes there are too many data values to be entered on a single line of the typewriter terminal. When this happens the data values may be entered on subsequent lines. An ampersand (&) must be used to indicate that a subsequent line of data will be entered. The ampersand must appear after the final data value in every line except the last. A new question mark will be printed at the start of each line.

Example 7.13

Suppose that the following 2 lines of input data have been typed in response to the MAT INPUT statement shown in Example 7.12.

        ?3,6,9,12,15,18,21,24,27,30&
        ?33,36,39,42,45,48,51,54,57,60

The question mark at the start of the second line, indicating a request for more data, was generated by the ampersand at the end of the first line. This procedure could have been continued if necessary (i.e., an ampersand could have been typed at the end of the second line, generating a request for a third line of data, and so on).

Execution of the program will be resumed after the second carriage return (following the second line of data). The 100-element vector A will then have the following values for its first 20 elements; $A(1)=1$, $A(2)=6$, $A(3)=9$, ..., $A(19)=57$, $A(20)=60$. The remaining elements of A will be unaffected.

It is sometimes desirable to know how many values have been entered from the typewriter terminal. The NUM library function allows us to answer this question. Whenever the NUM function is referenced it returns the number of data values entered in the most recent MAT INPUT statement. Arguments are not required.

Example 7.14

A portion of a BASIC program is shown below.

        10 DIM A(100)
           ...
        50 MAT INPUT A
        60 LET A(0)=NUM
           ...
        150 PRINT "THE LIST CONTAINS"; A(0); " VALUES"

When the program is executed an unspecified number of data values will be entered and assigned to the elements of A. Statement 60 causes the number of data values to be determined and stored in the zeroth element of A. Execution of statement 150 causes a message to be printed which indicates the effective size of the vector A.

Suppose, for example, that A had been assigned 20 values (as in Example 7.13). Then statement 150 would generate the message

        THE LIST CONTAINS 20 VALUES

since $A(0)$ was assigned a value of 20 in statement 60.

In some versions of BASIC the MAT INPUT statement can be used to enter matrix elements as well as vector elements. With a matrix, however, the number of elements to be entered must always be specified within the statement. (We will see how this is accomplished in Section 7.4.) Thus the MAT INPUT statement is less useful for entering matrix elements than for vector elements, since a *partial* set of matrix elements cannot be entered. For this reason, and because many versions of BASIC do not allow the MAT INPUT statement to be used at all with a matrix, we will not discuss this topic any further.

The next example illustrates the use of several matrix statements, including MAT READ and MAT PRINT, in a complete BASIC program. We will see a complete program that makes use of the MAT INPUT statement later in this chapter, in Example 7.22.

Example 7.15   Matrix Manipulation

Suppose that A and B are 3×3 matrices whose elements are assigned the following values.

$$A = \begin{bmatrix} 1 & 3 & 5 \\ 7 & 9 & 11 \\ 13 & 15 & 17 \end{bmatrix} \qquad B = \begin{bmatrix} 2 & 4 & 6 \\ 8 & 10 & 12 \\ 14 & 16 & 18 \end{bmatrix}$$

We wish to evaluate the matrix formula

$$F=5*(A+B)*(A-B)$$

This can be accomplished very easily by means of the matrix statements presented earlier in this chapter. (This problem can also be solved without using matrix statements, though the programming would be more complicated.)

Computational Procedure

Since the given formula cannot be evaluated with a single matrix statement, we must construct a sequence of simple matrix operations that will yield the desired result. This can be accomplished as follows.

        C=A+B
        D=A−B
        E=C*D
        F=(5)*E

Each operation can be carried out with a single matrix statement.

The Program Outline

Let us print out the elements of each matrix as soon as they are either read or calculated. This allows us to observe the outcome of each step in the overall computational procedure. Also, the results of the individual matrix statements will be readily apparent.

The computation will proceed as follows.

1. Read the elements of A and B.

2. Print the elements of A, followed by the elements of B.

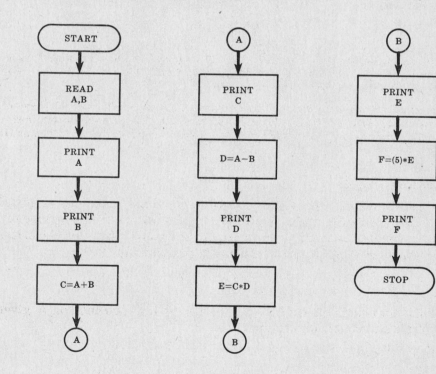

Fig. 7.1

3. Calculate the elements of C.

4. Print the elements of C.

5. Calculate the elements of D.

6. Print the elements of D.

7. Calculate the elements of E.

8. Print the elements of E.

9. Calculate the elements of F.

10. Print the elements of F.

11. Stop.

A corresponding flowchart is shown in Fig. 7.1.

The BASIC Program

In Fig. 7.2 we see a complete BASIC program for carrying out the computation. Notice that several different matrix statements are included. Also, note that a DIM statement is included, though its presence is not really necessary since this program requires only 3×3 arrays.

```
10  REM EVALUATION ØF THE MATRIX FØRMULA F=(5)*(A+B)*(A-B)
20  DIM A(3,3),B(3,3),C(3,3),D(3,3),E(3,3),F(3,3)
30  MAT READ A,B
40  PRINT "THE A-MATRIX IS:"
50  MAT PRINT A;
60  PRINT "THE B-MATRIX IS:"
70  MAT PRINT B;
80  MAT C=A+B
90  PRINT "THE C-MATRIX IS:"
100 MAT PRINT C;
110 MAT D=A-B
120 PRINT "THE D-MATRIX IS:"
130 MAT PRINT D;
140 MAT E=C*D
150 PRINT "THE E-MATRIX IS:"
160 MAT PRINT E;
170 MAT F=(5)*E
180 PRINT "THE F-MATRIX IS:"
190 MAT PRINT F;
200 DATA 1,3,5,7,9,11,13,15,17,2,4,5,8,10,12,14,16,18
210 END
```

Fig. 7.2

Figure 7.3 contains the output that is generated by this program. The elements of each matrix defined in the program are printed out in closely spaced, tabular form. We see the desired results (the calculated elements of the F-matrix) at the bottom of the figure.

Finally, we again remark that the matrix statements were not essential — we could have accomplished the same thing by including several FOR-TO loops in our program. (A program written in this manner is shown in Example 5.15.) However, the use of the matrix statements simplifies the programming considerably.

7.3 Special Matrices

When carrying out matrix operations we must sometimes make use of certain special matrices, such as the *identity* matrix, the *transpose* of a matrix or the *inverse* of a matrix. BASIC contains a number of matrix statements that allow these special matrices to be formed. Let us consider each of these statements individually.

MAT ZER

The MAT ZER statement is used to assign 0's to the elements of a given matrix. A typical MAT ZER statement might appear as

        10 MAT A=ZER

where A represents a matrix whose dimensions have been specified.

```
THE A-MATRIX IS:

 1    3    5
 7    9   11
13   15   17
THE B-MATRIX IS:

 2    4    6
 8   10   12
14   16   18
THE C-MATRIX IS:

 3    7   11
15   19   23
27   31   35
THE D-MATRIX IS:

-1   -1   -1
-1   -1   -1
-1   -1   -1
THE E-MATRIX IS:

-21  -21  -21
-57  -57  -57
-93  -93  -93
THE F-MATRIX IS:

-105  -105  -105
-285  -285  -285
-465  -465  -465
```

Fig. 7.3

MAT CON

The purpose of this statement is to assign 1's to the elements of a given matrix.   A MAT CON statement might typically be written as

        10 MAT B=CON

where B represents a matrix whose dimensions have been specified.

MAT IDN

This statement causes 0's to be assigned to all of the elements of a square matrix except those on the *principal diagonal* (i.e., the diagonal running from upper left to lower right), where 1's will be assigned.   A matrix whose elements are assigned these values is known as an *identity matrix*.

The MAT IDN statement might typically be written as

        10 MAT C=IDN

where C represents a square matrix whose dimensions have been specified.   (Note that C must have the same number of rows and columns if it is to be a square matrix.)

The identity matrix has the following important characteristic: if a square matrix D is multiplied by the identity matrix C, then the product will be simply the given matrix D. In other words,

$$C*D=D*C=D$$

(provided C and D conform to the rules of matrix multiplication). Hence we see that matrix multiplication involving the identity matrix is analogous to ordinary multiplication where one of the factors is the constant 1.

Example 7.16

A portion of a BASIC program is shown below.

```
10 DIM  A(2,3),B(4,2),C(3,3)
   . . .
70 MAT A=ZER
80 MAT B=CON
90 MAT C=IDN
```

Execution of this program will cause the matrices A, B and C to be defined as follows.

$$A = \begin{bmatrix} 0 & 0 & 0 \\ 0 & 0 & 0 \end{bmatrix} \qquad B = \begin{bmatrix} 1 & 1 \\ 1 & 1 \\ 1 & 1 \\ 1 & 1 \end{bmatrix} \qquad C = \begin{bmatrix} 1 & 0 & 0 \\ 0 & 1 & 0 \\ 0 & 0 & 1 \end{bmatrix}$$

MAT TRN

The MAT TRN statement causes the rows and columns of a given matrix to be transposed (i.e., interchanged). The statement might appear as

```
10  MAT B=TRN(A)
```

Thus if A is an $m \times n$ matrix then B will be an $n \times m$ matrix whose elements are determined as

$$B(I,J)=A(J,I)$$

The matrix B is called the *transpose* of the vector A.

Example 7.17

Consider a BASIC program that contains the following statements

```
10 DIM A(2,3),B(3,2)
20 MAT READ A
   . . .
50 MAT B=TRN(A)
   . . .
80 DATA 1,3,5,7,9,11
```

Statement number 20 causes the elements of A to be assigned the values shown below.

$$A = \begin{bmatrix} 1 & 3 & 5 \\ 7 & 9 & 11 \end{bmatrix}$$

Statement number 50 will therefore assign the following values to the elements of B.

$$B = \begin{bmatrix} 1 & 7 \\ 3 & 9 \\ 5 & 11 \end{bmatrix}$$

Notice that B has 3 rows and 2 columns, whereas A has 2 rows and 3 columns.

MAT INV

The *inverse* of a square matrix is itself a square matrix having the following important property: the product of a matrix and its inverse is equal to the identity matrix. In other words, if A is a square matrix and B is its inverse, then

$$A*B=B*A=C$$

where C is the identity matrix. A matrix must be square for its inverse to be defined. For some square matrices, however, it is not possible to calculate an inverse. Thus an inverse matrix may or may not exist for a given square matrix.

A matrix inverse may be calculated (if it exists) by means of the MAT INV statement. This statement might appear as

10 MAT B=INV(A)

where A and B are square matrices whose dimensions have been established.

Once the inverse of a matrix has been determined we may obtain the *determinant* of the original matrix by means of the DET library function. This function returns a single numerical value, and does not require an argument.

Among other things the DET function may be used to determine whether a given matrix has an inverse, since the determinant will be zero if the inverse does not exist. Remember, however, that the DET function can only be referenced *after* a MAT INV statement. If the DET function returns a value of zero for a given matrix, then the inverse determined by the preceeding MAT INV statement will not be meaningful.

Example 7.18

Shown below is a simple BASIC program that computes the inverse of a matrix, the determinant of the matrix and the product of the matrix and its inverse.

```
10 DIM A(3,3),B(3,3),C(3,3)
20 MAT READ A
30 MAT B=INV(A)
40 MAT C=A*B
50 MAT PRINT A,B,C
60 PRINT "DETERMINANT="; DET
70 DATA 5,3,1,3,7,4,1,4,9
80 END
```

Execution of this program should result in the following values for the elements of A, B and C:

$$A = \begin{bmatrix} 5 & 3 & 1 \\ 3 & 7 & 4 \\ 1 & 4 & 9 \end{bmatrix} \quad B = \begin{bmatrix} 0.274854 & -0.134503 & 0.0292398 \\ -0.134503 & 0.25731 & -0.0994152 \\ 0.0292398 & -0.0994152 & 0.152047 \end{bmatrix} \quad C = \begin{bmatrix} 1 & 0 & 0 \\ 0 & 1 & 0 \\ 0 & 0 & 1 \end{bmatrix}$$

Also, the determinant of A should equal 171.

The actual output produced by this program is shown below.

```
 5              3              1

 3              7              4

 1              4              9


 0.274854      -0.134503       2.92398E-2

-0.134503       0.25731       -9.94152E-2

 2.92398E-2    -9.94152E-2     0.152047


 1.            8.38190E-9      3.72529E-9

 5.58794E-9    1.             7.45058E-9

 0             7.45058E-9      1.

DETERMINANT= 171
```

Notice that some of the elements of C are only approximately correct, owing to numerical errors that occur in the calculation of C.   These errors result when we compute the difference between numbers that are very nearly equal.

Solution of Simultaneous Equations

The MAT INV statement allows us to solve a system of simultaneous, linear algebraic equations very easily.   To understand how the method works we must utilize the properties of both the inverse and the identity matrices.   Suppose, for example, that we are given the system of n equations

$$c_{11}x_1 + c_{12}x_2 + \cdots + c_{1n}x_n = d_1$$
$$c_{21}x_1 + c_{22}x_2 + \cdots + c_{2n}x_n = d_2$$
$$\cdots\cdots\cdots\cdots\cdots\cdots\cdots\cdots\cdots\cdots\cdots$$
$$c_{n1}x_1 + c_{n2}x_2 + \cdots + c_{nn}x_n = d_n$$

where the c's and d's represent known values and the x's are the unknown quantities.

We can write the given equations in matrix form as follows.

C*X=D

where C is a matrix containing the values of the coefficients, that is

$$C = \begin{bmatrix} c_{11} & c_{12} & \ldots & c_{1n} \\ c_{21} & c_{22} & \ldots & c_{2n} \\ \cdots & \cdots & \cdots & \cdots \\ c_{n1} & c_{n2} & \ldots & c_{nn} \end{bmatrix}$$

and D is a vector containing the right hand values, i.e.,

$$D = \begin{bmatrix} d_1 \\ d_2 \\ \cdot \\ \cdot \\ d_n \end{bmatrix}$$

and X is a vector containing the unknown quantities,

$$X = \begin{bmatrix} x_1 \\ x_2 \\ \cdot \\ \cdot \\ x_n \end{bmatrix}$$

Let us multiply our given matrix equation by E, where E represents the inverse of C. Then we have

E*C*X=E*D

However, the matrix product E*C is simply the identity matrix, which we will call I. Therefore we can write

I*X=E*D

Since I*X=X, our matrix equation simplifies to

X=E*D

which is the desired result.

The significance of this result is the following. *The solution to a system of simultaneous, linear algebraic equations is equal to the product of the inverse of the coefficient matrix and the right-hand side vector.* Example 7.19 illustrates how easily this idea can be incorporated into a BASIC program.

Example 7.19 Simultaneous Equations

Suppose we are given the following system of 5 equations and 5 unknowns.

$$
\begin{aligned}
11x_1 + 3x_2 \quad\quad + x_4 + 2x_5 &= 51 \\
4x_2 + 2x_3 \quad\quad + x_5 &= 15 \\
3x_1 + 2x_2 + 7x_3 + x_4 \quad\quad &= 15 \\
4x_1 \quad\quad + 4x_3 + 10x_4 + x_5 &= 20 \\
2x_1 + 5x_2 + x_3 + 3x_4 + 13x_5 &= 92
\end{aligned}
$$

We wish to determine the values for the unknowns x_1, x_2, x_3, x_4 and x_5.

Computational Procedure

Let us rewrite the equations in matrix form as

C*X=D

where

$$
C = \begin{bmatrix}
11 & 3 & 0 & 1 & 2 \\
0 & 4 & 2 & 0 & 1 \\
3 & 2 & 7 & 1 & 0 \\
4 & 0 & 4 & 10 & 1 \\
2 & 5 & 1 & 3 & 13
\end{bmatrix}
\qquad
D = \begin{bmatrix}
51 \\
15 \\
15 \\
20 \\
92
\end{bmatrix}
$$

and X will contain the values for x_1, x_2, x_3, x_4 and x_5. We can obtain these values simply by calculating the matrix product

X=E*D

where E is the inverse of C.

Once we have determined the values for x_1 through x_5 we can check the accuracy of our solution by calculating the product

F=C*X

If the elements of X have been determined correctly then the vector F will be the same as the specified vector D. Any differences in magnitude between the elements of F and the corresponding elements of D therefore provide a measure of the errors involved in calculating X.

The Program Outline

The computation can be carried out as follows.

1. Read the elements of C and D.

2. Print the elements of C and D.

3. Calculate E (the inverse of C).

4. Determine X by forming the matrix product E*D.

5. Print the elements of X.

6. Determine F by forming the product C*X.

7. Calculate the error vector G=D−F.

8. Print the elements of G.

9. Stop.

A corresponding flowchart is shown in Fig. 7.4.

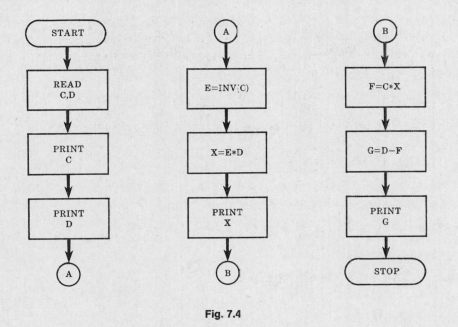

Fig. 7.4

The BASIC Program

A complete BASIC program is shown in Fig. 7.5. The structure of the program is very straight-forward, since branches and loops are not required. This simplicity results from the use of the matrix statements, which free the programmer from considering the logical details of matrix manipulation.

```
10   REM SØLUTIØN ØF SIMULTANEØUS LINEAR ALGEBRAIC EQUATIØNS
20   DIM C(5,5),D(5),E(5,5),F(5),G(5),X(5)
30   MAT READ C,D
40   PRINT "CØEFFICIENT MATRIX:"
50   MAT PRINT C
60   PRINT "RIGHT HAND SIDE:"
70   MAT PRINT D,
80   MAT E=INV(C)
90   MAT X=E*D
100  PRINT "SØLUTIØN VECTØR:"
110  MAT PRINT X,
120  MAT F=C*X
130  MAT G=D-F
140  PRINT "ERRØR VECTØR:"
150  MAT PRINT G,
160  DATA 11,3,0,1,2,0,4,2,0,1,3,2,7,1,0
170  DATA 4,0,4,10,1,2,5,1,3,13,51,15,15,20,92
180  END
```

Fig. 7.5

In Fig. 7.6 we see the output that is generated by the program, providing us with a solution to our system of 5 equations in 5 unknowns. Our desired solution is approximately $x_1 = 3.0$, $x_2 = 2.2$, $x_3 = 0.21$, $x_4 = 0.15$ and $x_5 = 5.7$. Notice also that the elements of the error vector, G, are all smaller (in magnitude) than 10^{-6}. This assures us that the solution is reasonably accurate.

7.4   Changing Dimensions

We have already seen that the MAT INPUT statement allows us to enter an unspecified number of vector elements from a typewriter terminal, thus providing us with a variable dimension feature. In addition, several of the matrix statements allow us to alter the dimensions of an array during program execution. In fact we can, if we wish, change the effective size of an array at different places within a program. This capability can be used to extend the generality of many BASIC programs that involve vectors and matrices.

```
CØEFFICIENT MATRIX:

11            3            0            1            2

0            4            2            0            1

3            2            7            1            0

4            0            4            10           1

2            5            1            3            13

RIGHT HAND SIDE:

51           15           15           20           92

SØLUTIØN VECTØR:

2.97917      2.2156       0.211284     0.152317     5.71503

ERRØR VECTØR:

-9.53674E-7  -2.38419E-7  -4.76837E-7  -7.15256E-7  -1.90735E-6
```

Fig. 7.6

The matrix statements that permit an array to be redimensioned are MAT READ, MAT ZER, MAT CON and MAT IDN. (Note that the MAT PRINT statement *is not* included.) This feature is implemented by enclosing the effective dimensions in parentheses, following the array name. In the case of a matrix the dimensions must be separated by a comma.

Example 7.20

A BASIC program contains the statements

```
10 DIM  A(24,24),B(24,24)
   ...
50 MAT A=IDN(20,20)
60 MAT B=CON(8,12)
```

When the program is executed a total of 625 elements (including the zeroth row and the zeroth column) will be reserved for each of the matrices A and B. Statement 50, however, will define A to be a 20×20 identity matrix, and statement 60 will establish B as an 8×12 matrix whose elements each have a value of 1.

Either constants or variables can be used to represent the effective dimensions of an array. However, the dimensions must be expressed as positive integer values, and they cannot exceed the maximum array sizes specified in a DIM statement. (If a DIM statement is not present then each effective dimension cannot exceed 10.)

Example 7.21

A portion of a BASIC program is shown below.

```
10 DIM  P(35),Q(50,50),R(50,50)
   ...
50 INPUT M,N
   ...
80 MAT READ P(M),Q(N,N)
90 MAT R=INV(Q)
   ...
200 DATA...
```

Statement 50 will cause values of M and N (the effective array sizes) to be entered from a typewriter terminal. Any positive integer values can be entered, provided they do not exceed 35 and 50, respectively.

When statement 80 is encountered the first M values in the data block will be assigned to the elements of P, and the next N × N (i.e., the next N↑2) values will be assigned to the elements of Q. In statement 90 the matrix R will *implicitly* be redimensioned as an N × N matrix, since the inverse of a matrix must have the same dimensionality as the given matrix.

Finally, statement 200 must be present in order to define the data block (there may actually be several DATA statements). Notice that the data block must contain at least N↑2+M data values (extra data values will be ignored). Also, note that a given value in the data block may be assigned to an element of P, an element of Q, or it may not be read at all — depending on the values assigned to M and N.

In the following example we will see that the generality of a BASIC program can be enhanced considerably by making use of the variable dimension feature.

Example 7.22 Least Squares Curve Fitting (Playing the Stock Market)

In this example we will write a BASIC program for fitting a curve to a set of data using the method of least squares. We will then apply this program to the problem of fitting an appropriate "trend curve" to the set of earnings data shown in Table 7.1 for a fictitious company known as Federated Mousetraps, Incorporated. Once we have obtained such a "trend curve," we can estimate what the per-share earnings will be at some future time, say in 1978. Based upon some average price-to-earnings ratio, we can then estimate what the price of the stock will be in 1978, using the formula

$$P = R \cdot E$$

where P = estimated price of one share of stock in 1978

R = average price-to-earnings ratio

E = estimated earnings, dollars per share, in 1978

This information might be used as a guide in determining whether or not to buy stock in the company at the current price.

Table 7.1 Yearly Earnings Per Share of Federated Mousetraps, Inc.

Earnings, $/Share	Year
$0.01	1957
0.02	1958
0.02	1959
0.03	1960
0.03	1961
0.04	1962
0.04	1963
0.09	1964
0.24	1965
0.38	1966
0.63	1967
0.93	1968
1.24	1969
1.48	1970
1.73	1971
2.07	1972
2.50	1973
3.12	1974
3.48	1975

The Least Squares Technique

The method of least squares is a common technique for fitting a curve

$$y = f(x)$$

to a set of data points (y_1, x_1), (y_2, x_2), ..., (y_M, x_M).   The method is based upon the concept of minimizing the sum of the square errors,

$$e_1^2 + e_2^2 + \cdots + e_M^2$$

where e_i is the ith error.   That is, for a given x_i, e_i is the difference between the data point y_i and a value $y = f(x_i)$ which is read from the fitted curve.   (See Fig. 7.7.)

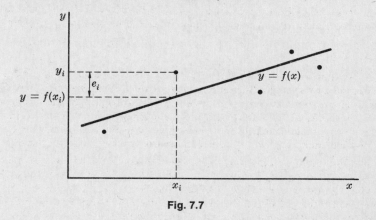

Fig. 7.7

The method is commonly applied to power functions, exponential functions and to polynomials.   In either case the method requires solving a set of simultaneous, linear algebraic equations, where the unknown quantities are the *constants* in the equation for the curve.

For example, suppose we wish to pass the power function

$$y = ax^b$$

through a set of M data points.   To do this we must solve the following two equations for a and b:

$$M \log a + \left\{ \sum_{i=1}^{M} \log x_i \right\} b = \sum_{i=1}^{M} \log y_i$$

$$\left\{ \sum_{i=1}^{M} \log x_i \right\} \log a + \left\{ \sum_{i=1}^{M} (\log x_i)^2 \right\} b = \sum_{i=1}^{M} (\log x_i)(\log y_i)$$

where $\sum$ indicates summation. $\left(\text{For instance, } \sum_{i=1}^{M} \log x_i = \log x_1 + \log x_2 + \cdots + \log x_M. \right)$ Notice that these are linear algebraic equations in terms of the unknowns $\log a$ and b.   Once $\log a$ has been determined, it is, of course, very simple to obtain the constant a.

Now suppose that we wish to pass the exponential curve

$$y = ae^{bx}$$

through a set of M data points.   The equations to be solved are

$$M \log a + \left\{ \sum_{i=1}^{M} x_i \right\} b = \sum_{i=1}^{M} \log y_i$$

$$\left\{ \sum_{i=1}^{M} x_i \right\} \log a + \left\{ \sum_{i=1}^{M} x_1^2 \right\} b = \sum_{i=1}^{M} x_i \log y_i$$

Again we solve two simultaneous, linear algebraic equations for $\log a$ and b.

If the curve is the polynomial

$$y = c_1 + c_2 x + c_3 x^2 + \cdots + c_{n+1} x^n$$

then we determine the coefficients $c_1, c_2, c_3, \ldots, c_{n+1}$ by solving the system of equations

$$Mc_1 + \left\{\sum_{i=1}^{M} x_i\right\} c_2 + \left\{\sum_{i=1}^{M} x_i^2\right\} c_3 + \cdots + \left\{\sum_{i=1}^{M} x_i^n\right\} c_{n+1} = \sum_{i=1}^{M} y_i$$

$$\left\{\sum_{i=1}^{M} x_i\right\} c_1 + \left\{\sum_{i=1}^{M} x_i^2\right\} c_2 + \left\{\sum_{i=1}^{M} x_i^3\right\} c_3 + \cdots + \left\{\sum_{i=1}^{M} x_i^{n+1}\right\} c_{n+1} = \sum_{i=1}^{M} x_i y_i$$

$$\cdots\cdots\cdots\cdots\cdots\cdots\cdots\cdots\cdots\cdots\cdots\cdots\cdots\cdots\cdots\cdots\cdots\cdots\cdots$$

$$\left\{\sum_{i=1}^{M} x_i^n\right\} c_1 + \left\{\sum_{i=1}^{M} x_i^{n+1}\right\} c_2 + \left\{\sum_{i=1}^{M} x_i^{n+2}\right\} c_3 + \cdots + \left\{\sum_{i=1}^{M} x_i^{2n}\right\} c_{n+1} = \sum_{i=1}^{M} x_i^n y_i$$

Since each of the above cases involves the solution of simultaneous, linear algebraic equations, we will incorporate several matrix statements in our program, in a manner similar to Example 7.19.

Design of the Program

In designing the program we will include a number of features which will extend its generality. For example, we will include a provision for fitting either the power function or the exponential curve discussed earlier, or a polynomial of up to ninth degree (10 terms). We will allow for as many as 100 pairs of data, and we will convert the values of x_i and y_i to log x_i and log y_i internally if these logarithms should be required. Since the number of data points to be entered and the type of curve to be fit will vary from one problem to another, we will make use of the variable dimension feature when writing the program.

The coefficients in the system of linear equations will be printed as a part of the output. This information may be helpful when debugging the program. Also included in the output will be the equation of the fitted curve, showing the numerical values obtained for the various constants; a list of the input values x_i and y_i, with the corresponding calculated values $y(x_i)$ (this will facilitate plotting the input data and the fitted curve); and the numerical value of the sum of the square errors. This latter quantity is useful in comparing the success of fitting several different curves to the same set of data (the smaller the sum, the better the fit).

The Program Outline

In order to outline the program let us define the following variables and arrays.

- X = 100-element vector containing the input values x_i
- Y = 100-element vector containing the input values y_i
- A = a 10×10 matrix containing the coefficients of the unknown constants in the system of linear equations
- B = the inverse of A
- C = a 10-element vector containing the unknown constants in the system of linear equations
- D = a 10-element vector containing the right-hand terms in the system of linear equations
- M = input quantity which indicates the number of pairs of data
- N = input quantity indicating the curve to be used:

  - N = 0 indicates the power function $y = ax^b$
  - N = 1 indicates the exponential function $y = ce^{bx}$

  - N = 2, 3, ..., 10 indicates the polynomial $y = \sum_{i=1}^{N} c_i x^{i-1}$.

  (For example, N = 3 indicates the second-degree polynomial $y = c_1 + c_2 x + c_3 x^2$.)

- N1 = number of simultaneous, linear algebraic equations
  - N1 = 2 if N = 0 or N = 1
  - N1 = N if N = 2, 3, ..., 10

The outline of the main program proceeds as follows:

1. Read the input data:

   (a) Read a value for N, thus specifying the particular curve to be fit.

   (b) Read M values for y_i followed by M values for x_i.

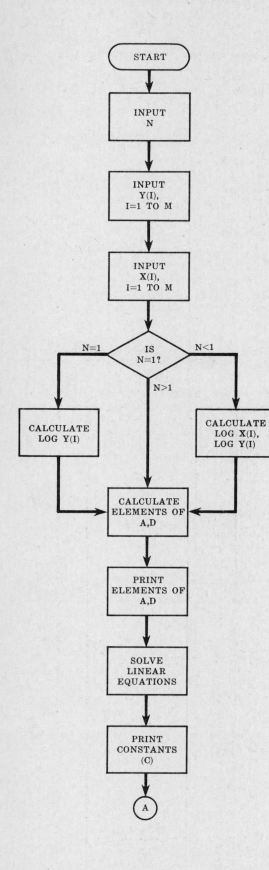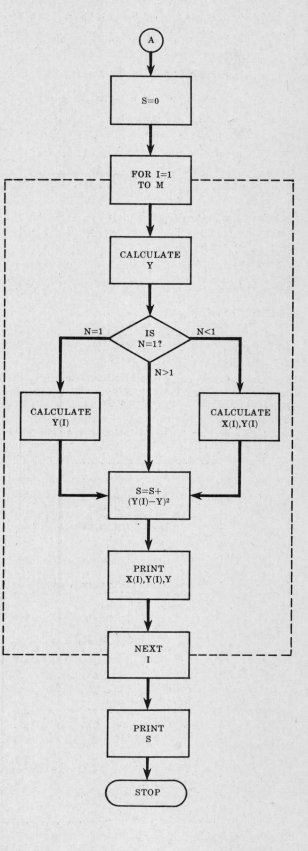

Fig. 7.8

2. Calculate $\log x_i$ and $\log y_i$ if $N = 0$, or calculate $\log y_i$ if $N = 1$, for $i = 1, 2, \ldots, M$.

3. Calculate the elements of the arrays A and D, using the appropriate formulas for the particular curve selected.

4. Print out the elements of A and D.

5. Solve the simultaneous, linear algebraic equations.

6. Print out the values obtained for the unknown constants (the elements of the array C), in a form that shows the equation of the curve selected.

7. Calculate $y(x_i)$ for $i = 1, 2, \ldots, M$.

8. Calculate the sum of the square errors

$$e_1^2 + e_2^2 + \cdots + e_M^2$$

9. Print out x_i, y_i and $y(x_i)$ for $i = 1, 2, \ldots, M$, and then print out the sum of the square errors. (Note that if $N = 0$ or $N = 1$ it will be necessary to convert $\log y_i$ and perhaps $\log x_i$ back to y_i and x_i.)

10. Stop.

Figure 7.8 shows a flowchart of the computational procedure.

The BASIC Program

The complete BASIC program is shown in Fig. 7.9. This program is somewhat lengthy and should therefore be examined carefully. A number of REM statements are included in order to break the program up into major logical blocks.

Notice that several matrix statements, as well as the NUM function, are included in the program (see lines 70, 75, 90, 95, 200, 205, 370 and 375). The MAT INPUT statements allow for a variable number of data points, and the MAT ZER statements cause the A-matrix and the D-vector to be redimensioned each time the program is executed. In statements 370 and 375 the B-matrix and the C-vector are *implicitly* redimensioned to correspond to the A-matrix and the D-vector, respectively.

```
5     REM          LEAST SQUARES CURVE FITTING
10    DIM X(100),Y(100)
15    PRINT "INPUT N=0 FOR A POWER FUNCTION, N=1 FOR AN EXPONENTIAL ";
20    PRINT "FUNCTION."
25    PRINT "FOR A POLYNOMIAL, LET N EQUAL THE NUMBER OF TERMS IN ";
30    PRINT "THE POLYNOMIAL."
35    PRINT "N=";
40    INPUT N
45
50    REM          ENTER DATA POINTS
55
60    PRINT
65    PRINT "ENTER THE Y-VALUES"
70    MAT INPUT Y
75    LET M=NUM
80    PRINT
85    PRINT "ENTER THE X-VALUES"
90    MAT INPUT X
95    IF NUM=M THEN 115
100   PRINT "THE NUMBER OF Y-VALUES DOES NOT CORRESPOND TO THE ";
105   PRINT "NUMBER OF X-VALUES"
110   STOP
115
120   REM          CALCULATE LOGARITHMS OF X- AND Y-VALUES IF NECESSARY
125
130   IF N>=2 THEN 170
135   FOR I=1 TO M
140       LET Y(I)=LOG(Y(I))
145   NEXT I
150   IF N=1 THEN 170
155   FOR I=1 TO M
160       LET X(I)=LOG(X(I))
165   NEXT I
170
175   REM          CALCULATE ELEMENTS OF A-MATRIX AND D-VECTOR
180
185   LET N1=N
190   IF N1>=2 THEN 200
195   LET N1=2
200   MAT A=ZER(N1,N1)
```

Fig. 7.9

```
205 MAT D=ZER(N1)
210 FØR I=1 TØ N1
215    FØR J=1 TØ N1
220       IF I+J>2 THEN 235
225       LET A(I,J)=M
230       GØ TØ 245
235       FØR K=1 TØ M
240          LET A(I,J)=A(I,J)+X(K)↑(I+J-2)
245       NEXT K
250    NEXT J
255    FØR K=1 TØ M
260       IF I>1 THEN 275
265       LET D(I)=D(I)+Y(K)
270       GØ TØ 280
275       LET D(I)=D(I)+Y(K)*X(K)↑(I-1)
280    NEXT K
285 NEXT I
290
295 REM        PRINT SIMULTANEØUS LINEAR EQUATIØNS
300
305 PRINT
310 PRINT "CØEFFICIENTS IN SYSTEM ØF LINEAR EQUATIØNS"
315 PRINT
320 FØR I=1 TØ N1
325    FØR J=1 TØ N1
330       PRINT A(I,J);
335    NEXT J
340    PRINT D(I)
345    PRINT
350 NEXT I
355
360 REM        SØLVE SIMULTANEØUS LINEAR EQUATIØNS
365
370 MAT B=INV(A)
375 MAT C=B*D
380
385 REM        PRINT EQUATIØN FØR CURVE FIT
390
395 IF N>1 THEN 430
400 LET C1=EXP(C(1))
405 IF N=1 THEN 420
410 PRINT "PØWER FUNCTIØN:   Y=";C1;"*X↑";C(2)
415 GØ TØ 490
420 PRINT "EXPØNENTIAL FUNCTIØN:   Y=";C1;"*EXP(";C(2);"*X)"
425 GØ TØ 490
430 IF C(2)>=0 THEN 445
435 PRINT "PØLYNØMIAL FUNCTIØN:   Y=";C(1);C(2);"X";
440 GØ TØ 450
445 PRINT "PØLYNØMIAL FUNCTIØN:   Y=";C(1);"+";C(2);"*X";
450 IF N=2 THEN 485
455 FØR I=3 TØ N
460    IF C(I)>=0 THEN 475
465    PRINT C(I);"*X↑";I-1;
470    GØ TØ 480
475    PRINT "+";C(I);"*X↑";I-1;
480 NEXT I
485 PRINT
490
455 REM         PRINT INPUT VALUES ØF X AND Y AND CALCULATED VALUES ØF Y
500
505 IF N>=2 THEN 545
510 FØR I=1 TØ M
515    LET Y(I)=EXP(Y(I))
520 NEXT I
525 IF N=1 THEN 545
530 FØR I=1 TØ M
535    LET X(I)=EXP(X(I))
540 NEXT I
545 PRINT
550 PRINT TAB(2);"X";TAB(16);"Y (ACTUAL)";TAB(30);"Y (CALCULATED)"
555 LET S=0
560 FØR I=1 TØ M
565    IF N>=2 THEN 595
570    IF N=1 THEN 585
575    LET Y1=C1*X(I)↑C(2)
580    GØ TØ 615
585    LET Y1=C1*EXP(C(2)*X(I))
590    GØ TØ 615
595    LET Y1=C(1)
600    FØR J=2 TØ N
605       LET Y1=Y1+C(J)*X(I)↑(J-1)
610    NEXT J
615    LET S=S+(Y(I)-Y1)↑2
620    PRINT X(I),Y(I),Y1
625 NEXT I
630 PRINT
635 PRINT "SUM ØF SQUARE ERRØRS=";S
640 END
```

Fig. 7.9 (cont.)

```
INPUT N=0 FØR A PØWER FUNCTIØN, N=1 FØR AN EXPØNENTIAL FUNCTIØN.
FØR A PØLYNØMIAL, LET N EQUAL THE NUMBER ØF TERMS IN THE PØLYNØMIAL.
N= ?0

ENTER THE Y-VALUES
 ?.01,.02,.02,.03,.03,.04,.04,.09,.24,.38,.63,.93,1.24,1.48,1.73&
 ?2.07,2.50,3.12,3.48

ENTER THE X-VALUES
 ?7,8,9,10,11,12,13,14,15,16,17,18,19,20,21,22,23,24,25

CØEFFICIENTS IN SYSTEM ØF LINEAR EQUATIØNS

 19   51.4244  -26.0334

 51.4244  141.871  -56.6213

PØWER FUNCTIØN:  Y= 2.26350E-7 *X↑ 5.14716

    X            Y (ACTUAL)      Y (CALCULATED)
    7.            0.01            5.06560E-3
    8             2.00000E-2      1.00722E-2
    9.            2.00000E-2      1.84678E-2
    10.           3.00000E-2      3.17640E-2
    11.           3.00000E-2      5.18788E-2
    12.           4.00000E-2      8.11884E-2
    13.           4.00000E-2      0.12258
    14.           9.00000E-2      0.179506
    15.           0.24            0.256038
    16            0.38            0.356922
    17.           0.63            0.487632
    18.           0.93            0.65443
    19.           1.24            0.864418
    20.           1.48            1.1256
    21.           1.73            1.44693
    22.           2.07            1.83839
    23.           2.5             2.31103
    24.           3.12            2.87701
    25.           3.48            3.54972

SUM ØF SQUARE ERRØRS= 0.614177
```

Fig. 7.10(a)

```
INPUT N=0 FØR A PØWER FUNCTIØN, N=1 FØR AN EXPØNENTIAL FUNCTIØN.
FØR A PØLYNØMIAL, LET N EQUAL THE NUMBER ØF TERMS IN THE PØLYNØMIAL.
N= ?1

ENTER THE Y-VALUES
 ?.01,.02,.02,.03,.03,.04,.04,.09,.24,.38,.63,.93,1.24,1.48,1.73&
 ?2.07,2.50,3.12,3.48

ENTER THE X-VALUES
 ?7,8,9,10,11,12,13,14,15,16,17,18,19,20,21,22,23,23,25

CØEFFICIENTS IN SYSTEM ØF LINEAR EQUATIØNS

 19   304  -26.0334

 304  5434  -213.6C7

EXPØNENTIAL FUNCTIØN:  Y= 8.53337E-4 *EXP( 0.356011 *X)

    X            Y (ACTUAL)      Y (CALCULATED)
    7             0.01            1.03137E-2
    8             2.00000E-2      1.47242E-2
    9             2.00000E-2      2.10205E-2
    10            3.00000E-2      3.00094E-2
    11            3.00000E-2      4.28422E-2
    12            4.00000E-2      6.11625E-2
    13            4.00000E-2      8.73170E-2
    14            9.00000E-2      0.124656
    15            0.24            0.177962
    16            0.38            0.254062
    17            0.63            0.362705
    18            0.93            0.517806
    19            1.24            0.739232
    20            1.48            1.05535
    21            1.73            1.50664
    22            2.07            2.15091
    23            2.5             3.07069
    24            3.12            4.38379
    25            3.48            6.25839

SUM ØF SQUARE ERRØRS= 10.395
```

Fig. 7.10(b)

```
INPUT N=0 FOR A POWER FUNCTION, N=1 FOR AN EXPONENTIAL FUNCTION.
FOR A POLYNOMIAL, LET N EQUAL THE NUMBER OF TERMS IN THE POLYNOMIAL.
N= ?3

ENTER THE Y-VALUES
 ?.01,.02,.02,.03,.03,.04,.04,.09,.24,.38,.63,.93,1.24,1.48,1.73&
 ?2.07,2.50,3.12,3.48

ENTER THE X-VALUES
 ?7,8,9,10,11,12,13,14,15,16,17,18,19,20,21,22,23,24,25

COEFFICIENTS IN SYSTEM OF LINEAR EQUATIONS

 19   304  5434  18.08

 304  5434  105184  394.84

 5434  105184  2151370  8773.92

POLYNOMIAL FUNCTION:  Y= 1.73884 -0.34583 X+ 1.65945E-2 *X↑ 2

    X           Y (ACTUAL)       Y (CALCULATED)
    7             0.01             0.131157
    8             0.02             3.42441E-2
    9             0.02            -2.94800E-2
    10            0.03            -6.00152E-2
    11            0.03            -5.73615E-2
    12            0.04            -2.15188E-2
    13            0.04             4.75128E-2
    14            0.09             0.149733
    15            0.24             0.285143
    16            0.38             0.453741
    17            0.63             0.655528
    18            0.93             0.890505
    19            1.24             1.15867
    20            1.48             1.46002
    21            1.73             1.79457
    22            2.07             2.1623
    23            2.5              2.56322
    24            3.12             2.99733
    25            3.48             3.46463

SUM OF SQUARE ERRORS= 8.91439E-2
```

Fig. 7.10(c)

```
INPUT N=0 FOR A POWER FUNCTION, N=1 FOR AN EXPONENTIAL FUNCTION.
FOR A POLYNOMIAL, LET N EQUAL THE NUMBER OF TERMS IN THE POLYNOMIAL.
N= ?5

ENTER THE Y-VALUES
 ?.01,.02,.02,.03,.03,.04,.04,.09,.24,.38,.63,.93,1.24,1.48,1.73&
 ?2.07,2.50,3.12,3.48

ENTER THE X-VALUES
 ?7,8,9,10,11,12,13,14,15,16,17,18,19,20,21,22,23,24,25

COEFFICIENTS IN SYSTEM OF LINEAR EQUATIONS

 19   304  5434  105184  2151370  18.08

 304  5434  105184  2151370  45723424  394.84

 5434  105184  2151370  45723424  9.98814E+8  8773.92

 105184  2151370  45723424  9.98814E8  2.22672E+10  197719

 2151370  45723424  9.98814E+8  2.22672E+10  5.04212E+11  4.50758E+6

POLYNOMIAL FUNCTION:  Y=-0.727783 + 0.330811 *X-4.78821E-2 *X↑ 2 +
2.56300E-3 *X↑ 3 -3.63439E-5 *X↑ 4

    X           Y (ACTUAL)       Y (CALCULATED)
    7             0.01             3.35158E-2
    8             0.02             1.76392E-2
    9             0.02             1.03749E-3
    10            0.03            -8.32534E-3
    11            0.03            -3.35775E-3
    12            0.04             2.21596E-2
    13            0.04             7.35737E-2
    14            0.09             0.15536
    15            0.24             0.271119
    16            0.38             0.423584
    17            0.63             0.614611
    18            0.93             0.845186
    19            1.24             1.11542
    20            1.48             1.42456
    21            1.73             1.77098
    22            2.07             2.15216
    23            2.5              2.56473
    24            3.12             3.00446
    25            3.48             3.4662

SUM OF SQUARE ERRORS= 6.42682E-2
```

Fig. 7.10(d)

The solution of the simultaneous equations is greatly simplified by the use of matrix statements (see statements 370 and 375). On the other hand, several FOR-TO loops are required in the program, despite the availability of the matrix statements. There are several reasons for this. First, the elements of A are generated internally (lines 185 through 285). Also, under certain conditions it is necessary to convert the input data into logarithmic form, and vice versa (lines 135-145, 155-165, 510-520 and 530-540). Finally, the format in which the results are printed requires the presence of several FOR-TO loops (lines 320-350, 455-480 and 560-625) in order to output the data.

Application of the Program

Returning to our stock market problem, let us fit a curve to the earnings vs. time data for Federated Mousetraps using a power function, an exponential curve, a second-degree polynomial ($N = 3$) and a fourth-degree polynomial ($N = 5$). Before proceeding with the calculation, however, we remark that in curve-fitting calculations it is desirable to prevent the x-values and the y-values from being too far apart in magnitude. Therefore we will subtract the number 1950 from each of the x-values. Thus, for example, the year 1957 will be represented as simply 7, and so on.

The results of the calculations are shown in Figs. 7.10(a) through 7.10(d) for $N = 0, 1, 3$ and 5 respectively. By examining the sum of the square errors in each case, we see that the best fit was obtained using the fourth-degree polynomial ($N = 5$), yielding the equation

$$y = -0.727783 + 0.330811\,x - 0.047882\,x^2 + 0.002563\,x^3 - 0.000036\,x^4$$

(Note that the second-degree polynomial resulted in a fit that is almost as good.) On the other hand, the worst fit was obtained using the exponential curve ($N = 1$), resulting in the expression

$$y = 0.000853\,e^{0.356011\,x}$$

Each of these equations is plotted with the original data in Fig. 7.11.

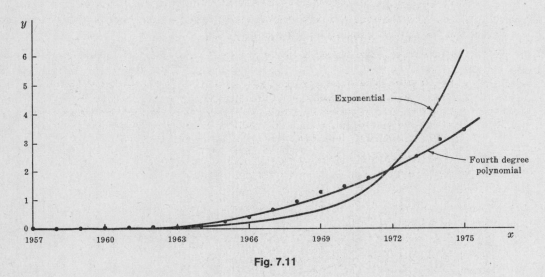

Fig. 7.11

In order to estimate the per-share earnings for the year 1978, we let 1978-1950 = 28. Substituting this value into the fourth-degree polynomial yields a value of $y = 4.92$. Thus we see that the estimated earnings per share of Federated Mousetraps, Inc., will be $4.92 for the year 1978.

Based upon an average price-to-earnings ratio of 30 (which is not unusual for a company growing this fast), we estimate that one share of Federated Mousetraps should sell for about $147.60 in 1978. If we were to buy the stock in 1974 at a price of $75.00 (corresponding to a price-to-earnings ratio of 24), it would be reasonable to expect almost to double our money by 1978. This is equivalent to a yield of about 19 percent a year, in terms of simple interest, compounded annually.

All of the examples in this chapter have been concerned with arrays whose elements represent numeric values. The reader is reminded, however, that BASIC will also accept string arrays, and that the matrix statements can also be used to carry out legitimate string array operations.

Review Questions

7.1   What is a vector? A matrix?

7.2   Is it necessary to use matrix statements to carry out vector and matrix operations? What advantage is there in the use of matrix statements?

7.3   What is the difference between scalar multiplication and matrix multiplication? What conditions must be satisfied in order to multiply one matrix by another?

7.4   Summarize the rules for writing each of the following matrix statements.
(*a*) Assignment   (*c*) Subtraction   (*e*) Matrix multiplication
(*b*) Addition   (*d*) Scalar multiplication

7.5   What is the purpose of the MAT READ statement? What other BASIC statement must be used in conjunction with MAT READ?

7.6   Summarize the rules for writing a MAT READ statement.

7.7   Suppose a MAT READ statement contains the name of one matrix. In what order will the values in the data block be assigned to the matrix elements?

7.8   How are the zeroth elements of a vector or matrix affected by a MAT READ statement?

7.9   Suppose a single MAT READ statement contains several array names. In what order will the values in the data block be assigned to the array elements?

7.10 What is the purpose of the MAT PRINT statement? Summarize the rules for writing this statement.

7.11 Suppose a MAT PRINT statement contains the name of one matrix. In what order will the matrix elements be printed? How can we distinguish one row of the matrix from another? How can the spacing of the matrix elements be altered?

7.12 Suppose a MAT PRINT statement contains the name of a vector. How can the vector elements be printed out in columnar form? In row form? How can the spacing of the vector elements be altered?

7.13 How are the zeroth elements of a vector or matrix affected by a MAT PRINT statement?

7.14 Suppose a single MAT PRINT statement contains several array names. In what order will the array elements be printed? How can the elements of one array be distinguished from the elements of another array?

7.15 Can formulas and function references be included in a MAT PRINT statement?

7.16 What is the purpose of the MAT INPUT statement? How does it differ from the MAT READ statement?

7.17 Summarize the rules for writing a MAT INPUT statement.

7.18 What happens when a MAT INPUT statement is executed? How are the input values transmitted to the computer?

7.19 How is the zeroth element of a vector affected by a MAT INPUT statement?

7.20 How can two or more lines of input data be read with a single MAT INPUT statement?

7.21 How can we determine the number of vector elements that have been entered by a MAT INPUT statement? Suggest a convenient place to store this number.

7.22 Can a MAT INPUT statement be used to enter matrix elements as well as vector elements? Are there any restrictions with matrices that are not present with vectors?

7.23 What is an identity matrix?

7.24 What is meant by the transpose of a matrix?

7.25 What is meant by the inverse of a matrix? Does an inverse always exist? Explain.

7.26 What relationship must exist between the number of rows and the number of columns of an identity matrix? An inverse matrix?

7.27 What relationship must exist between the number of rows and columns of a given matrix and its transpose? Can a vector have a transpose?

7.28 What is the result of multiplying a matrix by an identity matrix?

7.29 What is the result of multiplying a matrix by its inverse?

7.30 State the purpose and summarize the rules for writing each of the following matrix statements.
(a) MAT ZER
(b) MAT CON
(c) MAT IDN
(d) MAT TRN
(e) MAT INV

7.31 What is the purpose of the DET library function? For what kinds of matrices can the DET function be used? What matrix statement must always precede a reference to the DET function?

7.32 How can we determine whether or not a particular square matrix has an inverse?

7.33 How can we solve a system of simultaneous, linear algebraic equations using matrix statements? Is there a simple procedure to check the accuracy of the solution?

7.34 Which matrix statements allow an array to be redimensioned during program execution? How is the redimensioning accomplished?

7.35 Compare the concept of array redimensioning discussed in Section 7.4 with the variable dimension feature included in the MAT INPUT statement.

7.36 What operations can be performed on string arrays? Which matrix statements can be used for the manipulation of string arrays?

Solved Problems

7.37 Several BASIC statements, or groups of statements, are shown below. Some are written incorrectly. Identify all errors.

(a) 10 DIM P(12,20),Q(12,20),R(12,20)
. . .
50 MAT P=(.5)*(Q+R)

Matrix formulas cannot appear in a matrix statement.

(b) 10 DIM P(12,20),Q(12,20)
. . .
50 MAT P=((N+1)/2)*Q

Correct, provided N is an ordinary (scalar) variable.

(c) 30 MAT INPUT A,B,C

Most versions of BASIC allow only one vector name to appear in a MAT INPUT statement.

(d) 30 MAT INPUT N$

    Correct, provided N$ is a string vector.

(e) 200 MAT PRINT A,B,A+B,A−B

    Formulas cannot appear in a MAT PRINT statement.

(f) 10 DIM A(10,20),B(20,10)
     . . .
    30 MAT READ A
    40 MAT B=TRN(A)

    Correct.

(g) 10 DIM P(3,6),Q(8,10),R(5,5)
     . . .
    50 MAT R=P+Q

    Matrices cannot be added if their dimensions do not correspond.

(h) 10 DIM C(6,8),D(6,8),V(12)
     . . .
    60 MAT D=INV(C)
     . . .
    90 MAT V=IDN

    It is not possible to calculate an inverse for a nonsquare matrix. Also, a vector cannot appear in a MAT IDN statement.

7.38 Write one or more BASIC statements for each of the situations described below.

(a) Evaluate the formula

$$Y = X^T * A * X$$

where A is a 10×10 matrix, X is a 10-element vector (disregarding the zeroth row), and X^T is the transpose of X. What will be the dimensionality of Y?

```
100 MAT Z=TRN(X)
110 MAT B=Z*A
120 MAT Y=B*X
```
or
```
100 MAT Z=TRN(X)
110 MAT C=A*X
120 MAT Y=Z*C
```

    Y will represent a single value (i.e., Y will be an ordinary variable, not an array).

(b) Evaluate the formula

$$T = (N) * F^{-1} * G + H$$

where F, G and H are 50×50 matrices, N is an ordinary (scalar) variable and F^{-1} represents the inverse of F. What will be the dimensionality of T?

```
100 MAT A=INV(F)
110 MAT B=A*G
120 MAT C=(N)*B
130 MAT T=C+H
```

    T will be 50×50 matrix.

(c) Calculate the difference between I and $A^{-1} * A$, where A is a 10×10 matrix, A^{-1} represents the inverse of A and I is a 10×10 identity matrix. (Note that this difference should, in principle, be a matrix whose elements are zero. In reality the matrix elements may be different from zero because of numerical errors.)

```
100 MAT B=INV(A)
110 MAT C=B*A
120 MAT I=IDN
130 MAT D=I-C
```

(d) Print the answer obtained for part (c) above in matrix form, with the elements spaced as closely as possible.

```
140 MAT PRINT D;
```

(e) Suppose that A and B are 10×10 matrices whose elements are given in a data block. Read the elements of A, one *row* at a time, followed by the elements of B, one *column* at a time.

```
10 MAT READ A,C
20 MAT B=TRN(C)
```

(Note that A and C are each read row-by-row.)

(f) Suppose that X and Y are vectors whose elements are to be assigned values from a typewriter terminal. The number of values entered for X and Y will be stored in X(0) and Y(0), respectively.

```
10 MAT INPUT X
20 LET X(0)=NUM
30 MAT INPUT Y
40 LET Y(0)=NUM
```

(g) Suppose that P is a 5×12 matrix, T is a 6×6 matrix and X is 10-element vector. Print the values of P, T and X, with X appearing in row form.

```
200 MAT PRINT P,T,X,
```

(h) Repeat part (g) above, with the array elements spaced as closely as possible.

```
200 MAT PRINT P;T;X;
```

Supplementary Problems

7.39 Several BASIC statements, or groups of statements, are shown below. Some are written incorrectly. Identify all errors.

(a) ```
10 DIM L$(100),M$(100)
   ...
50 MAT INPUT M$
60 MAT L$=M$
```

(b)  ```
35 MAT Q=(A+B)*P
```

where A, B, P and Q are 10×10 matrices.

(c) ```
35 MAT Q=(A+B)*P
```

where A and B are ordinary (scalar) variables, and P and Q are $10 \times 10$ matrices.

(d)  ```
60 MAT H=(3)*H
```

where H is a 6×6 matrix.

(e)   60 MAT G=H*H

where G and H are 6×6 matrices.

(f)   60 MAT H=G*H

where G and H are 6×6 matrices.

(g)   10 DIM X(10,20),Y(10,20),Z(10,20)
       . . .
       50 MAT Z=X*Y

(h)   10 DIM V(100)
       . . .
       50 MAT INPUT V(50)

(i)   10 DIM C(100,50),D(100,50)
       20 INPUT M,N
       30 MAT READ C(M,N),D(M,N)

(j)   10 DIM C(100,50),D(100,50)
       20 INPUT M,N
       . . .
       100 MAT PRINT C(M,N),D(M,N)

(k)   10 DIM A(25,25)
       . . .
       50 MAT A=CON(12,24)

(l)   10 DIM A(20,5)
       . . .
       80 MAT A=ZER(10,6)

(m)   10 DIM F(10,20),G(10,20)
       . . .
       60 MAT G=INV(F)

(n)   10 DIM K(20,30)
       . . .
       50 MAT K=IDN(12,12)

7.40   Write one or more BASIC statements for each of the situations described below.

(a) Evaluate the formula

$$F=(2*N+1)*(A^T*A-I)$$

where A is a 10×10 matrix and A^T is its transpose, I is a 10×10 identity matrix and N is an ordinary (scalar) variable.   What will be the dimensionality of F?

(b) Suppose that A, B, C and D are 10×10 matrices.   Calculate the determinant of G, where

$$G=A*C-B*D$$

and print out its value.

(c) Modify part (b) above to print out the elements of G, followed by the inverse of G and the determinant of G.   Space the matrix elements as closely as possible.

(d) Suppose that A is a 20×30 matrix.   Assign zeros to the elements in the first 8 columns of the first 12 rows.

(e) Suppose that A and B are 20×30 matrices.   Read the elements in the first 12 columns of the first 8 rows of A, followed by the elements in the first 15 columns of the first 6 rows of B. How must the data be arranged in the data block?

(f) Suppose that A and B are 20×30 matrices.   Print the elements in the first 12 columns of the first 8 rows of A, followed by the elements in the first 15 columns of the first 6 rows of B. Compare with the solution to part (e) above.

Programming Problems

7.41   Modify the program given in Example 7.15 so that the transpose of F, the inverse of F and the determinant of F are calculated and printed. Explain the results that are obtained.

7.42   Modify the program given in Example 7.19 so that any system of N equations in N unknowns can be solved. Use the variable dimension feature described in Section 7.4. Include a provision for printing the determinant of the coefficient matrix.

7.43   When numerical errors are generated in solving the system of simultaneous equations C*X=D, it is often helpful to proceed as follows.

(a) Calculate the vector F=C*X.

(b) Calculate the error vector G=D−F. (If numerical errors are not present, then F will be the same as the given vector D, and the elements of G will be zeros.)

(c) If the elements of G are not all equal to zero, then solve the system of simultaneous equations

$$A*Y=G$$

for the values of Y(1), Y(2), ..., Y(N).

(d) Add the elements of Y to the corresponding elements of X to obtain an improved solution.

Modify the program given in Example 7.19 to include this error-correction feature. Include a provision for calculating the determinant of the coefficient matrix

Use the program to solve the following system of equations.

$$x_1 + \tfrac{1}{2}x_2 + \tfrac{1}{3}x_3 + \tfrac{1}{4}x_4 + \tfrac{1}{5}x_5 = \tfrac{1}{6}$$
$$\tfrac{1}{2}x_1 + \tfrac{1}{3}x_2 + \tfrac{1}{4}x_3 - \tfrac{1}{5}x_4 + \tfrac{1}{6}x_5 = \tfrac{1}{7}$$
$$\tfrac{1}{3}x_1 + \tfrac{1}{4}x_2 + \tfrac{1}{5}x_3 + \tfrac{1}{6}x_4 + \tfrac{1}{7}x_5 = \tfrac{1}{8}$$
$$\tfrac{1}{4}x_1 + \tfrac{1}{5}x_2 + \tfrac{1}{6}x_3 + \tfrac{1}{7}x_4 + \tfrac{1}{8}x_5 = \tfrac{1}{9}$$
$$\tfrac{1}{5}x_1 + \tfrac{1}{6}x_2 + \tfrac{1}{7}x_3 - \tfrac{1}{8}x_4 + \tfrac{1}{9}x_5 = \tfrac{1}{10}$$

Compare the answers obtained with and without the error-correction feature.

7.44   Modify the program given in Example 7.22 so that several different curves can be fit to the same set of data (i.e., the program can be run several different times) *without* rereading the data each time the program is repeated.

7.45   Write a BASIC program for each of the problems described below. Include a detailed outline or a flowchart for each problem.

(a) Starting with the matrix A given in Example 7.18, calculate a new matrix D, where each element of D is the reciprocal of the corresponding element of A, i.e., $d_{ij} = 1/a_{ij}$. Compare the elements of D with the elements of the inverse of A. (The inverse of A is shown as the matrix B in Example 7.18.)

(b) Calculate the inverse of the matrix B given in Example 7.18. Compare the elements of this matrix with the elements of the matrix A in Example 7.18.

(c) For the matrices A and B given in Example 7.15, show that A*B does not equal B*A.

(d) For the matrices A and B given in Example 7.6, show that $(A*B)^T = B^T*A^T$, where A^T represents the transpose of A, B^T represents the transpose of B, etc.

(e) Evaluate the matrix formula

$$Y=D^T*C^T*C*D$$

using the matrix C and the vector D given in Example 7.19. What will be the dimensionality of Y?

(f) Evaluate the matrix formula

$$P=I+A+A^2+A^3+A^4$$

using the matrix A in Example 7.18. (Note that I represents the identity matrix, $A^2=A*A$, $A^3=A*A*A$, etc.) What will be the dimensionality of P?

Chapter 8

Data Files

In computer jargon a *file* is an orderly, self-contained collection of information. Any type of information may be included. Hence a file may contain a sequence of BASIC statements, or it may consist of data values (i.e., numbers and strings). The first type of file is, of course, a BASIC program; the latter is called a *data file*.

Data files offer a convenient means of storing data sets, since data files can easily be read and updated by a BASIC program. This chapter is concerned with the creation and use of such data files.

We will see that BASIC includes a number of file manipulation statements, similar to the matrix statements presented in chapter 7. Unlike the matrix statements, however, there is some variation in the exact form of the file manipulation statements between one version of BASIC and another. Therefore this chapter will emphasize the *concepts* of data file manipulation rather than the details of the individual statements. (The particular file manipulation statements appearing in this chapter are a part of the BASIC language applicable to Digital Equipment Corporation's DECsystem-10 computer. They are *representative* of the file manipulation statements available in other versions of BASIC.)

8.1 Sequential Data Files

A *sequential file* is characterized by the fact that the individual items are arranged sequentially, one after another. Usually the items in this type of file correspond to separate lines of information on a typewriter terminal. Thus a BASIC program is stored as a sequential file, since each statement appears on a separate line and the statements are arranged in the order of increasing line numbers.

A sequential file can also represent sets of data. Such a file will consist of several lines of data, each line beginning with a line number. The lines will be arranged sequentially, in the order of increasing line numbers. The data items in a given line can be numbers, strings or a combination of the two, separated either by commas or by blank spaces. If a string contains a comma or a blank space, it must be enclosed in quotation marks.

Example 8.1

A sequential data file contains the name and exam scores of each student in a computer science class. The file appears as follows.

```
 10  "COMP SCI 100" "FALL, 1975"
 20  "ADAMS B F" 45 80 80 95 55
 30  "BROWN P" 60 50 70 75 55
 40  "DAVIS R A" 40 30 10 45 60
 50  "FISHER E K" 0 5 5 0 10
 60  "HAMILTON S P" 90 85 100 95 90
 70  "JONES J J" 95 90 80 95 85
 80  "LUDWIG C W" 35 50 55 65 45
 90  "OSBORNE T" 75 60 75 60 70
100  "PRINCE W F" 85 75 60 85 90
110  "RICHARDS E N" 50 60 50 35 65
120  "SMITH M C" 70 60 75 70 55
130  "THOMAS B A" 10 25 35 20 30
140  "WOLFE H" 25 40 65 75 85
150  "ZORBA D R" 65 80 70 100 60
```

We see that each line begins with a line number.   The first line contains two strings, identifying the course and the term, respectively. (Notice that the strings are enclosed in quotation marks, since commas and blank spaces are included within the strings.)   Each successive line contains the name of a student (a string), followed by five examination scores. Thus the file consists of 15 lines, though there are only 14 students in the class.

It should be understood that the sequencing of this data file is determined by the line numbers, not the names. The fact that the names are arranged alphabetically is immaterial.

Creating and Editing a Sequential File

Since a sequential data file is structured in the same way as a BASIC program, we can create and edit such a file in the same manner as a program. We can also print a sequential data file on a typewriter terminal if we wish.   These functions are carried out with the system commands presented in Chapter 3 (e.g., NEW, OLD, SAVE, LIST, etc.).

The rules for naming a data file are the same as for a BASIC program — typically one to six characters, beginning with a letter.

Example 8.2

Suppose that the sequential data file shown in Example 8.1 is to be entered into the computer via a typewriter terminal and saved under the name SCORES.   To do so we must log in, specify that SCORES will be a new file, type the data sets line by line, and then save the file. We can also list the file if we wish, after it has been entered and corrected.

Figure 8.1 shows the major portion of the timesharing session, beginning after the login procedure. Notice that three typing errors were made when entering the data (in lines 120, 130 and 150). These errors were corrected either through use of the DELETE key (lines 120 and 130) or by retyping the entire line (see line 150).

A complete listing of the data file is shown at the bottom of Fig. 8.1. This listing was produced in response to the LIST command, shown in the middle of the figure. As in Chapter 3, all system commands entered by the user have been underlined.

A sequential data file can also be created directly by a BASIC program. We will see how to do this in Example 8.4.

Reading a Sequential Data File

In many applications the information stored in a data file will be read and then processed by a BASIC program. The data items in a sequential data file must be read in the same order they are stored, starting at the beginning of the data file. All of the information that is read will be preserved for subsequent use.

In order to read data from a sequential data file under program control, we will make use of the file manipulation statements FILES, INPUT and IF END.   The following example illustrates how this is accomplished.

```
NEW ØR ØLD-->NEW
NEW FILE NAME-->SCØRES
>10   "CØMP SCI 100" "FALL, 1975"
>20   "ADAMS B F" 45   80   80   95   55
>30   "BRØWN P" 60   50   70   75   55
>40   "DAVIS R A" 40   30   10   45   60
>50   "FISHER E K" 0   5   5   0   10
>60   "HAMILTØN S P" 90   85   100   95   90
>70   "JØNES J J" 95   90   80   95   85
>80   "LUDWIG C W" 35   50   55   65   45
>90   "ØSBØRNE T" 75   60   75   60   70
>100  "PRINCE W F" 85   75   60   85   90
>110  "RICHARDS E N" 50   60   50   35   65
>120  "SMITH M C" 70   60   7%\%5   70   55
>130  "THØN\N\MAS C\C\B A" 10   25   35   20   30
>140  "WØLFE H" 25   40   65   75   85
>150  "ZØRBA 65   80   70   100   60
>150  "ZØRBA D R" 65   80   70   100   60
> SAVE
> LIST


SCØRES

10   "CØMP SCI 100" "FALL, 1975"
20   "ADAMS B F" 45   80   80   95   55
30   "BRØWN P" 60   50   70   75   55
40   "DAVIS R A" 40   30   10   45   60
50   "FISHER E K" 0   5   5   0   10
60   "HAMILTØN S P" 90   85   100   95   90
70   "JØNES J J" 95   90   80   95   85
80   "LUDWIG C W" 35   50   55   65   45
90   "ØSBØRNE T" 75   60   75   60   70
100  "PRINCE W F" 85   75   60   85   90
110  "RICHARDS E N" 50   60   50   35   65
120  "SMITH M C" 70   60   75   70   55
130  "THØMAS B A" 10   25   35   20   30
140  "WØLFE H" 25   40   65   75   85
150  "ZØRBA D R" 65   80   70   100   60
>BYE
JØB 25, USER [115421,160531]  LØGGED ØFF TTY41     1238  16-DEC-73
CPUTIME 0:01    DISK R+W=131+11   CØNNECT=14 MIN    UNITS=0.0135
```

Fig. 8.1

Example 8.3

Let us return to the list of names and exam scores shown in Fig. 8.1. Suppose we want to carry out the following operations for each student in the class.

1. Read the first five exam scores from data file SCORES.

2. Enter a sixth exam score from a typewriter terminal.

3. Calculate an average of all six exam scores.

4. Print the average on the typewriter terminal.

The computation will cease when the end of the data file has been reached.

A BASIC program which will carry out these operations is shown in Fig. 8.2. The variables in this program are defined as follows.

N = line number of each line in data file SCORES

$T\$$ = course title

$Y\$$ = term

$N\$$ = student name

$C1, C2, C3, C4, C5$ = exam scores for each student in data file SCORES

$C6$ = exam score to be entered from the typewriter terminal for each student

A = calculated average of all six exams for each student.

An explanation of the file manipulation statements appearing in this program is given below.

```
10   FILES SCØRES
20   INPUT #1,N,T$,Y$
30   PRINT "CØURSE:";T$,"TERM:";Y$
40   PRINT
50   INPUT #1,N,N$,C1,C2,C3,C4,C5
60   PRINT N$,"SCØRE=";
70   INPUT C6
80   LET A=(C1+C2+C3+C4+C5+C6)/6
90   PRINT "AVERAGE=";A
100  PRINT
110  IF END #1,THEN 130
120  GØ TØ 50
130  END
```

Fig. 8.2

A transfer of information between a data file and a BASIC program always takes place over a *data channel*. Statement number 10 (FILES) assigns the data file SCORES to data channel number 1. This must be done before any information can be transferred to or from the data file. All subsequent file manipulation statements will then refer to the data file by channel number, not by name.

Statement 20 reads the line number (N), the course title (T$) and the term (Y$) from the first line of the data file assigned to channel number 1 (i.e., data file SCORES). Statement 50 reads a line number, a student's name and 5 examination scores from a line in SCORES. (Notice that the line numbers must be read from the data file, even though they are not used.)

Statement number 110 tests for an end of the data file. If there are no more data (end of file), then control is transferred to statement 130 (END); otherwise, control passes to the next executable statement (statement 120). Thus we see that this statement is very similar to our familiar IF-THEN statement, although it is used only to test for an end-of-file condition.

The remaining statements in this program are ordinary BASIC statements, as discussed in earlier chapters of this book. Their meaning should be straightforward.

Figure 8.3 shows the output which is generated by this program and data file SCORES. (A listing of the data file is shown in Fig. 8.1. Note that the only information entered directly from the typewriter terminal is a single exam score for each student. The remaining data was either transferred to the typewriter terminal from the data file, or else generated by the program.

```
COURSE:COMP SCI 100          TERM:FALL, 1975

ADAMS B F      SCORE= ?75
AVERAGE= 71.6667

BROWN P        SCORE= ?80
AVERAGE= 65

DAVIS R A      SCORE= ?55
AVERAGE= 40

FISHER E K     SCORE= ?5
AVERAGE= 4.16667

HAMILTON S P   SCORE= ?90
AVERAGE= 91.6667

JONES J J      SCORE= ?80
AVERAGE= 87.5

LUDWIG C W     SCORE= ?70
AVERAGE= 53.3333

OSBORNE T      SCORE= ?80
AVERAGE= 70

PRINCE W F     SCORE= ?100
AVERAGE= 82.5

RICHARDS E N   SCORE= ?70
AVERAGE= 55

SMITH M C      SCORE= ?75
AVERAGE= 67.5

THOMAS B A     SCORE= ?10
AVERAGE= 21.6667

WOLFE H        SCORE= ?95
AVERAGE= 64.1667

ZORBA D R      SCORE= ?95
AVERAGE= 78.3333
```

Fig. 8.3

Writing a Sequential Data File

Information can be written onto a data file by a BASIC program, in much the same manner that information is read from a data file. When writing onto a sequential data file the new information will automatically be located beyond any existing data, thus protecting whatever information may already be in the file. If the old data are to be deleted prior to writing the new data, then the file must explicitly be erased and repositioned to its starting point.

In the following example we will see how information can be read from both a sequential data file and a typewriter terminal, processed, and the results written out onto the typewriter terminal and a new sequential data file. To accomplish this we will utilize the file manipulation statements FILES, QUOTE, SCRATCH, INPUT, PRINT and IF END. The purpose of each statement will be discussed in the example.

Example 8.4   Processing Student Examination Scores

In this example we will continue with the problem situation described in Examples 8.2 and 8.3 – namely, recording and processing a set of exam scores for a class of students. Let us now develop a more comprehensive program which can perform the following operations for each student.

1. Read a set of exam scores from an existing data file (e.g., SCORES).

2. Enter a new exam score from a typewriter terminal.

3. Calculate an average for all of the exam scores.

4. Print the calculated average on the typewriter terminal.

5. Write the new set of data (i.e., the original exam scores, the new exam score and the calculated average) onto a new data file.

At the completion of the computation the new data file will contain all of the information in the original data file, plus an additional exam score and an average grade for each student.

Computational Procedure

We will write the program so that we can simply add a new exam score to each student's record, without calculating an average, if we wish. This allows us to use the program *during* the school term to record additional data (exam scores), and at the *end* of the school term to process the data (i.e., calculate an average score which will be used to determine each student's final grade).

In order that our program be as general as possible, let us enter all of the exam scores for each student into the array C. Thus C(1) will refer to the first exam score, C(2) the second exam score, etc. We will allow for as many as 15 individual exam scores for each student.

The variable K will refer to the particular exam being entered from the typewriter terminal, e.g., if the scores are being entered for the sixth exam, then K will be assigned a value of 6. Also, J$ will represent either "YES" or "NO", depending upon whether or not an average score is to be calculated for each student. All other variables will be as defined in Example 8.3.

The computation will proceed as follows.

1. Assign the data file SCORES to data channel 1, and UPDATE to data channel 2. (SCORES will be the input file and UPDATE the output file.)

2. Erase any old data that may appear on UPDATE and reposition the file to its starting point, in preparation for writing output.

3. Read a line number (N), the course title (T$) and the term (Y$) from SCORES.

4. Print the course title and the term on the typewriter terminal.

5. Write the line number, the course title and the term onto UPDATE.

6. Enter a value for K (the exam number) from the typewriter terminal.

7. Enter a value for J$ (either "YES" or "NO") from the typewriter terminal, indicating whether or not an average score is to be calculated for each student.

8. Read a line number (N), a student's name (N$), and K-1 exam scores from SCORES.

9. Enter the K*th* exam score from the typewriter terminal.

10. Write the line number, the student's name and all K exam scores onto UPDATE.

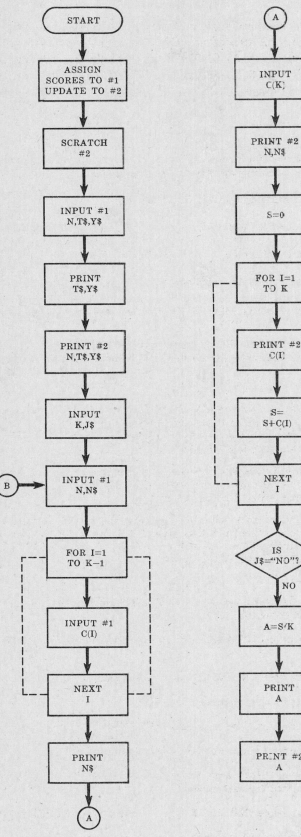
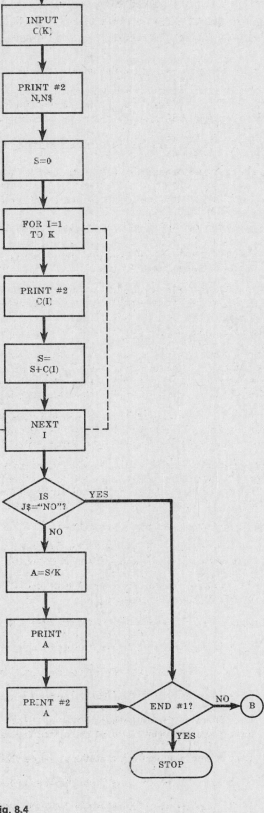

Fig. 8.4

11. If J$="NO", then proceed to step 13 below. Otherwise, calculate an average exam score, A, using the formula

$$A = \frac{C(1)+C(2)+\cdots+C(K)}{K}$$

12. Print the average exam score on the typewriter terminal and write this value onto UPDATE.

13. Test to see if there are additional data sets in SCORES. If so, return to step 8; otherwise, terminate the computation.

A corresponding flowchart is shown in Fig. 8.4.

The BASIC Program

Figure 8.5 contains the actual BASIC program. Notice that several file manipulation statements are included.

The FILES statement (line 50) assigns the data files SCORES and UPDATE to data channels 1 and 2, respectively. This statement must always precede all other file manipulation statements. Once the data files have been assigned to their respective data channels, then all references to these files will be by channel number rather than file name.

Statement number 60 (QUOTE) specifies that all strings that are written onto UPDATE will be enclosed in quotation marks. This is necessary if the strings are to be read by a BASIC program at some later time. The SCRATCH statement (line 70) causes UPDATE to be erased and reset to its starting point, in preparation for writing data.

Data are read from SCORES at several places within the program (lines 80, 180 and 200). Similarly, data are written onto UPDATE at several places (lines 100, 240, 270, 330 and 340). Notice that the line numbers are read and written, even though they are not used by the program. Also, we see that the variables appearing in the PRINT #2 statements are followed by semicolons. This causes the data in each line of UPDATE to be spaced as closely as possible.

Finally, in line 360 we examine SCORES for an end of file. Control is transferred to line 380 (END) if an end of file is found, thus terminating the computation. Otherwise control is transferred to the next executable statement (line 370), in preparation for processing the next student's grades.

```
10   REM PRØGRAM TØ PRØCESS STUDENT EXAMINATIØN SCØRES
20   REM      USING SEQUENTIAL DATA FILES
30
40   DIM C(15)
50   FILES SCØRES, UPDATE
60   QUØTE #2
70   SCRATCH #2
80   INPUT #1,N,T$,Y$
90   PRINT "CØURSE:";T$,"TERM:";Y$
100  PRINT #2,N;T$;Y$
110  PRINT
120  PRINT "EXAM NUMBER";
130  INPUT K
140  PRINT
150  PRINT "CALCULATE AVERAGES (YES ØR NØ)";
160  INPUT J$
170  PRINT
180  INPUT #1,N,N$
190  FØR I=1 TØ K-1
200     INPUT #1,C(I)
210  NEXT I
220  PRINT N$,"SCØRE=";
230  INPUT C(K)
240  PRINT #2,N;N$;
250  LET S=0
260  FØR I=1 TØ K
270     PRINT #2,C(I);
280     LET S=S+C(I)
290  NEXT I
300  IF J$="NØ" THEN 340
310  LET A=S/K
320  PRINT "AVERAGE=";A
330  PRINT #2,A;
340  PRINT #2
350  PRINT
360  IF END #1, THEN 380
370  GØ TØ 180
380  END
```

Fig. 8.5

Application of the Program

In Fig. 8.6 we see how the program can be used to add an additional exam score for each student, without calculating averages. Each new exam score is entered via the typewriter terminal.

The new data file (UPDATE), containing 6 exam scores for each student, is shown at the bottom of Fig. 8.6. The data file was generated from the original data file SCORES, which is shown in Fig. 8.1. The system command LIST was used to produce a listing of UPDATE on the typewriter terminal, after the program execution had been completed.

```
COURSE:COMP SCI 100         TERM:FALL, 1975

EXAM NUMBER ?6

CALCULATE AVERAGES (YES OR NO) ?NO

ADAMS B F       SCORE= ?75

BROWN P         SCORE= ?80

DAVIS R A       SCORE= ?55

FISHER E K      SCORE= ?5

HAMILTON S P    SCORE= ?90

JONES J J       SCORE= ?80

LUDWIG C W      SCORE= ?70

OSBORNE T       SCORE= ?80

PRINCE W F      SCORE= ?100

RICHARDS E N    SCORE= ?70

SMITH M C       SCORE= ?75

THOMAS B A      SCORE= ?10

WOLFE H         SCORE= ?95

ZORBA D R       SCORE= ?95


TIME:  0.80 SECS.
>OLD
OLD FILE NAME-->UPDATE
>LIST

UPDATE

10    "COMP SCI 100" "FALL, 1975"
20    "ADAMS B F" 45  80  80  95  55  75
30    "BROWN P" 60  50  70  75  55  80
40    "DAVIS R A" 40  30  10  45  60  55
50    "FISHER E K" 0  5  5  0  10  5
60    "HAMILTON S P" 90  85  100  95  90  90
70    "JONES J J" 95  90  80  95  85  80
80    "LUDWIG C W" 35  50  55  65  45  70
90    "OSBORNE T" 75  60  75  60  70  80
100   "PRINCE W F" 85  75  60  85  90  100
110   "RICHARDS E N" 50  60  50  35  65  70
120   "SMITH M C" 70  60  75  70  55  75
130   "THOMAS B A" 10  25  35  20  30  10
140   "WOLFE H" 25  40  65  75  85  95
150   "ZORBA D R" 65  80  70  100  60  95
```

Fig. 8.6

Suppose that, at some later time, the new data file is to be used as an *input* file for this same BASIC program. Then it will be necessary to change the name of this data file from UPDATE to SCORES. This can be accomplished by using the system commands SCRATCH (to delete the original data file SCORES) and RENAME (to change the name of UPDATE to SCORES). The procedure is shown in Fig. 8.7. (Do not confuse the BASIC *system command* SCRATCH with the *file manipulation statement* SCRATCH, e.g., SCRATCH #2.)

```
>OLD
>OLD FILE NAME-->SCORES
>SCRATCH
>OLD
>OLD FILE NAME-->UPDATE
>RENAME SCORES
```

Fig. 8.7

Now let us see how this program can be used to enter a new exam score and then calculate an average score for each student. The new exam scores and the calculated averages are shown in Fig. 8.8. (This output was generated using the *original* data file SCORES, shown in Fig. 8.1.)

Notice the similarity between Fig. 8.8 and Fig. 8.3 (the latter was generated using the program in Example 8.3). Now, however, we have not only a record of each student's average exam score shown on the typewriter terminal, but also a complete record of the individual exam scores and the averages in data file UPDATE. A listing of UPDATE is shown at the bottom of Fig. 8.8.

```
         COURSE:COMP SCI 100           TERM:FALL, 1975

         EXAM NUMBER ?6

         CALCULATE AVERAGES (YES OR NO) ?YES

         ADAMS B F      SCORE= ?75
         AVERAGE= 71.6667

         BROWN P        SCORE= ?80
         AVERAGE= 65

         DAVIS R A      SCORE= ?55
         AVERAGE= 40

         FISHER E K     SCORE= ?5
         AVERAGE= 4.16667

         HAMILTON S P   SCORE= ?90
         AVERAGE= 91.6667

         JONES J J      SCORE= ?80
         AVERAGE= 87.5

         LUDWIG C W     SCORE= ?70
         AVERAGE= 53.3333

         OSBORNE T      SCORE= ?80
         AVERAGE= 70

         PRINCE W F     SCORE= ?100
         AVERAGE= 82.5

         RICHARDS E N   SCORE= ?70
         AVERAGE= 55

         SMITH M C      SCORE= ?75
         AVERAGE= 67.5

         THOMAS B A     SCORE= ?10
         AVERAGE= 21.6667

         WOLFE H        SCORE= ?95
         AVERAGE= 64.1667

         ZORBA D R      SCORE= ?95
         AVERAGE= 78.3333


         TIME:  0.92 SECS.
        >OLD
         OLD FILE NAME-->UPDATE
        >LIST


         UPDATE

         10   "COMP SCI 100" "FALL, 1975"
         20   "ADAMS B F" 45  80  80  95  55  75  71.6667
         30   "BROWN P" 60  50  70  75  55  80  65
         40   "DAVIS R A" 40  30  10  45  60  55  40
         50   "FISHER E K" 0  5  5  0  10  5  4.16667
         60   "HAMILTON S P" 90  85  100  95  90  90  91.6667
         70   "JONES J J" 95  90  80  95  85  80  87.5
         80   "LUDWIG C W" 35  50  55  65  45  70  53.3333
         90   "OSBORNE T" 75  60  75  60  70  80  70
         100  "PRINCE W F" 85  75  60  85  90  100  82.5
         110  "RICHARDS E N" 50  60  50  35  65  70  55
         120  "SMITH M C" 70  60  75  70  55  75  67.5
         130  "THOMAS B A" 10  25  35  20  30  10  21.6667
         140  "WOLFE H" 25  40  65  75  85  95  64.1667
         150  "ZORBA D R" 65  80  70  100  60  95  78.3333
```

Fig. 8.8

Sequential data files are particularly useful for storing sets of data which will be processed by a BASIC program at some later time.   There are two reasons for this.   First, a sequential data file can be edited using the BASIC system commands, without altering the program.   Furthermore, it is possible to include both strings and numeric data within a sequential data file.

On the other hand, some applications require that information be transferred to or from a data file without regard for the order in which the data are stored.   The use of a sequential data file is relatively inefficient in such situations, since considerable computer time may be wasted by repeatedly searching along the data file for the desired information. In the next section we will consider a different kind of data file that is better suited for applications of this type.

8.2   Random Data Files

Whereas a sequential data file contains data sets that are arranged in the order of increasing line numbers, a *random data file* consists of individual data items that are not arranged in any particular order.   Each data item can be read directly from or written directly onto a random data file, without proceeding sequentially along the data file from the beginning.   Therefore it is faster to transfer information to or from a random data file than a sequential data file.

Random data files can consist of either numeric data or strings, but not both.   The type of file (i.e., numeric or string) is specified by placing either a percent sign (%) or a dollar sign ($) after the file name.   The % sign signifies a numeric file, the $ sign a string file.   A positive integer quantity (ranging from 1 to 132) must follow a $ sign.   This quantity specifies the maximum number of characters that may appear in each string.

Example 8.5

A BASIC program contains the statement

        10 FILES SALES%,MASTER%,ITEMS$20,CUSTMR$72

The files SALES and MASTER, assigned to data channels 1 and 2, are numeric random data files, as indicated by the % sign following each file name.   ITEMS and CUSTMR, assigned to data channels 3 and 4, are string random data files with maximum string lengths of 20 and 72 characters per string, respectively.

Note that the % sign, or the $ sign followed by a positive integer, is not a part of the actual file name.   Rather, it is a suffix.   (Recall that each file name, exclusive of suffixes, cannot exceed 6 characters.)

Random data files, unlike sequential data files, cannot be listed directly on a typewriter terminal.   Neither can they be edited using the BASIC system commands.   However we can easily write a BASIC program that will carry out either or both of these tasks. We will see how this is accomplished later in this chapter.   First we must consider how the individual items in a random data file can be accessed.

Pointer Control

Although the data items in a random data file are not arranged in any special order, the *locations* of the data items are numbered sequentially from the start of the file (beginning with location number 1 and increasing by one unit for each consecutive data item).   A *pointer* is used to indicate the location of the individual data items.   The pointer must always be properly positioned before a data item can be transferred to or from the data file.

Example 8.6

A random data file contains eight numeric values, arranged in the order shown below.

location	value
1	433
2	256
3	307
4	180
5	75
6	224
7	609
8	52

Suppose we want to read the fifth, the second and the seventh data items, in that order. We first position the pointer to location 5 and read a value of 75. Then we reposition the pointer to location 2 and read a value of 256. Finally, we move the pointer to location 7 and read a value of 609.

The pointer is automatically advanced one location every time a data item is read from or written onto the file. Thus it is possible to read and write data items sequentially from a random data file. We can reposition the pointer whenever we wish, however, by means of the SET statement (the RESET statement, in some versions of BASIC). This statement permits us to access data items in whatever order we may desire.

Closely associated with the SET statement are the library functions LOC and LOF. The LOC function allows us to determine the position of the pointer, and the LOF function indicates the last storage location in the file. We see an illustration of the use of the SET statement and the LOC and LOF functions in the next example.

Example 8.7

Shown below is the skeletal structure of a BASIC program that accesses data from a numeric random data file.

```
10 FILES VALUES%
   . . .
40 SET :1,K
   . . .
80 IF LOC(1)>LOF(1) THEN 200
   . . .
110 SET :1,LOC(1)+3
   . . .
150 SET :1,(1+LOF(1))/2
```

Statement 10 assigns the numeric random data file VALUES to data channel 1. In statement 40 the pointer for data channel 1 is positioned at the location indicated by the variable K (we assume that K has been assigned a positive integer value). Statement number 80 causes a transfer of control to statement 200 if the pointer for data channel 1 is positioned at any location beyond the end of the file.

In statement 110 we reposition the pointer for data channel 1 three locations beyond its present position. Finally, in statement 150 we reset the pointer to the midpoint of the file, determined as the average of the first and last locations in the file.

Notice that the pointer position in statements 110 and 150 are determined by the formulas LOC(1)+3 and (1+LOF(1))/2, respectively. A formula is permitted in a SET statement provided its value is positive but does not exceed the last location in the file. Noninteger values are automatically truncated.

Observe also that the channel number in the SET statement is preceded by a colon (:) instead of a pound sign (#). This is how we distinguish a random data file from a sequential data file. All of the file manipulation statements that refer to a channel number make use of this sign convention.

We will see a complete BASIC program that makes use of the SET statement and the LOC and LOF functions in Example 8.13.

COMPUTERS TO GO
3673 E. THOUSAND OAKS BLVD.
WESTLAKE VILLAGE, CA 91362
(805) 496-2868 (213) 707-0393

CUSTOMER'S ORDER NO.						DATE 11/21 1981		
NAME VOLK								
ADDRESS 1021 TAPEZE								
					N.P.			

SOLD BY Rich	CASH ✓	C.O.D.	CHARGE	ON ACCT.	MDSE. RETD.	PAID OUT

QUAN.	DESCRIPTION	PRICE	AMOUNT
1	Programing w/Basic		5 95
			5 95
		TAX	36
		TOTAL	6 31

ALL CLAIMS AND RETURNED GOODS MUST BE ACCOMPANIED BY THIS BILL.

36110

5R320 REDIFORM ®   REC'D BY_____

Reading a Random Data File

We have already seen that a random data file can be read either sequentially or randomly. If the data are to be read sequentially then the position of the pointer need not be considered, since the FILES statement places the pointer at the first location in the file and the pointer is automatically advanced one location each time a new data item is read.

Example 8.8

The random data file STATES contains the names of the 50 states in the U.S.A., arranged alphabetically. Figure 8.9 presents a BASIC program that will read the name of each state from the data file and then print the name on the typewriter terminal. The data will be read sequentially, in the same order they are stored within the file.

```
10 FILES STATES$15
20 FØR I=1 TØ 50
30    READ :1,NS
40    PRINT NS
50 NEXT I
60 END
>RUN


ALABAMA
ALASKA
ARIZØNA
ARKANSAS
CALIFØRNIA
CØLØRADØ
CØNNECTICUT
DELAWARE
FLØRIDA
GEØRGIA
HAWAII
IDAHØ
ILLINØIS
INDIANA
IØWA
KANSAS
KENTUCKY
LØUISIANA
MAINE
MARYLAND
MASSACHUSETTS
MICHIGAN
MINNESØTA
MISSISSIPPI
MISSØURI
MØNTANA
NEBRASKA
NEVADA
NEW HAMPSHIRE
NEW JERSEY
NEW MEXICØ
NEW YØRK
NØRTH CARØLINA
NØRTH DAKØTA
ØHIØ
ØKLAHØMA
ØREGØN
PENNSYLVANIA
RHØDE ISLAND
SØUTH CARØLINA
SØUTH DAKØTA
TENNESSEE
TEXAS
UTAH
VERMØNT
VIRGINIA
WASHINGTØN
WEST VIRGINIA
WISCØNSIN
WYØMING
```

Fig. 8.9

The FILES statement accomplishes several things in this program. First, it assigns the string random data file STATES to data channel 1, and it specifies that each string will consist of no more than 15 characters. Furthermore, it positions the pointer to the first location in the file.

Notice that we use the file manipulation statement READ rather than INPUT when reading a random data file. (In many versions of BASIC the READ and WRITE statements are used for random data files, and the INPUT and PRINT statements for sequential data files.)

The output that is generated by this program (i.e., the listing of the data file) is shown at the bottom of Fig. 8.9.

If the items in a data file are to be read randomly, then we must move the pointer to the proper location before reading each item. We use the SET statement for this purpose, as shown in the next example.

Example 8.9

Let us again consider the random data file STATES, as described in Example 8.8. We now wish to write a BASIC program that will perform the following steps.

1. Enter from the typewriter terminal the location of a string in STATES. (Each location will be specified by an integer constant having a value between 1 and 50.)

2. Read the string (i.e., the name of a state) contained in that location.

3. Print the string on the typewriter terminal.

This procedure will be repeated until a location is specified whose value is less than 1 or greater than 50.

Figure 8.10 presents the desired BASIC program. The variables L and N$ represent the specified location and the string contained in that location, respectively. Notice that the SET statement precedes the READ statement, thus placing the pointer at the proper location prior to reading each data item.

```
10    FILES STATES$15
20    PRINT "LØCATIØN";
30    INPUT L
40    IF L<1 THEN 110
50    IF L>50 THEN 110
60    SET :1,L
70    READ :1,N$
80    PRINT N$
90    PRINT
100   GØ TØ 20
110   END
>RUN


LØCATIØN ?38
PENNSYLVANIA

LØCATIØN ?23
MINNESØTA

LØCATIØN ?50
WYØMING

LØCATIØN ?11
HAWAII

LØCATIØN ?8
DELAWARE

LØCATIØN ?45
VERMØNT

LØCATIØN ?0
```

Fig. 8.10

The lower part of Fig. 8.10 shows the output that is generated in response to several input quantities. Note that the names of the states are listed in the order specified by the input data rather than the order in which they are stored in the data file.

Writing a Random Data File

A data item can be written onto a random file in much the same manner that it is read, except that we now use the file manipulation statement WRITE instead of READ. As before, the pointer must be positioned at the proper location before the data item is written. The new data item will replace whatever was previously stored in that location.

Example 8.10   Inventory Control

A warehouse maintains an inventory of many different items. The quantity of each item will fluctuate from one day to another, as orders are filled for customers (thus decreasing the inventory), and as shipments are received from suppliers (increasing the inventory). We wish to maintain a record of the exact inventory for each item. To do so we must adjust the inventory level after every individual transaction.

Computational Procedure

The inventory level for each item can be recorded most conveniently in a numeric random data file. We will use the data file INVTRY for this purpose.

Each item will be assigned a unique *stock number* (a positive integer) which will identify that item. The stock number will also be used to indicate the location of the inventory record in the data file. Thus if we should want to know how many units of item 86 are currently in the warehouse we would examine the contents of storage location 86 in the data file.

The computation will proceed as follows.

1. Assign the data file INVTRY to data channel 1.

2. Print the size of the data file (i.e., the value of the last storage location) on the typewriter terminal.

3. Enter a value for the stock number (P) from the typewriter terminal.

4. If P has a value that is less than 1 or greater than the last location in the data file, then terminate the computation. Otherwise proceed with step 5 below.

5. Set the pointer for the data file to location P.

6. Read the inventory level (N) from the data file.

7. Print the current value for N on the typewriter terminal.

8. Enter the change in the inventory level (N1), in terms of number of units, from the typewriter terminal. (Note that a decrease in the inventory level must be indicated by entering a negative value for N1.)

9. Calculate a new inventory level, i.e., let

    $$N=N+N1$$

10. If new value for N is negative (which is physically impossible), then set N equal to zero.

11. Print the new values for N on the typewriter terminal.

12. Reset the pointer to location P. (Note that the pointer will have advanced to location P+1 after step 6.)

13. Write the new value for N onto the data file.

14. Return to step 3.

A corresponding flowchart is shown in Fig. 8.11.

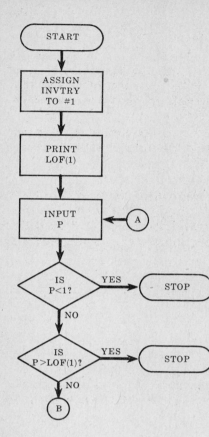
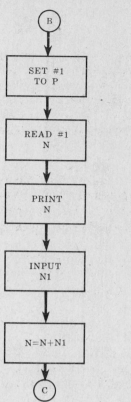
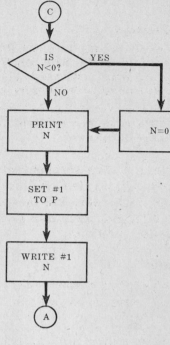

Fig. 8.11

```
10   REM INVENTØRY CØNTRØL PRØGRAM
20   FILES INVTRY%
30   PRINT "STØCK NUMBERS RUN FRØM 1 TØ ";LØF(1)
40   PRINT
50   PRINT "STØCK NUMBER";
60   INPUT P
70   IF P<1 THEN 220
80   PRINT
90   SET :1,P
100  READ :1,N
110  PRINT "ØRIGINAL INVENTØRY=";N;" ITEMS"
120  PRINT "CHANGE IN INVENTØRY LEVEL";
130  INPUT N1
140  LET N=N+N1
150  IF N>=0 THEN 170
160  LET N=0
170  PRINT "NEW INVENTØRY=";N;" ITEMS"
180  PRINT
190  SET :1,P
200  WRITE :1,N
210  GØ TØ 50
220  END
>RUN

STØCK NUMBERS RUN FRØM 1 TØ   2000

STØCK NUMBER ?1186

ØRIGINAL INVENTØRY= 346  ITEMS
CHANGE IN INVENTØRY LEVEL ?-45
NEW INVENTØRY= 301  ITEMS

STØCK NUMBER ?708

ØRIGINAL INVENTØRY= 368  ITEMS
CHANGE IN INVENTØRY LEVEL ?200
NEW INVENTØRY= 568  ITEMS

STØCK NUMBER ?84

ØRIGINAL INVENTØRY= 147  ITEMS
CHANGE IN INVENTØRY LEVEL ?16
NEW INVENTØRY= 163  ITEMS

STØCK NUMBER ?1400

ØRIGINAL INVENTØRY= 78  ITEMS
CHANGE IN INVENTØRY LEVEL ?-50
NEW INVENTØRY= 28  ITEMS

STØCK NUMBER ?0
```

Fig. 8.12

The BASIC Program

Figure 8.12 contains the actual BASIC program. We see that the program contains the file manipulation statements FILES, SET, READ and WRITE, as well as the library function LOF. Notice that the READ and WRITE statements are each preceded with a SET statement, thus positioning the pointer to the proper location before transferring information to or from the data file.

The lower portion of Fig. 8.12 shows a typical set of data resulting from execution of the program. Both input and output data are shown. Note that the program execution is terminated by entering a value of zero for a stock number.

We can include several output items in a single WRITE statement if we wish. In such cases the first data item will be placed in the location designated by the pointer, and the subsequent data items will be stored in the following consecutive locations. As with the PRINT statement, each data item can be represented by a constant, a variable, a formula or a function reference.

Example 8.11

A BASIC program contains the statements

        10 FILES DATA%
        . . .
        100 SET :1,P
        110 WRITE :1,C1,(A+B)/2,SQR(X)

Suppose that P has been assigned a value of 39. Then the value assigned to C1 will be placed in location 39 of the numeric data file DATA. Location 40 will contain the value represented by the formula $(A+B)/2$, and location 41 will contain SQR(X).

Creating a Random Data File

A random data file cannot be created using the BASIC system commands. We must therefore write a special BASIC program to create a random data file. The procedure for doing this is presented in the next example.

Example 8.12

Suppose that we wish to create the random data file STATES by means of the BASIC program FILGEN. The BASIC program and its associated system commands are shown in Fig. 8.13. The user-added system commands have once again been underlined.

Note that the first 3 lines define and save the file STATES, even though data have not yet been entered into STATES. This is required so that the file name specified in the FILES statement (line 10) will be recognized by the system.

When the program FILGEN is executed a sequence of strings will be entered from the typewriter terminal and written onto STATES, beginning in location 1 and continuing in consecutive storage locations. The computation will be terminated when the word END is typed, after all of the data have been entered.

```
>NEW
NEW FILE NAME-->STATES
>SAVE
>NEW
NEW FILE NAME-->FILGEN
>10 FILES STATES$15
>20 INPUT N$
>30 IF N$="END" THEN 60
>40 WRITE :1,N$
>50 GO TO 20
>60 END
>SAVE
```

Fig. 8.13

8.3 Run Time File Specifications

In many applications we may wish to write a BASIC program that makes use of data files but does not specify any particular file names. Rather, we would enter the required file names as input data whenever the program is executed. A program that is written in this manner will be much more general than a program that requires specific data files.

It is quite simple to enter the required file names at run time (i.e., during program execution) if we wish. To do so we must make use of the FILE statement rather than FILES. (Note that FILE and FILES are two different file manipulation statements, as we will see in the example below.)

Example 8.13   Searching a Data File

This example presents an efficient technique for locating a particular data item in a random data file containing strings. We will assume that the strings are stored alphabetically within the file. The method, known as *binary search*, is very similar to the scheme presented in Example 6.6 for finding the maximum of a function.

Computational Procedure

Let us consider a search interval consisting of several consecutive storage locations within the file. Initially the search interval will consist of the entire file. Our overall strategy will be to compare the string at the middle of the search interval with the desired string. One of three results will be obtained.

1. The string at the midpoint will be the desired string, in which case the computation will cease.

2. The desired string will be in the first half of the search interval. Hence the second half of the search interval will be eliminated, and the desired string will be compared with the string at the middle of the remaining subinterval.

3. The desired string will be in the second half of the search interval. In this case we eliminate the first half of the search interval, and compare the desired string with the string located at the middle of the remaining subinterval.

This procedure is repeated until either the desired string has been found, or it has been determined that this string is not contained within the data file.

The Program Outline

In order to outline the procedure let us define the following variables.

F\$ = the name of the string random data file, including the suffix.

N\$ = the string which is to be located within the data file.

M\$ = a string which is read from the data file and compared with N\$.

P1 = pointer indicating the start of the search interval.

P2 = pointer indicating the midpoint of the search interval.

P3 = pointer indicating the end of the search interval.

The computation will proceed as follows.

1. A file name is entered from the typewriter terminal and assigned to F\$.

2. The file represented by F\$ is associated with data channel 1.

3. A string is entered from the typewriter terminal and assigned to N\$. If N\$=END, then the program execution will end; otherwise the computation continues with step 4 below.

4. The pointers P1 and P3 are assigned initial values of 1 and LOF(1), respectively. This defines the initial search interval.

5. If the search interval has been narrowed down to such an extent that P1 and P3 point to adjacent locations, then a value for M\$ is read from location P1 and compared with N\$.

   (*a*) If N\$=M\$, then control is transferred to step 8 below.

   (*b*) If N\$ and M\$ are different, then a new value for M\$ is read from location P3 and compared with N\$.

   (*c*) If N\$=M\$, then control is transferred to step 8 below.

   (*d*) If neither value of M\$ is the same as N\$, then a message is printed on the typewriter terminal which indicates that the desired string cannot be found. We then return to step 3 above.

6. If P1 and P3 do not point to adjacent locations, then a value is determined for P2 using the formula

   $$P2=INT((P1+P3)/2)$$

7. A value for M\$ is read from location P2 and compared with N\$.

   (*a*) If N\$=M\$, then control is transferred to step 8 below.

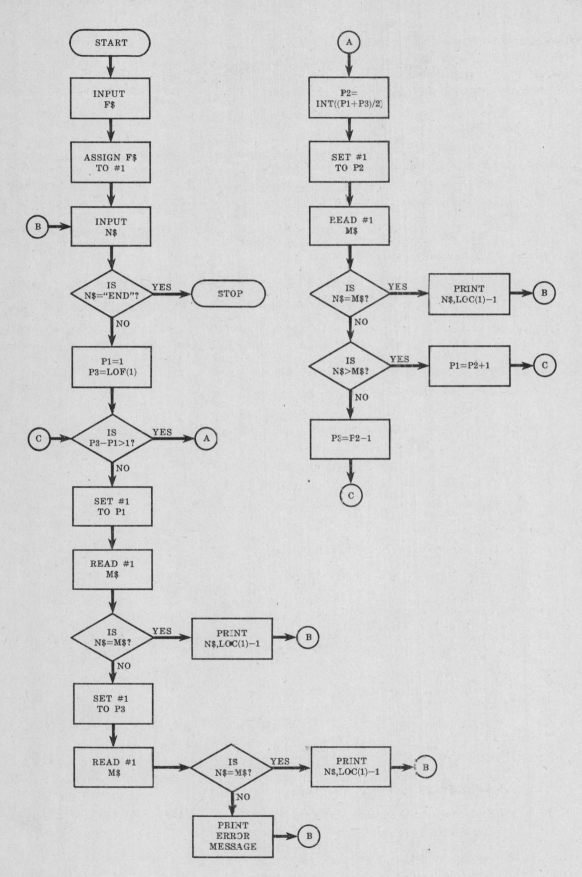

Fig. 8.14

(b) If N\$<M\$, then we retain the first half of the search interval. Hence a new value for P3 is computed as

$$P3 = P2 - 1$$

and control is transferred back to step 5 above.

(c) If N\$>M\$, we retain the second half of the search interval. We therefore calculate a new value for P1 as

$$P1 = P2 + 1$$

Control is then transferred back to step 5 above.

8. A message is printed on the typewriter terminal indicating that the desired string is stored in location LOC(1)−1. (Note that we use LOC(1)−1 rather than LOC(1) because the pointer will have advanced one unit when the most recent value of M\$ was read.)

9. We then return to step 3 above, thus repeating the search for a new string.

A corresponding flowchart is presented in Fig. 8.14.

The BASIC Program

Figure 8.15 contains a complete BASIC program for this problem. Three file manipulation statements are included in the program — namely, FILE (line 40), SET (lines 180 and 290) and READ (lines 190, 210 and 300). The LOC and LOF statements are also present, in lines 460 and 130, respectively. Notice that the customary FILES statement, which assigns a specific data file to a data channel, is not present. Rather, the program *reads in* a file name from the typewriter terminal (line 30), and then assigns this file name to data channel 1 by means of the FILE statement in line 40.

```
10   REM          BINARY SEARCH PROCEDURE
20   PRINT "FILE NAME";
30   INPUT F$
40   FILE :1,F$
50
60   REM          ENTER STRING AND ESTABLISH INITIAL SEARCH INTERVAL
70
80   PRINT
90   PRINT "DESIRED STRING";
100  INPUT N$
110  IF N$="END" THEN 480
120  LET P1=1
130  LET P3=LOF(1)
140
150  REM          TEST FOR SMALL INTERVAL
160
170  IF P3-P1>1 THEN 260
180  SET :1,P1
190  READ :1,M$
200  IF N$=M$ THEN 440
210  READ :1,M$
220  IF N$=M$ THEN 440
230  PRINT N$;" IS NOT IN THE DATA FILE"
240  GO TO 60
250
260  REM          LOCATE MIDPOINT AND COMPARE
270
280  LET P2=INT((P1+P3)/2)
290  SET :1,P2
300  READ :1,M$
310  IF N$=M$ THEN 440
320  IF N$>M$ THEN 390
330
340  REM          RETAIN FIRST HALF OF SEARCH INTERVAL
350
360  LET P3=P2-1
370  GO TO 150
380
390  REM          RETAIN LAST HALF OF SEARCH INTERVAL
400
410  LET P1=P2+1
420  GO TO 150
430
440  REM          DESIRED STRING HAS BEEN LOCATED - PRINT OUTPUT
450
460  PRINT N$;" IS STORED IN LOCATION";LOC(1)-1
470  GO TO 60
480  END
```

Fig. 8.15

The output that is generated by running this program is shown in Fig. 8.16. We see that the data file STATES, discussed in Examples 8.8, 8.9 and 8.12, is to be searched in this example. Notice that the suffix (i.e., $15) is entered along with the file name.

```
FILE NAME ?STATES$15

DESIRED STRING ?PENNSYLVANIA
PENNSYLVANIA IS STORED IN LOCATION 38

DESIRED STRING ?FLORIDA
FLORIDA IS STORED IN LOCATION 9

DESIRED STRING ?OHIO
OHIO IS STORED IN LOCATION 35

DESIRED STRING ?ALASKA
ALASKA IS STORED IN LOCATION 2

DESIRED STRING ?PUERTO RICO
PUERTO RICO IS NOT IN THE DATA FILE

DESIRED STRING ?CALIFORNIA
CALIFORNIA IS STORED IN LOCATION 5

DESIRED STRING ?MASSACHUSETTS
MASSACHUSETTS IS STORED IN LOCATION 21

DESIRED STRING ?END
```

Fig. 8.16

Finally, it should again be emphasized that this program, unlike the programs presented in earlier examples, can be run with *any* string data file. The particular data file to be searched is specified as an input quantity rather than as a part of the program. This method of file specification greatly increases the generality of the program.

Some file manipulation statements, such as RESTORE, MARGIN and PAGE, have not been discussed in this chapter. (Many versions of BASIC also include a set of matrix file manipulation statements.) The reason for this, as mentioned earlier, is the variability of the file manipulation statements between one version of BASIC and another. The reader who may wish to make use of data files should determine the exact nature of the file manipulation statements available at his particular installation.

Review Questions

8.1   What is a file? What kinds of information can be contained within a file?

8.2   What is the difference between a sequential data file and a random data file?

8.3   What are the advantages of a sequential data file compared with a random data file?

8.4   What are the advantages of a random data file compared with a sequential data file?

8.5   How are the data sets ordered in a sequential data file?

8.6   Can numbers and strings both be included in a sequential data file? A random data file?

8.7   How are the individual data items separated from one another in a sequential data file? What special rule applies to strings that contain commas or blank spaces?

8.8   Can the BASIC system commands be used to create and edit a sequential data file? A random data file?

8.9   What rule applies to naming a data file?

8.10   For which type of file must the file name be followed by a suffix? What information is provided by the suffix?

8.11   Must the data items in a sequential data file be read in any particular order?

8.12   How can we test for the end of a sequential data file?

8.13   What is a data channel? How is a particular data file assigned to a data channel?

8.14   Where on a sequential data file must new information be written?

8.15   How can a sequential data file be erased and repositioned to its starting point?

8.16   When writing a data set onto a sequential data file, how can the spacing of the individual data items be controlled?

8.17   How can a sequential data file be renamed?

8.18   How are the data items arranged in a random data file? How can a specific data item be accessed?

8.19   What is a pointer? How can the location of a pointer be established? How can a pointer be repositioned?

8.20   How are data items read from a random data file? Can a random data file be read sequentially? Explain.

8.21   How are data items written onto a random data file? Can a random data file be written sequentially? Explain.

8.22   When a data item is written onto a random data file, what happens to the information that was previously stored in that location?

8.23   How can a random data file be created?

8.24   How can a program be written so that the name of a data file can be specified during run time? Which file manipulation statements must be utilized in order to accomplish this?

8.25   When a random data file is specified at run time, must the suffix be included with the file name?

8.26   Summarize the purpose of each of the following file manipulation statements: FILES, FILE, INPUT, READ, PRINT, WRITE, IF END, QUOTE, SCRATCH, SET.

8.27   How do the file manipulation statements INPUT and PRINT differ from READ and WRITE?

8.28   How do the file manipulation statements FILES and FILE differ from one another?

8.29   What is the purpose of the library functions LOC and LOF?

Solved Problems

8.30   Several BASIC statements, or groups of statements, are shown below. Some are written incorrectly. Identify all errors.

     (*a*)   10 FILES DATAOLD,DATANEW

           A file name cannot exceed 6 characters in most versions of BASIC.

     (*b*)   50 PRINT #3,N,N$,P+Q,LOG(T)

           Correct, provided a sequential data file has been assigned to data channel 3.

(c)   25 READ :2,N$,M$,C1,C2

> A random file cannot contain both strings and numeric constants.

(d)   150 IF END #1, THEN STOP

> The word STOP must be replaced with a statement number.

(e)   10 FILES DATA1%,DATA2%
> . . .
> 40 READ :1,C1,C2
> . . .
> 80 WRITE :2,C1,C2

> Correct.

(f)   10 FILES SALES
> . . .
> 75 SET #1,P
> 80 INPUT #1,A,B,T$,G

> The SET statement is used only with random data files.

(g)   60 IF P=LOF(2) THEN 175

> Correct, provided a random data file has been assigned to data channel 2.

8.31 Write one or more BASIC statements or system commands for each of the situations described below.

(a)   Create the sequential data file SALES. Save and list the file after it has been entered.

```
NEW OR OLD --> NEW
NEW FILE NAME --> SALES
   10 ...
   20 ...          Data file SALES
   ...
  200 ...
SAVE
LIST
```

(b)   Assign the sequential data file SALES to data channel 1.

```
10 FILES SALES
```

(c)   Assign the sequential data file represented by the variable F$ to data channel 1.

```
10 INPUT F$
20 FILE #1,F$
```

(d)   Each line in the sequential data file FILE1 consists of a line number, followed by the values for the variables A, B, P$ and Q$. For each value of A and B we wish to calculate a value for C, where

$$C=SQR(A*B)$$

and write the values for A, B, C, P$ and Q$ onto another sequential data file called FILE2. Assume that the data sets are read from channel 2 and written onto channel 4.

```
10 FILES,FILE1,,FILE2
20 QUOTE #4
30 SCRATCH #4
40 INPUT #2,N,A,B,P$,Q$
50 LET C=SQR(A*B)
60 PRINT #4,N,A,B,C,P$,Q$
70 IF END #2, THEN 90
80 GO TO 40
90 END
```

(e)   A program reads data from the sequential data file MASTER and writes up-dated data onto the sequential data file REVISE.   At some later time we wish to use this same program to read the data file REVISE.   Since the program will not be altered, we wish to change the name of REVISE (the new output file) to MASTER (the old input file).   Show how this can be accomplished.

```
OLD
OLD FILE NAME ––> MASTER
SCRATCH
OLD
OLD FILE NAME ––> REVISE
RENAME MASTER
```

(f)   A program will write data onto the random data file MASTER.   Show how a blank file called MASTER can be defined and saved in preparation for running the program.

```
NEW
NEW FILE NAME ––> MASTER
SAVE
```

(g)   Determine the current location of the pointer for a random data file on channel 3. Transfer control to the end of the program if the pointer is positioned at the last location in the data file.

```
100 LET P=LOC(3)
110 IF P=LOF(3) THEN 250
    . . .
250 END
```

(h)   Read a positive integer quantity from the typewriter terminal.   Position the pointer for data channel 5 to the location indicated by the input quantity.

```
510 INPUT P5
160 SET :5,P5
```

Supplementary Problems

8.32   Determine which of the following file manipulation statements are available at your particular installation: FILES, FILE, INPUT, READ, PRINT, WRITE, IF END, QUOTE, SCRATCH, SET (or RESET), RESTORE, MARGIN, PAGE.   Are other file manipulation statements also available?

8.33   Review the purpose of each of the file manipulation statements available at your particular installation.   Summarize the grammatical rules for writing each statement.

8.34 Several BASIC statements, or groups of statements, are shown below. Some are written incorrectly. Identify all errors.

- (a) 35 READ #1,N,A,B,C,P$,Q$

- (b) 160 WRITE :2,X,Y,X+Y,X−Y,P$

- (c) 80 SET :2,LOC(1)+2
      90 WRITE :2,X1,X2,X3

- (d) 10 FILES NAMES$20,ACCTS%

- (e) 10 FILES MASTER
      20 SCRATCH MASTER
      30 QUOTE MASTER

- (f) 10 INPUT F$
      20 FILES F$

- (g) 100 SET :1,LOF(1)+3
      110 READ :1,L,M,N

- (h) 10 FILES NAMES$20,ACCTS%
      . . .
      75 SET :1,P1
      80 READ :1,N$
      85 SET :2,P2
      90 WRITE :2,N$

8.35 Write one or more BASIC statements or system commands for each of the situations described below.

- (a) Assign the sequential data files LIST1 and LIST2 to data channels 1 and 3, respectively.

- (b) Assign the string random data file NAMES to data channel 1, and assign the numeric random data file ACCTS to data channel 2. Assume that each string in NAMES will consist of 25 or fewer characters.

- (c) Assign the random data files represented by the variables F$ and G$ to data channels 2 and 5, respectively.

- (d) Create the sequential data file TAPE1. Save and list the file after it has been entered.

- (e) A program will write data onto the random data file ITEMS. Show how a blank file called ITEMS can be defined and saved in preparation for running the program.

- (f) A program reads data from the sequential data files OLD1 and OLD2 and writes updated data onto the sequential data files NEW1 and NEW2. At some later time we may want to use this same program to read the data files NEW1 and NEW2. How can the names of the previous output files (NEW1 and NEW2) be changed so that they can be used as input files?

- (g) How can the program described in part (f) above be rewritten so that the output files need not be renamed before they can be read? Assume that the input files will be assigned to data channels 1 and 2, and the output files to channels 3 and 4.

- (h) Each line in the sequential data file assigned to data channel 5 consists of a line number, followed by the values for the variables F$, X, Y, Z and G$. Suppose that we want to write the values of Z, F$ and G$ onto a sequential data file assigned to data channel 3. Show how this can be accomplished.

- (i) Copy the numeric random data file assigned to data channel 5 onto the file assigned to data channel 3.

- (j) Read a positive integer quantity from the typewriter terminal. Position the pointer for data channel 6 to the location indicated by the input quantity. Read a value of X from this location, and write the value of X onto the corresponding location for data channel 2.

- (k) Determine the location of the pointer for the random data files assigned to data channels 1 and 4. Transfer control to statement number 200 if both pointers have the same value (i.e., indicate the same respective locations). Otherwise set the pointer for data channel 2 to the greater of the two values.

(*l*) Determine the last locations of the random data files assigned to data channels 3 and 5. Transfer control to statement number 25 if the last locations are not the same.

Programming Problems

8.36 Modify the program given in Example 8.4 so that the file names can be entered from the typewriter terminal during program execution. Also, include an option which will cause the data sets to be stored in the order of decreasing class averages rather than by alphabetical order of the students' names.

8.37 Modify the program given in Example 8.10 so that any of the following options can be carried out.

(*a*) Simply print the inventory level for a given stock number.

(*b*) Define a "block" of stock numbers by reading in the first and last stock numbers in the block. Print the inventory level for each stock number within the block.

(*c*) Print the inventory level for each stock number within the data file.

(*d*) Print the stock numbers and the corresponding inventory levels for all items having less than some specified inventory level.

(*e*) Print the stock numbers and the corresponding inventory levels for all items having greater than some specified inventory level.

8.38 Modify the program given in Example 8.13 so that any of the following options can be carried out.

(*a*) The entire data file can be listed on the typewriter terminal.

(*b*) All of the strings beginning with a specified letter will be printed on the typewriter terminal.

(*c*) All of the strings which precede a specified string will be printed.

(*d*) All of the strings that are located beyond a specified string will be printed.

8.39 For each problem listed below rewrite the program so that the data are read from or written onto a data file. (*Note*: some problems will require reading the data from a data file and printing the calculated results on the typewriter terminal. Other problems will accept input from the typewriter terminal and write the output onto a data file. In a few cases it may be desirable to read the input data from one data file and write the output onto another data file.)

(*a*) Example 4.16, page 64.

(*b*) Example 4.18, page 68.

(*c*) Problem 4.46(*e*), page 78.

(*d*) Example 5.5, page 82.

(*e*) Problem 5.48, page 103.

(*f*) Problem 5.49, page 103.

(*g*) Problem 5.50, page 103.

(*h*) Problem 5.51, page 103.

(*i*) Problem 5.52, page 104.

(*j*) Problem 5.53(*a*), page 104.

(*k*) Problem 5.53(*b*), page 105.

(*l*) Problem 5.53(*c*), page 105.

(*m*) Problem 5.53(*d*), page 105.

(*n*) Problem 5.53(*e*), page 105.

(*o*) Problem 5.53(*g*), page 106.

(*p*) Problem 5.53(*j*), page 107.

(*q*) Example 6.26, page 133.

(*r*) Example 6.28, page 140.

(*s*) Problem 6.48, page 154.

(*t*) Problem 6.52(*e*), page 155.

(*u*) Problem 6.52(*i*), page 156.

APPENDIX

Appendix A

BASIC Statement Summary

Statement	Example	Reference
CHANGE	10 CHANGE N$ TO N	Section 6.4, page 121.
DATA	10 DATA 12,SEVENTEEN,−5	Section 5.5, page 88.
DEF	10 DEF FNR(A,B,C)=SQR(A↑2+B↑2+C↑2	Section 6.1, page 113.
DIM	10 DIM A(10,20),X(20),F$(60)	Section 5.4, page 87.
END	10 END	Section 2.11, page 22.
FNEND	10 FNEND	Section 6.3, page 118.
FOR-TO	10 FOR J=1 TO 99 STEP 2	Section 4.5, page 62.
GO TO	10 GO TO 50	Section 2.14, page 24.
GOSUB	10 GOSUB 300	Section 6.9, page 132.
IF-THEN	10 IF I>=100 THEN 80	Section 4.2, page 53.
INPUT	10 INPUT A,B,C,M$,N$	Section 2.9, page 18.
LET	10 LET A=3.141593*R↑2	Section 2.8, page 17.
NEXT	10 NEXT I	Section 4.6, page 63.
ON-GO TO	10 ON K GO TO 15,40,25,40,60	Section 4.3, page 57.
PRINT	10 PRINT "X=";X,"Y=";Y	Section 2.10, page 19.
RANDOMIZE	10 RANDOMIZE	Section 6.7, page 127.
READ	10 READ K,N$,Z(1)	Section 5.5, page 88.
REM	10 REM AREA OF A CIRCLE	Section 2.13, page 24.
RESTORE	10 RESTORE	Section 5.6, page 96.
RETURN	10 RETURN	Section 6.8, page 131.
STOP	10 STOP	Section 4.4, page 58.
MAT =	10 MAT C=A	Section 7.1, page 157.
MAT +	10 MAT C=A+B	Section 7.1, page 157.
MAT −	10 MAT C=A−B	Section 7.1, page 157.
MAT (K)*	10 MAT C=(10)*A	Section 7.1, page 157.
MAT *	10 MAT C=A*B	Section 7.1, page 157.
MAT CON	10 MAT B=CON	Section 7.3, page 167.
MAT IDN	10 MAT C=IDN	Section 7.3, page 167.
MAT INPUT	10 MAT INPUT A	Section 7.2, page 161.
MAT INV	10 MAT B=INV(A)	Section 7.3, page 167.
MAT PRINT	10 MAT PRINT A	Section 7.2, page 161.

Statement	*Example*	*Reference*
MAT READ	10 MAT READ A	Section 7.2, page 161.
MAT TRN	10 MAT B=TRN(A)	Section 7.3, page 167.
MAT ZER	10 MAT A=ZER	Section 7.3, page 167.
FILE	10 FILE :1,F$	Section 8.3, page 205.
FILES	10 FILES SCORES	Section 8.1, page 190.
IF END-THEN	10 IF END #1, THEN 130	Section 8.1, page 190.
INPUT	10 INPUT #1,N,T$,Y$	Section 8.1, page 190.
PRINT	10 PRINT #2,N;N$	Section 8.1, page 190.
QUOTE	10 QUOTE #2	Section 8.1, page 190.
READ	10 READ :1,L	Section 8.2, page 199.
SCRATCH	10 SCRATCH #2	Section 8.1, page 190.
SET (RESET)	10 SET :1,L	Section 8.2, page 199.
WRITE	10 WRITE :1,N	Section 8.2, page 199.

Arithmetic Operators:	+	−	*	/	↑	
Relational Operators:	=	<>	<=	<	>=	>

Appendix B

BASIC Library Functions

Function	Example	Reference
ABS	10 LET Y=ABS(X)	Section 5.1, page 80.
ATN	10 LET Y=ATN(X)	Section 5.1, page 80.
ASC	10 LET N=ASC(T)	Section 6.5, page 123.
CHR$	10 LET N$=CHR$(N)	Section 6.5, page 123.
COS	10 LET Y=COS(X)	Section 5.1, page 80.
COT	10 LET Y=COT(X)	Section 5.1, page 80.
DET	10 LET X=DET	Section 7.3, page 167.
EXP	10 LET Y=EXP(X)	Section 5.1, page 80.
INT	10 LET Y=INT(X)	Section 5.1, page 80.
LOC	10 LET N=LOC(1)	Section 8.2, page 199.
LOF	10 LET N1=LOF(3)	Section 8.2, page 199.
LOG	10 LET Y=LOG(X)	Section 5.1, page 80.
NUM	10 LET N(0)=NUM	Section 7.2, page 161.
RND	10 LET X=RND	Section 6.6, page 126.
SGN	10 LET Y=SGN(X)	Section 5.1, page 80.
SIN	10 LET Y=SIN(X)	Section 5.1, page 80.
SQR	10 LET Y=SQR(X)	Section 5.1, page 80.
TAB	10 PRINT TAB(N);X	Section 5.1, page 80.
TAN	10 LET Y=TAN(X)	Section 5.1, page 80.

Appendix C

BASIC System Commands

Command	Purpose
Command	*Purpose*
BYE	Terminate timesharing session.
CATALOG	List names of all files being saved.
GOODBYE	Same as BYE.
LIST	Produces a listing of the current file.
NEW	Specifies that a new file will be created.
OLD	Accesses an existing file.
RENAME	Allows the name of the current file to be changed.
REPLACE	Causes the current file to be saved (stored) in place of the file previously stored with the same name. (The old file will be deleted.)
RUN	Causes the current program to be compiled and executed.
SAVE	Causes the current file to be saved (stored).
SCRATCH	Erases (deletes) the current file.
SYSTEM	Transfers control from BASIC to the system monitor.
UNSAVE	Cancels storage of a file.

References

The BASIC Language

1. Gottfried, B. S.: *BASIC Programmer's Reference Guide,* Quantum Publishers, New York, 1973.

   A concise review and summary of the statements and commonly used features of BASIC.

2. Gruenberger, F.: *Computing with the BASIC Language,* Canfield Press, San Francisco, 1969.

   A well-written, complete text describing the BASIC language.

3. Kemeny, J. G., and T. E. Kurtz: *BASIC Programming,* 2nd ed., Wiley, New York, 1971.

   An elementary, easy-to-read text containing a large number of interesting programming examples.

   The serious programmer should also consult the BASIC programmer's reference manual that is published by the manufacturer of his particular computer.

Related Programming Languages

4. Gottfried, B. S.: *Programming with Fortran IV,* Quantum Publishers, New York, 1972.

   This book contains Fortran versions of most of the programming examples presented in the present text.

5. Gottfried, B. S.: *A Comparison of Programming Languages — Programmer's Reference Guide,* Quantum Publishers, New York, 1973.

   A concise, comparative summary illustrating common programming operations in BASIC, Fortran IV, ALGOL-60, PL/I and COBOL.

Numerical and Statistical Applications

6. Barrodale, I., F. D. K. Roberts, and B. L. Ehle: *Elementary Computer Applications,* Wiley, New York, 1971.

7. Conte, S. D.: *Elementary Numerical Analysis,* McGraw-Hill, New York, 1965.

8. Dorn, W. S., and D. D. McCracken: *Numerical Methods with Fortran IV Case Studies,* Wiley, New York, 1972.

9. Freund, J. E.: *Mathematical Statistics,* 2nd ed., Prentice-Hall, Englewood Cliffs, N. J., 1971.

10. Grove, W. E.: *Brief Numerical Methods,* Prentice-Hall, Englewood Cliffs, N. J. 1966.

Computer Applications—General

11. Gruenberger, F., and G. Jaffray: *Problems for Computer Solution,* Wiley, New York, 1965.

12. Weiss, E. A. (ed.): *Computer Usage/Applications,* McGraw-Hill, New York, 1970.

Answers to Selected Supplementary Problems

1.18 (a) Calculate the area of a triangle whose base and height are given.

(b) Calculate the circumference of a rectangle whose length and width are given.

(c) Evaluate

$$w = u + v$$
$$x = u - v$$
$$y = uv$$
$$z = u/v$$

where u and v are specified.

(d) Evaluate

$$y = 1 + x + \frac{x^2}{2} + \frac{x^3}{6}$$

where x is specified.

1.19 (a)
```
10 INPUT R
20 LET C=2*3.141593*R
30 PRINT R,C
40 END
```

Statement number 20 can also be written as

```
20 LET C=6.283186*R
```

(b)
```
10 INPUT B,H
20 LET L=(B↑2+L↑2)↑.5
30 PRINT B,H,L
40 END
```

(c)
```
10 INPUT U,V
20 LET W=(U−V)/(U+V)
30 PRINT U,V,W
40 END
```

(d)
```
10 INPUT X
20 LET Y=100*(1+X+2*X↑2+3*X↑3)
30 PRINT X,Y
40 END
```

1.20 The following errors are present.

1. The second line contains 2 statements. (Only 1 statement is allowed per line.)

2. The third line does not contain the keyword LET. (This is permitted in some versions of BASIC.)

3. The numbers of the successive program statements do not increase. (The fourth line should have a statement number that is greater than 35 but less than 40.)

2.43 (a) 5

     (b) 8000 or 8E+3

     (c) −1.8033E−9

     (d) 0.33333333

     (e) −7328500 or −7.3285E+6

     (f) 2851 or 0.2851E+4

     (g) 0.2851E+10 or 2851E+6, etc.

     (h) −16752.47 or −1.675247E+4

2.44 (a) Correct.

     (b) Correct.

     (c) Correct.

     (d) Exponent cannot contain a decimal point.

     (e) Correct.

     (f) Commas not allowed.

     (g) Exponent is too large in magnitude.

     (h) Correct.

     (i) Too many significant figures.

     (j) Correct.

     (k) Letter E must be followed by a numerical exponent.

     (l) Exponent is written incorrectly (should read E−2).

2.45 (a) Correct.

     (b) Correct.

     (c) Too long for some versions of BASIC.

     (d) Correct.

     (e) Quotation marks are not allowed.

     (f) Correct.

2.46 (a) Numeric (correct).

     (b) Numeric (correct).

     (c) String (correct).

     (d) The dollar sign cannot be followed by an integer.

     (e) The first character must be a letter.

     (f) Some versions of BASIC do not allow an integer to be included in a string variable.

     (g) Too many characters.

     (h) Too many integers.

     (i) Too many letters.

     (j) String (correct).

     (k) The first character must be a letter.

     (l) Second character, if present, must be an integer or a dollar sign.

     (m) Numeric (correct).

     (n) Numeric (correct).

2.47 (a) $T\uparrow(N+1)$

     (b) $(X+3)\uparrow(1/K)$

     (c) $2*(A/B)\uparrow.33333333$ or $2*(A/B)\uparrow(1/3)$

     (d) $1.87*(U+V)-5.088*(X/Y+2*Z\uparrow2)$

     (e) $1-X+X\uparrow2/2-X\uparrow3/6+X\uparrow4/24-X\uparrow5/120$

     (f) $(2*(P/Q)\uparrow(K-1))/((R-3*T)\uparrow(1/M))$

(g) $(I+J-1)\uparrow 2/5$ or $0.2*(I+J-1)\uparrow 2$

(h) $(((X1+X2)\uparrow M*(Y1+Y2)\uparrow N)/((X1/Y1)\uparrow (M+N)*(X2/Y2)\uparrow (M-N)))\uparrow (1/(M*N))$

2.48 Each variable that appears on the right side of the equal sign in a LET statement must previously have been assigned an appropriate numerical or string value.

2.49 (a) 10 LET P=758.33

(b) 20 LET B=A

(c) 30 LET F$="PITTSBURGH, PA."

(d) 40 LET N$=M$

(e) 50 LET Y3=X/(A+B−C)

(f) 60 LET K=K−2

(g) 70 LET C5=2*C5

(h) 80 LET B=C=(A↑2+B↑2)↑.5

2.50 (a) 10 LET W=((A+3)*B↑N)/(2.7*(C−D/B)+1)

(b) 20 LET F=(((A/B)↑N/(C−D)↑M)/(D/(B−A)↑(N+M)))↑(1/(N+M))

(c) 30 LET Y=(A1−A2*X+A3*X↑2−A4*X↑3+A5*X↑4)/(C1−C2*X+C3*X↑2−C4*X↑3)

(d) 40 LET P=R*A*(1+R)↑N/((1+R)↑N−1)

2.51 (a) 10 LET W1=(A+3)*B↑N
            15 LET W2=2.7*(C−D/B)+1
            20 LET W=W1/W2

(b) 50 LET F1=(A/B)↑N/(C−D)↑M
     55 LET F2=D/(B−A)↑(N+M)
     60 LET F=(F1/F2)↑(1/(N+M))

(c) 100 LET Y1=A1−A2*X+A3*X↑2−A4*X↑3+A5*X↑4
     105 LET Y2=C1−C2*X+C3*X↑2−C4*X↑3
     110 LET Y=Y1/Y2

(d) 200 LET Q=(1+R)↑N
     205 LET P=R*A*Q/(Q−1)

2.52 (a) $f = a + 2b/\sqrt{c}$

(b) $f = a + \sqrt{2b/c}$

(c) $f = (a + 2)\sqrt{b/c}$

(d) $f = \sqrt{(a + 2)b/c}$

(e) $g = (pq/r)(s/t)$

2.53 If $(Y - Z)$ represents a negative quantity, then difficulty will be encountered since a negative quantity cannot be raised to a fractional power in BASIC.

2.54 $P=-(2\uparrow 4)=-16$

2.55 $P=(-2)\uparrow 4=16$

2.56 (a) 10 INPUT A,B,C,M$,N$

(b) 10 INPUT A,N$,B
     15 INPUT M$,C

(c) 10 INPUT A
     12 INPUT B
     14 INPUT C
     16 INPUT M$
     18 INPUT N$

(d) 10 PRINT "ENTER VALUES FOR A,B,C,M$ AND N$";
     20 INPUT A,B,C,M$,N$

(e) 10 PRINT "ENTER VALUES FOR A,B,C,M$, AND N$"
     20 INPUT A,B,C,M$,N$

(f) 100 PRINT A,B,C,M$,N$

(g) 100 PRINT A;B;C;M$;N$

(h) 120 PRINT A;B;C;

(i) 200 PRINT A;B;C;(A+B+C)/3;(A*B*C)↑(1/3);(A↑2+B↑2+C↑2)↑.5
     210 PRINT
     220 PRINT M$,,,,N$

(j) 300 PRINT "A=";A,"B=";B,"C=";C
     or
     300 PRINT "A=";A;"B=";B;"C=";C

(k) 500 PRINT ,"NAME: ";M$
     510 PRINT
     520 PRINT ,"SOCIAL SECURITY NUMBER: ";N$

2.57 (a) ?6.2E−6,27.5E−12,−1000
               ?SHARON,GAIL

               The first line of data can also be typed as

               ?.0000062,.275E−10,−1000

          (b) ?−743.08,.00987,SUSAN
               or
               ?−.74308E+3,.987E−2,SUSAN

          (c) ?"NEW YORK","CHICAGO","SAN FRANCISCO"

               (The quotation marks are required around NEW YORK and SAN FRANCISCO because of
               the inclusion of a blank space. In the case of CHICAGO, the quotation marks are optional.)

          (d) ?2770543,"DECEMBER 29, 1963",48.8E+9,"ELEVEN O' CLOCK"

               (The strings must be enclosed in quotation marks because of the blank spaces and the comma.)

2.58 (a) 6.20000E−6   2.75000E−11 −1000   2770543 −743.08   9.87000E−3
               4.88000E+10

          (b) 6.20000E−6   2.75000E−11   −1000   2770543   −743.08
               9.87000E−3   4.88000E+10

          (c) 6.17250E−6   5.67734E−5   −75286.7

          (d) SHARON   DECEMBER 29, 1963   ELEVEN O' CLOCK

2.59 (a) 10 REM AVERAGING OF AIR POLLUTION DATA

          (b) 250 REM BEGIN LOOP TO CALCULATE CUMULATIVE SUM

          (c) 80 LET A=S/N 'CALCULATE AVERAGE VALUE

          (d) 20 INPUT X,T 'READ A DATA POINT

2.60 (a) Correct.

          (b) The statement number to which control is transferred must be a positive integer, not a formula.

          (c) A GO TO statement cannot transfer control to itself.

          (d) Correct.

          (e) The quotation marks cannot appear.

2.61   The flowchart is shown in Fig. P-2.61.

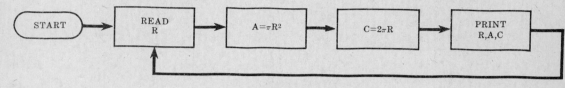

Fig. P-2.61

2.62   (a)   10 REM TEMPERATURE CONVERSION PROBLEM
            20 PRINT "TEMPERATURE IN DEGREES FAHRENHEIT=";
            30 INPUT F
            40 LET C=5*(F−32)/9
            50 PRINT "DEGREES F=";F,"DEGREES C=";C
            60 END

   (b)   10 REM PIGGY-BANK PROBLEM
            20 PRINT "NUMBER OF HALF-DOLLARS=";
            30 INPUT N1
            40 PRINT "NUMBER OF QUARTERS=";
            50 INPUT N2
            60 PRINT "NUMBER OF DIMES=";
            70 INPUT N3
            80 PRINT "NUMBER OF NICKELS=";
            90 INPUT N4
           100 PRINT "NUMBER OF PENNIES=";
           110 INPUT N5
           120 LET S=.5*N1+.25*N2+.1*N3+.05*N4+.01*N5
           130 PRINT "TOTAL AMOUNT OF MONEY=";S;" DOLLARS"
           140 END

   Note that the END statement can be replaced with an appropriate GO TO statement in each of the above problems.   This will allow each program to process multiple sets of data in succession.

2.63   Presented below is a complete BASIC program for each problem.   It should be understood, however, that the actual programming should not begin until a detailed outline or flowchart has been prepared.   Each program is written in such a manner that multiple sets of data can be processed sequentially.

   (a)   10 REM VOLUME AND AREA OF A SPHERE
            20 LET P=3.1415927
            30 PRINT "RADIUS=";
            40 INPUT R
            50 LET V=4*P*R↑3/3
            60 LET A=4*P*R↑2
            70 PRINT "R=";R,"V=";V,"A=";A
            80 PRINT
            90 GO TO 30
           100 END

   (b)   10 REM COMPUTATION OF MASS OF AIR IN A TIRE
            20 PRINT "P=";
            30 INPUT P
            40 PRINT "V=";
            50 INPUT V
            60 PRINT "T=";
            70 INPUT T
            80 LET M=P*V/(.37*(T+460))
            90 PRINT "M=";M
           100 PRINT
           110 GO TO 20
           120 END

    (c)   10 REM GEOMETRIC PROPERTIES OF A TRIANGLE

```
        20 PRINT "A=";
        30 INPUT A
        40 PRINT "B=";
        50 INPUT B
        60 PRINT "C=";
        70 INPUT C
        80 LET S=(A+B+C)/2
        90 LET A0=(S*(S—A)*(S—B)*(S—C))↑.5
       100 LET R1=A0/S
       110 LET A1=3.14159*R1↑2
       120 LET R2=A*B*C/(4*A0)
       130 LET A2=3.14159*R2↑2
       140 PRINT "AREA OF TRIANGLE=";A0
       150 PRINT "AREA OF LARGEST INSCRIBED CIRCLE=";A1
       160 PRINT "AREA OF SMALLEST CIRCUMSCRIBED CIRCLE=";A2
       170 PRINT
       180 GO TO 20
       190 END
```

    (d)   10 REM COMPOUND INTEREST PROBLEM

```
        20 PRINT "P=";
        30 INPUT P
        40 PRINT "I=";
        50 INPUT I
        60 PRINT "N=";
        70 INPUT N
        80 LET A=P*(1+I)↑N
        90 PRINT "A="; A
       100 PRINT
       110 GO TO 20
       120 END
```

If the interest is compounded quarterly rather than annually, statement number 80 must be changed to read

```
        80 LET A=P*(1+I/4)↑(4*N)
```

    (e)   10 REM GROWTH OF A BACTERIA POPULATION

```
        20 PRINT "T=";
        30 INPUT T
        40 LET C=.0289*T
        50 LET F=1+C+C↑2/2+C↑3/6+C↑4/24+C↑5/120+C↑6/720+C↑7/5040+C↑8/40320
        60 LET F=F+C↑9/362880
        70 PRINT "P/P0=";F
        80 PRINT
        90 GO TO 20
       100 END
```

Notice that the computation of the multiplication factor (F) requires 2 statements because a single statement would exceed a 72-character line.

4.32   (a) Correct.

    (b) This condition can never be satisfied.

    (c) Correct.

    (d) Correct.

    (e) A numeric variable cannot be compared with a string variable.

    (f) Correct.

4.33   The string represented by P$ must come earlier in alphabetical order than the string represented by Q$.

4.34   (a) Correct.

    (b) Incorrect grammatical structure (THEN can be followed only by a statement number).

    (c) Not all versions of BASIC allow use of GO TO in place of THEN.

    (d) Correct.

    (e) The statement number to which control is transferred must be a positive integer, not a variable.

    (f) Correct.

    (g) The condition can never be satisfied.

4.35   (*a*)   40 IF K<15 THEN 50

        (*b*) 100 IF N\$="OPTION A" THEN 70
             110 GO TO 150

        (*c*)   60 ...
             ...
             150 IF X>=100 THEN 200
             160 LET J=J+1
             170 INPUT X
             180 GO TO 60
             ...
             200 ...

        (*d*) 20 ...
             ...
             80 IF J=0 THEN 150
             90 LET S=S+J
             100 GO TO 20
             ...
             150 ...

4.36   (*a*) Correct.

        (*b*) The loop will continue indefinitely, since the value of J will always be reset to 1. (If statement number 80 is changed to

                    80 GO TO 40

            then the loop will be executed correctly.)

        (*c*) Control will always be transferred to statement 200.

        (*d*) The loop will continue indefinitely, since the value of X will never exceed 100.

        (*e*) Correct.

4.37   (*a*) A string variable cannot appear in an ON-GO TO statement.

        (*b*) Correct.

        (*c*) An ON-GO TO statement cannot transfer control to itself.

        (*d*) The statement numbers to which control is transferred must be positive integers, not variables.

        (*e*) Correct.

        (*f*) Not all versions of BASIC allow use of THEN in place of GO TO.

        (*g*) Incorrect grammatical structure (ON must precede GO TO).

4.38   (*a*) An error message will result (execution cannot proceed because J−K=−1).

        (*b*) Control will be transferred to statement number 20.

        (*c*) Control will be transferred to statement number 50.

        (*d*) An error message will result (execution cannot proceed because J−K=5).

        (*e*) Control will be transferred to statement number 100.

4.39   (*a*) Correct.

        (*b*) A formula cannot appear in place of a running variable.

        (*c*) String variables cannot appear in a FOR-TO statement.

        (*d*) Correct. (Note that V(1), V(2) and V(3) are subscripted variables, which are discussed in Chapter 5.)

        (*e*) Correct.

        (*f*) Illogical statement (the running variable is required to decrease in value, but cannot do so because of the positive STEP size).

4.40 (a) 10 FOR I=1 TO 200

      . . .

      70 NEXT I

      (Statement numbers are arbitrary.)

  (b) 10 FOR I=1 TO 200

      . . .

      50   IF X<.001 THEN 175

      . . .

      70 NEXT I

      . . .

      175 . . .

  (c) 10 FOR I=1 TO 73 STEP 3

      . . .

      70 NEXT I

  (d) 10 FOR C=.5 TO A↑3−10 STEP A+B

      . . .

      70 NEXT C

4.41 (a) The value of the running variable is altered within the loop.

  (b) Correct.

  (c) The loops overlap.

  (d) The inner and outer loops use the same running variable (X). Also, both loops end with the same NEXT statement.

  (e) Correct, providing numerical values have been assigned to the variables T and T1.

  (f) The running variable in the NEXT statement (C) is not the same as the running variable in the FOR-TO statement (X).

5.40 (a) 10 LET Y=SQR(SIN(X)−COS(X))

  (b) 10 LET P=Q*EXP(−Q*T)

  (c) 10 LET C=LOG(SQR(ABS(A+B)))+LOG(SQR(ABS(A−B)))

  (d) 10 LET W=ABS(ABS(U−V)−ABS(U+V))

  (e) 10 LET Z=COS(X+ATN(Y))

5.41 (a) 10 ON SGN((A*B−C*D)/(F+G))+2 GO TO 135,260,75

  (b) 100 PRINT TAB(4);"X=";X;TAB(28);"Y=";Y;TAB(52);"Z=";Z

  (c) 100 IF (N/2)=INT(N/2) THEN 200

      Control will be transferred to statement number 200 if N is even-valued.

  (d) Control will continue to be transferred to statement number 200 if N is even.

5.42 (a) N$ is a string list.

  (b) A is a numeric table, A$ a string table, B a numeric list and C$ a string list.

  (c) P$ is a string list, P is a numeric table.

  (d) Z is a numeric table.

5.43 (a) Correct.

  (b) Correct.

  (c) The quantities enclosed in parentheses in the DIM statement must be positive integers; variables are not allowed.

  (d) A DIM statement cannot contain nonsubscripted variables (in this case, the variables C1 and C2).

  (e) A subscript cannot have a negative value.

  (f) Correct.

5.44 (*a*)   10 LET S=0
                 20 FOR I=1 TO 199 STEP 2
                 30   LET S=S+X(I)↑2
                 40 NEXT I
                 50 LET S1=SQR(S)

       (*b*)   10 FOR I=1 TO 8
                 20   FOR J=1 TO 12
                 30   LET H(I,J)=1/(I+J−1)
                 40   NEXT J
                 50 NEXT I

       (*c*)   100 FOR I=1 TO N
                110   IF K(I)>15 THEN 130
                120   PRINT TAB(8);"I=";I;TAB(44);"K=";K(I)
                130 NEXT I

       (*d*)   100 LET P=1
                110 FOR I=1 TO K
                120   LET P=P*W(I,I)
                130 NEXT I

       (*e*)   100 FOR I=1 TO M
                110   PRINT TAB(10);M$(I,4)
                120 NEXT I

       (*f*)   100 FOR I=1 TO M
                110   PRINT M$(I,4);" ";
                120 NEXT I

       (*g*)   100 FOR J=1 TO N
                110   PRINT M$(5,J);" ";
                120 NEXT J

5.45 (*a*)   10 READ L$(1),L$(2),L$(3),L$(4),P,Q,R,H$
                 20 READ T(1,1),T(1,2),T(1,3),T(1,4),T(2,1),T(2,2),T(2,3),T(2,4)
                    . . .
                200 DATA WHITE, YELLOW, ORANGE, RED
                210 DATA 2.25E+5,6.08E−9,−1.29E+12,RESTART
                220 DATA 1,−3,5,−7,−2,4,−6,8

       The READ and DATA statements can be combined or expanded if desired.

       (*b*)   10 FOR I=1 TO 4
                 20   READ L$(I)
                 30 NEXT I
                 40 READ P,Q,R,H$
                 50 FOR I=1 TO 2
                 60   FOR J=1 TO 4
                 70   READ T(I,J)
                 80   NEXT J
                 90 NEXT I

       The DATA statements will be the same as in part (*a*).

       (*c*)   10 FOR I=1 TO 4
                 20   READ L$(I)
                 30 NEXT I
                 40 READ P,Q,R,H$
                 50 FOR I=1 TO 2
                 60   FOR J=1 TO 4
                 70   READ T(I,J)
                 80   NEXT J
                 90 NEXT I
                    . . .
                150 RESTORE*
                160 READ P1,Q1,R1

       The DATA statements will be the same as in part (*a*).

(d) The solution is the same as in part (c), except that statement number 150 must be replaced by either

150 RESTORE

or

150 RESTORE$

and statement number 160 must be replaced by

160 READ A1$,A2$,A3$,A4$

6.41 (a) 10 DEF FNY(A,B,X)=A*X↑B

(b) 10 DEF FNQ(R)=C0+C1*R+C2*R↑2+C3*R↑3+C4*R↑4

The values for C0 through C4 must be specified elsewhere in the program, before the function is referenced.

(c) 10 DEF FNI(J,K)=(J+K)↑(J+K)

(d) 10 DEF FNR(A,B,C)
20 IF B↑2<4*A*C THEN 50
30 LET FNR=SQR(B↑2−4*A*C)
40 GO TO 60
50 LET FNR=SQR(4*A*C−B↑2)
60 FNEND

6.42 (a) 10 DEF FNZ(Z)=INT(Z+.5)

(b) 10 DEF FNP(N)
20 LET P=1
30 FOR I=1 TO N
40   LET P=P*T(I)
50 NEXT I
60 LET FNP=P
70 FNEND

(c) 10 DEF FNR(A,B)
20 LET FNR=0
30 FOR I=1 TO 5
40   LET X=A+(B−A)*RND
50   IF X<=R THEN 70
60   LET FNR=X
70 NEXT I
80 FNEND

(d) 10 DEF FNW$(X)
20 ON SGN(X)+2 GO TO 30,50,70
30 LET FNW$="NEGATIVE"
40 GO TO 80
50 LET FNW$="ZERO"
60 GO TO 80
70 LET FNW$="POSITIVE"
80 FNEND

(e) 10 DEF FNL$(N$)
20 CHANGE N$ TO L
30 LET N=90
40 FOR I=1 TO L(0)
50   IF N<=L(I) THEN 70
60   LET N=L(I)
70 NEXT I
80 LET FNL$=CHR$(N)
90 FNEND

Note that the constant 90 is equivalent to the letter Z in the 7-bit ASCII code (see Table 6.1, page 121).

6.43   (a) 100 LET T=FNY(C1+C2,3,X+Y)

            [See the solution given for Problem 6.41(a).]

       (b) 100 LET Q=FNQ(LOG(X))

            [See the solution given for Problem 6.41(b).]

       (c) 100 PRINT FNI(A−B,C)

            [See the solution given for Problem 6.41(c).]

       (d) 100 LET D=ABS(X−FNZ(X))

            [See the solution given for Problem 6.42(a).]

       (e) 10 FOR I=1 TO 60
            20   IF FNP(I)>1000 THEN 40
            30 NEXT I
            40 PRINT "N"; I

            [See the solution given for Problem 6.42(b).]

       (f) 10 FOR I=1 TO 20
            20   PRINT "I=";I,"LARGEST R=";FNR(2,5)
            30 NEXT I

            [See the solution given for Problem 6.42(c).]

6.44   (a) The number of arguments in the function reference does not agree with the number of arguments in the function definition.

       (b) This example contains two errors:

            (i) The function name (FNC) is not assigned a value within the function.

            (ii) A RETURN statement cannot appear in a function definition.

       (c) This example contains two errors:

            (i) Control cannot be transferred into a subroutine by a GO TO statement.

            (ii) An FNEND statement cannot appear in a subroutine.

       (d) This example contains two errors:

            (i) The function is named incorrectly.

            (ii) Formulas cannot appear as dummy arguments.

       (e) Arguments are not present in the function reference.

       (f) Control cannot be transferred out of a subroutine by means of an IF-THEN statement.

       (g) The program logic is incorrect. (The function references the subroutine, which in turn references the function.)

7.39   (a) Correct.

       (b) Matrix formulas cannot appear in a matrix statement.

       (c) Correct.

       (d) Correct.

       (e) Correct.

       (f) A matrix cannot be updated by means of matrix multiplication.

       (g) Matrix multiplication cannot be carried out unless the number of columns of the first matrix (X) is the same as the number of rows of the second matrix (Y). In this example X has 20 columns but Y has only 10 rows.

       (h) The MAT INPUT statement should be written

                 50 MAT INPUT V

       (i) Correct, provided M and N are assigned positive integer values not exceeding 100 and 50, respectively.

(j) The variable dimension feature cannot be used with a MAT PRINT statement.

(k) Correct.

(l) One of the dimensions specified in the MAT ZER statement exceeds the corresponding dimension in the DIM statement.

(m) A nonsquare matrix cannot have an inverse.

(n) Correct.

7.40 (a) 100 MAT I=IDN
110 MAT B=TRN(A)
120 MAT C=B*A
130 MAT D=C−I
140 MAT F=(2*N+1)*D

F will be a 10×10 matrix.

(b) 100 MAT E=A*C
110 MAT F=B*D
120 MAT G=E−F
130 MAT H=INV(G)
140 LET D1=DET
150 PRINT "DETERMINANT OF G=";D1

(c) Add the statement

145 MAT PRINT G;H;

to part (b) above.

(d) 100 MAT A=ZER(12,8)

(e) 100 MAT READ A(8,12),B(6,15)

The data block must contain the elements of A, in a row-by-row order, followed by the elements of B, row-by-row.

(f) 100 FOR I=1 TO 8
110   FOR J=1 TO 12
120   PRINT A(I,J);
130   NEXT J
140   PRINT
150 NEXT I
160 PRINT
170 FOR I=1 TO 6
180   FOR J=1 TO 15
190   PRINT B(I,J);
200   NEXT J
210   PRINT
220 NEXT I

The FOR-TO loops are required because the variable dimension feature is not available with the MAT PRINT statement.

8.34 (a) Most versions of BASIC make use of the INPUT statement rather than the READ statement when reading a sequential data file.

(b) A random data file cannot contain both strings and numeric constants.

(c) Correct, provided random data files have been assigned to data channels 1 and 2.

(d) Correct.

(e) The SCRATCH and QUOTE statements must include data channel numbers, not file names.

(f) The FILES statement must include a file name, not a string variable.

(g) A pointer cannot be positioned beyond the end of the file.

(h) A string cannot be written onto a numeric random data file.

8.35   (a)   10 FILES LIST1,,LIST2

    (b)   10 FILES NAMES$25,ACCTS%

    (c)   10 FILE :2,F$
        20 FILE :5,G$

    (d)   NEW OR OLD --> <u>NEW</u>
        NEW FILE NAME --> <u>TAPE1</u>
        10 ...
        20 ...
        ...   } Data file TAPE1
        300 ...
        <u>SAVE</u>
        <u>LIST</u>

    (e)   NEW OR OLD --> <u>NEW</u>
        NEW FILE NAME --> <u>ITEMS</u>
        <u>SAVE</u>

    (f)   <u>OLD</u>
        OLD FILE NAME --> <u>OLD1</u>
        <u>SCRATCH</u>
        <u>OLD</u>
        OLD FILE NAME --> <u>OLD2</u>
        <u>SCRATCH</u>
        <u>OLD</u>
        OLD FILE NAME --> <u>NEW1</u>
        <u>RENAME OLD1</u>
        <u>OLD</u>
        OLD FILE NAME --> <u>NEW2</u>
        <u>RENAME OLD2</u>

    (g)   Presumably, the program described in Problem 8.35(f) will contain the statement
                10 FILES OLD1,OLD2,NEW1,NEW2
        This statement should be replaced by the following sequence of statements.
                10 INPUT A$,B$,C$,D$
                20 FILE #1,A$
                30 FILE #2,B$
                40 FILE #3,C$
                50 FILE #4,D$
        When the program is executed the names of the input files will be assigned to A$ and B$, and the names of the output files to C$ and D$.

    (h)   10 INPUT A$,B$
        20 FILE #5,A$
        30 FILE #3,B$
        40 QUOTE #3
        50 SCRATCH #3
        60 INPUT #5,N,F$,X,Y,Z,G$
        70 PRINT #3,N,Z,F$,G$
        80 IF END #5, THEN 100
        90 GO TO 60
      100 END

(i) 10 INPUT A$,B$
     20 FILE :5,A$
     30 FILE :3,B$
     40 READ :5,X
     50 WRITE :3,X
     60 IF LOC(5)=LOF(5) THEN 80
     70 GO TO 40
     80 END

(j) 50 INPUT P
     60 SET :6,P
     70 READ :6,X
     80 SET :2,P
     90 WRITE :2,X

(k) 100 LET P1=LOC(1)
    110 LET P4=LOC(4)
    120 IF P1=P4 THEN 200
    130 LET P2=P1
    140 IF P4<=P1 THEN 160
    150 LET P2=P4
    160 SET :2,P2

(l) 100 IF LOF(3)<>LOF(5) THEN 25

Index